P9-CLK-187

ILLINOIS CENTRAL COLLEGE
PR453.H8 1970
STACKS
Brief literary criticisms

A12900 373150

PR
453
.H8
1970

HUTT
Brie
criticisms

PR
453
.H8
1970

42988

HUTTON
Brief literary
criticisms

WITHDRAWN

Illinois Central College
Learning Resource Center

EGLI

F. Hollyer, photo. Swan Electric Engraving Co.

Richard H. Hutton.

BRIEF
LITERARY CRITICISMS

BY THE LATE

RICHARD HOLT HUTTON

SELECTED FROM THE *SPECTATOR*

AND EDITED BY HIS NIECE

ELIZABETH M. ROSCOE

ILLINOIS CENTRAL COLLEGE
LEARNING RESOURCES CENTER

KENNIKAT PRESS
Port Washington, N. Y./London

42988

PR
453
, H8
1970

BRIEF LITERARY CRITICISMS

First published in 1906
Reissued in 1970 by Kennikat Press
Library of Congress Catalog Card No: 71-111311
SBN 8046-0932-2

Manufactured by Taylor Publishing Company   Dallas, Texas

ESSAY AND GENERAL LITERATURE INDEX REPRINT SERIES

Upon the publication of a second selection from the essays contributed to the *Spectator* by my uncle, the late Mr. R. H. Hutton, I have again to acknowledge the great kindness of Mr. Meredith Townsend and Mr. St. Loe Strachey, as well as to thank the Proprietors of the *Economist* for kindly allowing me to reprint from that journal his article on the death of its late editor, Mr. Walter Bagehot.

As a newspaper article is necessarily very brief, I have thought that it might be more interesting and a greater convenience to the reader if, ignoring the chronological sequence, I placed several of those touching on the same, or similar subjects together.

The essays cover a great number of years, and here and there a little repetition may be noticed, but, in spite of this, it has seemed better to publish them just as they left the hands of Mr. Hutton.

E. M. R.

CONTENTS

BOOKISHNESS AND LITERATURE

Sir John Lubbock, in his panegyric on the pleasures of reading to the Wimbledonians the other day, guarded himself against its being supposed that he wished the English people to become mere book-worms, adding : "Of that, indeed, I think there is not much fear. Englishmen happily combine with the love of literature a keen and healthy delight in fresh air and field sports." Well, on that I should remark that I doubt if there ever was a people less imbued with a general love of literature than the English ; and that, so far from that fact being at all unfavourable to the character of English literature, it is, I suspect, the very reason why our literature is as great as it is. A bookish people do not make great books. The Germans are, I suppose, the most bookish people in the world ; and though they make magnificent encyclopedias, the most learned of disquisitions, and scientific treatises beyond all praise ; though they edit classics as few but German scholars ever edited them ; though they master the principles of comparative grammar, and exhaust the views which can be taken on the philosophy of history, and treat "the categories" of all things nameable with a thoroughness that both bewilders and enraptures less masterly logicians ;

1

though their dry prolegomena to drier studies enlarge our conceptions of the range of human industry ; and their revisions, which they characteristically term "belabourings" (*Bearbeitungen*), of former works betray not only their extraordinary fidelity of diligence, but their immense humility ;—yet when all is said that you can say of the vast merits of this literary people, you certainly cannot say that they have a literature to compare with the English. And the reason is, as I believe, simply this, that a bookish people cannot produce the greatest books, if we mean by the greatest books something more than monuments of investigation or learning, — namely, living powers, powers that stir the heart, books whose words have, as Luther, the most unbookish of men, called it, "hands and feet" that can wring us in their living grasp.   That is where Homer beats even the tragedians of the great Athenian age : he was not bookish, but for that very reason wrote a book that had the life of a whole world in it; while Euripides, Sophocles, and possibly even Æschylus, were in a sense bookish, and made you feel that the life they dealt with was, as it were, the distilled water of life, not the water of life as it bubbled up from the fresh earth.   So Virgil and Horace were in the highest sense literary men ; they saw life as reflected in a polished surface, not in its primitive vigour and simplicity.   And yet it is certain that in proportion as the modifying process goes on by which life becomes subdued to the literary type and manner, in that proportion we lose that special charm of freshness which constitutes the chief difference between the books of bookish men and the books of out-of-doors people who are not bookish at all.   Consider only the greatest English writers. One of the greatest, Milton, was perhaps in the main a bookish man, a man who had lived on books, and whose imagination was schooled even more by books than by actual contact with life. But where would Milton stand beside Shakespeare, who is the most unbookish man who ever wrote great books, whose greatest charm was but very inadequately described even in Milton's own beautiful phrase, when he contrasted " Jonson's learned sock " with the delights to be experienced when

> . . . sweetest Shakespeare, Fancy's child,
> Warbles his native woodnotes wild ?

That Shakespeare must have concerned himself more or less with books no one doubts, or he could not have accumulated the material he did. But his great charm consists in his power to make us believe that we are in direct contact with human life, with the clowns, the rustics, the men-at-arms, the travelling players, the courtiers, the lovers, the ambitious statesmen, the more ambitious women, the dreamers of dreams, the plotters of revenge, the dull burgesses, the stately nobles, and the shrewd fools, who move about in that majestic imagination with as much ease and sureness as if they trod the solid earth itself. If ever there were a writer who could not have been what he was, if he had been in the main a bookish man, it was Shakespeare; and yet there is hardly even a French or German, or an Italian or a Spanish writer of any worth, who will not put Shakespeare far above the great authors of his own country. And who comes next to Shakespeare in our literature ? Probably either Chaucer or Scott; and whether you put Chaucer above Scott, or, as I should do, Scott above Chaucer, again you have that very same distinguishing note, that the freshness of the contact with life is precisely of the kind which indicates a man who was not bookish, and could write great books just because he was not bookish. I am not, of course, denying that there are great levels in literature which are appropriate to men of the literary type. Sophocles was in some sense such a writer, and, as I said, Virgil and Horace. Bacon, again, was a man of the desk. One of the most amazing of the mad criticisms of the world is the criticism which professes to find in Shakespeare's plays hints of Bacon's genius. Just conceive those stately bookish essays proceeding from the voice which "warbled his native woodnotes wild"! Conceive Shakespeare beginning a work with the equivalent of the sentence, "Franciscus Baconus sic cogitavit!" Ben Jonson, again, was a poet of the desk. And still more was Pope, and even Dryden. But then, as men of literature, all these belong to the writers who do not touch the hearts of common Englishmen. If you come, even in the eighteenth century, on a book that is eagerly read by the unbookish world, like Burns's songs, you may be sure that its popularity is due to that savour of the "clods fresh-cloven by the plough" which distinguishes it from the works of men of letters. Or go to prose. *Robinson Crusoe* is read by unbookish men with a wonderful eagerness. And is it not because De Foe had so strange a power of giving to his earthy imaginations the very impress of real clay? Or come to our own day. What is the book which in our own times has probably appealed to the hearts of the largest number of human beings who find reading, as a rule, hard work? Perhaps *Uncle Tom's Cabin*, a book of fresh out-of-doors genius if ever there were one; or perhaps *Oliver Twist*, or *Nicholas Nickleby*, or some other production of that strange genius which was always bringing the microscope of the human naturalist and the quaintly distorting lens of the humourist to bear upon the minutest fragments of city life, and then was always interpolating among the inimitable effects so produced patches of screamy melodrama or excruciating pathos. Still, it is the contact with real external fact, the unbookishness of Dickens, that gives him almost all his vast popularity.

And may we not say the same of those writers who have here and there carried the British world by storm with some masterly book of travels or some vivid ballad of human suffering? What, for instance, is the great charm of *Eothen*, the most delightful of all books of Eastern travel, except that it contains in it a flash of unbookish, buoyant life, as different as possible from the elaborate art of the historian of the Crimean war? Why were Kingsley's "Sands of Dee" and his fishermen's and poachers' ballads so fascinating to those who never read, except that there was the same breath of out-of-doors life, of direct sympathy with unbookish woes, in all of them? Why does *Tom Brown's Schooldays* rivet boys as it does, except because it conveys in a book the strong impulses of a fresh, unbookish mind? Why, again, have Stevenson and Rider Haggard fascinated the modern world of boys and men alike as few authors since the days of *Robinson Crusoe* ever fascinated them, except that neither of these men rise to their best until they are breathing the free air of wild and daring enterprise ? I believe most profoundly that it takes a nation which is not bookish in its habits to produce the greatest and most living books. Only a descendant of the wild Borderers, with more Borderers' than authors' blood in his veins, could have achieved the great successes in making Scotland what she now is to us, which have placed Scott perhaps second in the long roll of British literature. Only the profoundly vernacular sympathies of the great Dorsetshire writers, Barnes and Hardy, could have given to these two singularly unbookish writers the power which they have certainly achieved of charming unbookish men with their books. Indeed, I believe I might say that although there will always be a field for highly cultivated genius,—for instance, for a students' poet like Milton, or Herbert, or Henry Vaughan, or Words-worth (who had, however, in him a streak of the hardy shepherd and mountaineer), or Coleridge, or Keats, or Tennyson, or Matthew Arnold,—the men who will make the great popular books of the world, the books which dominate the unbookish, will always be fed chiefly on first-hand experience of men and things, and only by accident, as it were, on literary studies.

LITERATURE AND ACTION

IN a letter contributed to the *Spectator* Mr. Alfred
Austin, who has a very large knowledge both of
English literature and English politics, gives a
variety of reasons why a man who is, in his own
estimation and that of his friends, equally well
fitted for literature and politics, should on the
whole choose the former and eschew the latter. I
heartily agree with him, that there are not many of
those really fitted to exert a considerable influence
in the higher walks of literature who are also fitted
to exert a considerable influence in the higher walks
of politics. There is, as a rule, in genuine literary
men—though there are great exceptions to the rule
—a warning instinct against the *mêlée* of political
life, without the protection of which they could
never really produce the great works they do
produce. Literature in its higher forms almost
always requires a certain amount of solitude, of
separateness of spirit, of imaginative brooding,
which is extremely uncongenial to the political
life. Goethe felt this, and felt it not only to the
extent of a strong repulsion to the grind and
racket of political life, but to the extent of an
almost equally strong repulsion to the exacting ties
of domestic life, by which he probably suffered

morally more than he gained intellectually. Sir
Walter Scott felt it, and never intervened in
politics without something of injury to his imaginative nature, for which there was no adequate
compensation of any kind. Even the great French
poets have all felt this, and though their sociable
French nature has often decoyed them into politics,
as the flame of the candle draws the moth into it,
we have seen in the lives of Chateaubriand, of
Lamartine, and of Victor Hugo, that their interference with politics was never very durable, and
hardly of a kind to reflect lustre on themselves.
At the same time, it is certain that there are, here
and there, men of very considerable literary power
who seem to be destined for politics, and who find
in politics the exact sphere of their literary genius.
Canning was one such. Probably Burke was
another, though his peculiar sphere was rather what
we may call the sheath or membrane of the political
life,—the work of the political reviewer and
pamphleteer,—than the most vital processes of the
State. Macaulay was a third whose influence on
politics was still less direct than Burke's; while
Mr. Disraeli, on the contrary, never really found
his highest *literary* gifts—and even as a politician
almost all his successors were literary—till he
found them in the actual thrust and parry of
Parliamentary debate. Thus, it can certainly not
be said that a true gift for literature necessarily
wards off the minds of men from politics. In its
higher imaginative forms it is very apt to do so.
The Muses are jealous mistresses, and will not lend
their higher gifts of song to any one who plunges
very deep into the *mêlée* of the world. Even the
greater imaginative politicians, like Burke, cannot

help crying to the eager crowd of active partisans, "What shadows we are, and what shadows we pursue!" And the true poets feel this shadowiness of practical aims so deeply, that if by chance they get drawn into the eddy, they are only too thankful when at last they find themselves once more stranded on the *terra firma* of ideal life. But still, there are kinds of literary power, not precisely poetic, but involving a good deal of the detachment of imaginative insight, which seem to find their natural expression in political life, though they might also find a very adequate expression in the field of pure literature ; and can we say of such kinds of literary power as this that they are the worse for that "baptism of fire" which they receive in the fierce struggles of the political world ?

Mr. Austin says they are, on the ground, first, that literary men with anything of the true imaginative power in them can find a higher joy and a more glorifying radiance in the world of their own thoughts, than any they can obtain in that curious mixture of admiration and contempt which besets the politician's stormy life ; and next, that in literature, at all events, the man with any gift for it can, if he pleases, be pretty sure to do no harm, while the politician, whether he eats his heart out in the fray or not, can never be quite sure that he has not done more harm than good. I cannot accept either plea. Of course, I heartily concede that a literary man who is warned by his own instincts, as he often is, that he loses his true self, instead of finding it, in the field of politics, is justified, nay, enjoined, by that instinct of self-preservation to keep out of an angry world in which he is unable to be his truest self. But it is not of

such that I am speaking, rather of those who in
the field of political struggle find themselves at least
as clear and strong as they do out of it.   Now, for
such as these, is either of Mr. Austin's pleas valid ?
As for the first, is it not a purely selfish plea ?
Admit, if you like, that an imaginative brain may
dream a happier dream in the retirement to which
Pope invited St. John than in the struggles of the
political field,—though this is not always true, for
the battle-cry sometimes strikes a kind of fire out
of a man which nothing else elicits,—yet does it
count for much whether he dreams a happier dream
or not ?   Surely the man who has the instincts of a
warrior is not the better for suppressing them, even
though he have other gifts which enable him to
suppress them without losing general influence.   I
never had any but a literary respect for Lord
Beaconsfield, but I doubt whether Lord Beaconsfield
was not at his very best when he was "educating his
party,"—setting them the example of his fortitude
and nonchalance in defeat, dealing about his blows
to his innumerable assailants with all the coolness
of true courage, and appealing to the monarchical
and aristocratic sympathies of the democracy at the
very moment when he was showing his own vast
superiority to thrones and dukes.   Surely he was a
far greater man in doing work like that, than when
he was pouring forth the biting sneers of *Vivian
Grey* or *Ixion in Heaven*, to say nothing of the
balderdash of the *Revolutionary Epic* (for there, of
course, as I do not regard the *Revolutionary Epic* as
true literature at all, he was neither on political
nor on literary ground).   And so far as regards the
politician's right to be content with himself,—for
that is the point on which Mr. Austin dwells first,

and on which I am now following him,—has not
such a man as Mr. John Morley more right to be
content with himself in striking a blow, as he
thinks, for an oppressed race like the Irish, than
when he has just succeeded in giving the world a
rather truer and rather less repulsive conception of
a foul genius such as that of Diderot, or of a witty
scoffer like Voltaire? So far as I can judge, Mr.
John Morley—to take him as the kind of example
least likely to attract me because I mourn over his
policy—is engaged in work which should give him
a better right to think well of himself now, than
when he was pouring out his wealth of knowledge
concerning Vauvenargues, or even dilating for us
on the principles which should guide and limit
Compromise.

Of course, the second plea is a very much more
important one,—that a literary man may be able
to limit his influence to what is purely good, while
even the greatest of politicians can never be sure
that he is not doing harm. But there I think
that Mr. Austin is probably contemplating literature of a very special kind. He speaks first of
the great lyric poetry of the country, and we may
be very sure that a lyric poet of any genius—and
Mr. Austin knows what lyric poetry really is, for
he has produced beautiful lyrics—is almost as
certain to be, on the whole, repelled from politics
by the very bent of that genius, as a lark is to be
repelled from the earth when his song possesses
him. But can Mr. Austin honestly say that the
great bulk of the dramatic poetry of this country
—Dryden's, for example, to take a famous poet not
the most licentious of the dramatists—has done
nothing but good? And as regards the rest of

literature, is not a great deal of it of the most dubious tendency, good in the eyes of one man, evil in the eyes of another? What would Christians say of the literary labours of a writer like Bolingbroke, or even of Frederic Harrison? What would Positivists say of the productions of a preacher like Cardinal Newman, or even a thinker like Dr. Martineau? Nay, what are we to deem the moral profit of Byron's genius, of the great poem, for instance, of "Don Juan"? Again, how are we to esteem the effect of satirical literature as a whole—the influence, for example, of Swift on the world? How are we to judge the net result of such writings as those of George Sand, or Balzac, or the modern realist school of Zola? Of course, if you lay down that a man of literature need not write anything that is not purely good, you lay down in effect that a good many writers shall not write what their literary instincts impel them to write, and that is only saying in effect that they ought to be silent altogether. Surely there never was anything farther from the truth than the assertion that, on the whole, literature has not seriously misguided men,—an assertion, which, of course, I do not impute to Mr. Austin, though it seems needful to his position. And unless politics have done as much harm as good,—which I doubt whether even Mr. Austin believes,—I should be strongly disposed to hold that politics, including the evil it has done,—sometimes rectified by subsequent experience and sometimes not,—has done as much to discipline the minds of average men, and to raise the moral level of communities, as literature itself.

But the central point of the controversy is,

I think, here, that the politician—who might be a
purely literary man, but yields to the attraction
of politics, *not*, of course, against his own better
instincts—throws more of his true self into his
life than the literary man who, feeling the same
attraction to politics, abstains only in order to
avoid the racket of his own imaginative nature.
There is something heroic in the devotion of the
man who, feeling the literary instinct strong and
the political instinct also strong, prefers to
surrender his literary fame to the hope of partially
embodying in actual life ideals which will benefit
others.   And, even though something of the
truest self should disappear in the din and passion
of the conflict, I suspect that the choice, if made
sincerely and honestly, will justify itself on the
same principle on which it was once said that they
who would keep their life should lose it, while they
who would lose their life for the sake of Him who
was above life, should find it.

THE STORING OF LITERARY POWER

MR. GLADSTONE, in replying for "The Interests of Literature" at the Royal Academy on Saturday,[1] intimated that we must not expect to see soon again so great a literary period as that which commenced with the Peace of 1815; but beyond intimating that the immediate future was likely to be an age of research rather than one of expression, he gave no hint of the reasons which were likely, in his opinion, to prevent the present day from becoming a day of great literary splendour. Yet one reason, at all events, is conspicuous why this should not be so, and one, I fear, which is not likely to diminish, but rather to increase in influence; I mean—and my reason will only seem paradoxical to those who have not thought much on those subjects—the very great and increasing facilities for literary expression, which prevent anything like large reserves of feeling and thought from accumulating till they acquire sufficient mass to produce great individual effects. Yet almost every great literary period in the world has been one following a long period of repression, and consequently of accumulation. When Athens first opened the sluices of literary life and power, the

[1] May 5, 1877.

14

world awoke almost for the first time to the conception of literary freedom and to the full power
of human thought and language.   The revival of
learning was a period of similar awakening after
a long pressure of the yoke of ecclesiastical restraint.
The glory of the Elizabethan literature was the
fruit of the long brooding life of the Middle Ages.
And the great literary era to which Mr. Gladstone
referred was chiefly due to that sudden break up
of the conventionalisms of the eighteenth century
caused by the French Revolutions; for the long
reign of a literary oligarchy or aristocracy, and
the habit which such an aristocracy forms of constraining into fixed channels the life and taste of
the rising generations, are at least as effective for
a considerable period in restricting and, as it were,
banking up many kinds and moods of feeling,
as that direct discouragement of all literary expression which precedes the first burst of a new
literature.   But in our own day the enormous
facilities for expressing everything that is felt,
and for fostering much that is not really felt, but
only fancied as possible to be felt, useful as they
are for spreading equally among all classes the
culture hitherto attained, are positive premiums
on literary diffuseness, feebleness, and attenuation.
Just as a perfect system of drainage, if completed
without proper arrangements for storing rain,
carries back far too soon all the water - supply
through millions of rivulets to the great streams,
and through the great streams to the ocean, so a
perfect organisation of facilities for expression
carries off far too soon everything in the shape of
literary feeling and thought into the public mind,
without giving it time to grow to what is great

and forcible. And this tendency to multiply the runlets, the dwindling runlets of literary power, instead of multiplying those great reservoirs of the imagination by which alone the highest life can be fed, is increased to a very great extent by the gradual relaxation of that stern discipline of childhood and youth which marked almost all the ages up to our own. I am far from pleading for that stern discipline, for it is certain that many good effects of this relaxation—perhaps better in their total result than this one evil effect—could be adduced. The young people who are thus relieved from the high pressure of the discipline imposed on former generations certainly grow up in many respects more amiable and more reasonable, less moody, less self-willed, less passionate than their fathers. But they too often grow up less strenuous also, and with much less stored power. It is the damming up of driblets of feeling and thought which really creates great supplies of such feeling and thought. It is the resistance to cherished purposes which accumulates these purposes into something capable of striking the eye and the imagination. As Dr. Newman long ago said :

> Prune thou thy words, the thoughts control,
>   That o'er thee swell and throng,
> They will condense within thy soul,
>   And swell to purpose strong.
>
> But he who lets his feelings run
>   In soft luxurious flow,
> Shrinks when hard service must be done,
>   And faints at every woe.

And what is true of moral purpose is equally true of literary impressions. It is the age of reserve

which prepares the way for the age of literary
splendour ; it is the youth of brooding thoughts
and emotions which prepares the way for the man-
hood of great genius. And unquestionably the
lighter pressure under which children are now
placed during the time of discipline,—the larger
amount of sympathy which they now attract,—that
cultus of children which makes the loneliness of
children and of childhood and youth so comparatively
rare, while they produce a great number of good
effects, do also produce this bad effect,—that there
is far less opportunity than there was for the silent
maturing of strong purposes and deep feelings.

It is curious to note in the lives of Miss
Martineau and Miss Brontë how the very conditions
which seem to have produced the peculiar strength
they had, are just those which it is the tendency of
the feelings excited by their writings to render
rarer and feebler for the future. Miss Martineau
complains of the want of sympathy for children
manifested in her home in her youth, and the terrible
aggravation of those evils caused later by the
unwise mode in which her deafness was treated, so
as to isolate her even more completely from her
fellow-creatures than she would otherwise have
been isolated. Yet I strongly believe that these
were just the conditions which enabled powers of
not very much more than ordinary calibre to
produce really good results of their kind. No
doubt she "kept silence, yea, even from good
words," and "it was pain and grief" to her ; but it
was during this enforced silence that the "fire
kindled," and when at last she spoke with her
tongue, she spoke with the accumulated force of
years of brooding, and if my judgment is worth

anything, it was much more this, than the natural power and breadth of her imagination and understanding which made her what she undoubtedly was—a very remarkable woman of her kind, who, with less repression in childhood and less deprivation in youth, might have been but a clever woman and nothing more. Yet the remarkable effect produced by repression, reticence, and reserve, in accumulating power is still more curiously illustrated in the lives of the Brontës, especially Emily and Charlotte. Of course, reserve and slow accumulation will do little for powers which are from the beginning commonplace, as was apparently the case with Anne Brontë. But how much they will do for women of real genius who are yet not women of such great breadth and luxuriance of imagination that, spread themselves as they may, their imagination would still work vividly, the very interesting story which Mr. Reid has told us of the Brontës, by way of supplement to Mrs. Gaskell's biography of Charlotte, shows with very great force. The highest power of reserve which was probably ever concentrated in any human life whose outlines are well known to us, was that under the steady stress of which Emily Brontë's short career was passed. She, like her sisters, lived with a father of whom they were afraid, amidst wild and gloomy moors, where they had no companions but themselves, yet, unlike her sisters, she could hardly tell even to them the imaginations of her own heart. We are told by Mr. Reid how hopeless her efforts proved to enter into anything like the ordinary intercourse with her fellow-creatures,—how again and again she returned home after efforts to gain her own bread, which failed solely from her complete failure to open easy re-

lations with her kind,—how in her last illness she
would not admit, even to her sisters, her illness till
within two hours of her death, but then whispered
faintly, "If you send for a doctor, I will see him
now," when she was almost in the agonies of death.
In Emily Brontë the restraining power of reserve
assuredly amounted to something very near mental
disease. Yet what a wonderful force it gave to
her genius! Highly as Mr. Reid appreciates
Wuthering Heights, he almost makes one laugh at
him as if he were thoroughly unable to appreciate it,
when he compares it, even for a moment, with such
trash as Lord Lytton's *Strange Story*. The passage
he quotes, for instance, from *Wuthering Heights* as
to the way in which Catherine's image haunted
Heathcliff after her death, is, when compared with
anything Lord Lytton ever achieved, like a stroke
of lightning to the glimmer of a rushlight. There
is more concentrated fire and power in that weird,
wild tale, not merely than in all the pinchbeck
novels Lord Lytton ever wrote (which is saying
nothing), but than in any single story known to
me in the English language. The capacity for expressing imaginative intensity surpasses, to my
mind, any achievement in the same space in the
whole of our prose literature. I should rank
Wuthering Heights, eccentric and lurid as it is, as
an effort of genius far above not only *Villette*,
which seems to me Charlotte Brontë's greatest effort,
but the *Bride of Lammermoor*, which is the nearest
thing to it in Sir Walter Scott's imaginative
writings. In *Wuthering Heights* the concentrated
power of a great imagination gave one brilliant
flash and disappeared. No doubt the repressive
force of Emily Brontë's reserve was something like

a disease, but it had the effect of storing imaginative power as nothing else in the world could have stored it; and no one who reads all that is told of her could suppose for a moment that, had her reserve been less than it was, we should ever have had that one great flash of genius. Doubtless she would have been broader, happier, in many respects a truer woman than she was, if she had had more channels of communication with her kind, but her genius could hardly have effected any one thing so great; she might have been far wider, she could not have been so intense; she would never have gazed so deeply into those evil eyes of Heathcliff's— eyes seen only in her reveries, and never in real life—which she so finely describes as "the cloudy windows of Hell," if she had not stored up all the elastic force of her reveries into that one single creative effort. And so with Charlotte Brontë's genius; it certainly reached its acme when her life was at its loneliest, when she was robbed of the sympathy of both her sisters. *Villette* is almost as much greater than *Shirley* or *Jane Eyre* as the *Bride of Lammermoor*, written in pain and under stress of illness, was greater than *Ivanhoe* or *Kenilworth*.

I hold, then, that the great facilities for expression —the great stimulus given to expression by our intensely literary age, and to expression which anticipates the proper ripening of the feeling and thought to be expressed—are really considerable obstacles to the development of that high literary power, for which Mr. Gladstone is compelled to look back to a generation when the intellectual life was far more sharply kept under, and far less constantly fostered than it is now.

SAYINGS OF GREAT MEN

In turning over the admirably edited and amusing book which Mr. Samuel Arthur Bent has just given us on the *Sayings of Great Men*, nothing, perhaps, strikes me more than the interest attaching to the sayings of persons of very poor capacity, so long as that poor capacity has been weighted with sufficient self-confidence to make it measure itself coolly against the world. The most memorable quality attaching to the sayings of eminent men is not usually the wit, or the wisdom, or the truth of the saying, but the stamp of a distinct personality upon it. A hundred wise or witty sayings go astray in the world, and get fathered upon wrong parents, for every one sharply marked characteristic saying that thus goes astray. For example, Goethe's sayings are, very many of them, really wise and instructive, but it is often difficult—extremely difficult—to remember from whom they proceeded, because they are not stamped with a distinct personality. "Stupidity is without anxiety," or "Architecture is petrified music," or "Mastery is often considered a kind of egotism," for instance, are all sayings of interest, but not sayings which shed much light on the character of the sayer, and, therefore, not closely associated with the sayer.

But when George III. said, "Was there ever such
stuff as great parts of Shakespeare? Is there not
sad stuff? But one must not say it," it is
impossible to forget this courageous attempt of the
poor old King to cut himself out, as it were, in a
bas-relief on the background of Shakespeare, and
to mark even his British deference to a widespread
admiration which he did not in the least share.
Mr. Bent might also have recalled King George's
remark, when he was asked to give preferment to
Archdeacon Paley, and replied, with reference to
Paley's celebrated illustration of the artificial
character of the institution of property taken from
the demeanour of a crowd of pigeons scrambling for
their share of a heap of corn,—"What, Paley, Paley,
pigeon-Paley? No, no, no, no." George III.
gained from his crown only the ability, which most
dull people lack, to have confidence in himself,—to
hold his own opinion against the universe, however
"infinitely little" that opinion may have been; and
it is this power to annex an opinion, to make it part
of a man's own character, much more even than the
greatness or truth of it, or even the brilliant manner
in which it is expressed, which makes it memorable
for us. George III.'s sayings are, like his own image,
stamped on copper, poor in expression, but very
strongly stamped. It was the same with Madame
de Pompadour's celebrated expression of recklessness,—"*Après nous, le déluge,*" a saying which has
become part of history, partly from its truth, partly
from its vivid expression of the selfishness and
recklessness which made it historical. And it is
this quality of personal expressiveness which, when
the character so stamped is not poor, but has
anything magnificent or noble in it, that makes a

great saying take rank with a good deed. Louis
XIV.'s declaration on his death-bed to Madame de
Maintenon, "I imagined it more difficult to die," as
though *his* departure at least must have involved a
convulsion of nature ; and Pitt's grand farewell to
power, when he returned, dying, from Bath, "Fold
up the map of Europe," are excellent specimens of
the sort of sayings which, though containing no
thought at all, nothing but a great consciousness of
power, yet impress us more than the most vivid
wisdom or the most poignant wit. This is why
dignity tells for so much in a saying of this kind,—
for so much more, indeed, than even truth. Burke's
grand sentence on the hustings, when referring to
the death of another candidate, "What shadows we
are, and what shadows we pursue !" makes an even
greater impression on the imagination than the
other sentence, "I do not know how to draw up an
indictment against a whole people," not because it
embodies half the political wisdom of the second
sentence, but because it recalls Burke and his soaring imagination more impressively to the mind.
Even Lord Chesterfield, with all his thinness and
superficiality, makes his mark upon us, directly he
begins to delineate himself. "There is a certain
dignity to be kept up in pleasures as well as in
business," and, "Knowledge may give weight, but
accomplishments give lustre, and many more people
see than weigh," paint so exactly a man thoughtfully
and consistently anxious about appearances, that
they impress us almost as much as one of Dr.
Johnson's vivid self-portraitures of a much nobler
kind. Indeed, they impress us not only almost as
much, but for nearly the same reason, that by
imagining the man who lived in appearances, they

throw up in strong relief on our minds the recollection of men to whom mere appearances were naught.

Sayings, however excellent, which do not convey in them any self-portraiture are seldom vividly associated with their true authors. How many people will remember who it was that said— "Nothing is certain but death and taxes," or, "We must all hang together, else we shall all hang separately," or even "It is better to wear out than rust out," which last does represent the energy of a certain kind of temperament, but energy so common that it marks rather a class than an individual? Benjamin Franklin said the two first sayings, and Bishop Cumberland the last; but I should be surprised to find any one in a company of literary men who could have pronounced on the spot to whom any one of the three was to be attributed. On the other hand, we seldom misappropriate sayings containing much less that it is worth while to remember, if only they vividly portray a memorable figure, — like Frederick the Great's indignant, "Wollt ihr immer leben?" ("Do you fellows want to live for ever?"), when his soldiers showed some disinclination to being shot down (a saying which Mr. Bent has forgotten, though he has included several by the same speaker much less remarkable); or Gambetta's peremptory "Il faudra ou se soumettre ou se démettre," of Marshal MacMahon's "Government of Combat." Thus, the most impressive of all sayings are probably those of great rulers who contrived to embody the profound confidence they felt that a life of command was before them in a few weighty words. Julius Cæsar's "Veni, vidi, vici," and his question to the skipper who feared for the loss of his boat, "What dost thou fear, when Cæsar is on board?" or his disdainful apology for an unjust divorce, "Cæsar's wife ought to be free even from suspicion," are likely to be in every one's mouth as long as the world lasts. And so, perhaps, is Napoleon's "I succeeded not Louis ₁IV. but Charlemagne," and the same great man's remark, "Imagination rules the world," and, "I ought to have died at Waterloo."

But the most influential of all great sayings are those which combine great force and weight of character with a precept, express or implied. Thus, Cavour's remarkable prophecy, written seven-and-twenty years before its fulfilment, "In my dreams I see myself already Minister of the Kingdom of Italy,"—the most impressive of all precepts to have faith in great national cravings; or, again, his expressive saying, "In politics nothing is so absurd as rancour;" or, "I will have no state of siege; any one can govern with a state of siege," will do more to keep Italy united, to keep her Governments statesmanlike, and to keep her people free, than reams of argument from men less memorable and less potent. Has not Danton's "Let us be terrible, to prevent the people from becoming so," and his still more celebrated, "De l'audace, encore de l'audace, et toujours de l'audace!" done more to excite an unfortunate enthusiasm for deeds of terror done in the name of the people, than all the windy eloquence of the Gironde or the Mountain? When a man once manages to compress a strong character, —good or bad—into a pithy sentence which claims to regulate the conduct of others, he lives after death in a sense denied to the great majority, even of men of genius, though his posthumous life may be either for evil or for good.

Indeed, the essence of the grandest sayings appears to be that in such sayings the speaker flings down his glove to all the forces which are fighting against him, and deliberately regards himself as the champion in some dramatic conflict the centre of which he is. Cromwell's "Paint me as I am," and the more elaborate though not more memorable, "I have sought the Lord night and day that He would rather slay me than put me upon the doing of this work," or his reputed saying of Charles, "We will cut off his head with the crown on it," all implied his supreme conviction that he was the involuntary Minister of a great series of providential acts. It is the same with Mirabeau's contemptuous thrusting aside of the part taken by Lafayette with the scornful remark, "He would fain be a Grandison-Cromwell!" and still more with his inflated, but still genuinely sincere, avowal in the Constitutional Assembly, "When I shake my terrible locks, all France trembles," and his brushing away of the thought "Impossible,"—"Never mention that stupid word again." Even Voltaire in his flippant way regarded himself as the one personal enemy of the Roman Catholic Church, when he said in reply to a friend who had noticed his reverence as the Host passed, and who asked whether he had been reconciled to the Church, "We bow, but do not speak." It is true that many such sayings acquire their dramatic meaning by the artificial moderation rather than the emphasis of their language, as when the Duke of Wellington spoke of the battle of Navarino simply as "an untoward event;" but this, too, was supreme assumption in disguise, for it meant that he was able entirely to ignore its drift as a battle, and to concentrate his attention and the attention of the world solely on its tendency to unsettle "the balance of power." The perfect silence in which he passed over the commonplace view of Navarino, and insisted on looking at it solely in the attitude of a diplomatist, indicated in the most graphic manner how completely indifferent he felt to the class of consequences which would first strike the popular mind. His supreme indifference to the Turkish disaster as a disaster was quite Olympian. Perhaps the finest thing ever said was Burke's answer to Pitt, who declared that England and the British Constitution were safe till the Day of Judgment,—"It is the day of *no* judgment I am afraid of"; but it is not certain that Burke meant to convey all that the words do convey. Possibly he meant it chiefly as a sarcasm on Pitt's want of judgment; but the larger sense of the saying, in which it means that it is not the day of divine judgment that is to be feared, so much as the day when the reality of divine judgment is hidden from men, and human beings go on in the frivolous, irresponsible pursuit of their own wishes, is quite worthy of Burke, and conveys a grander conception of the spiritual scales in which political negligence will be judged, than any other saying which even Burke himself has uttered.

MR. MORLEY ON APHORISMS

MR. JOHN MORLEY'S delightful lecture on "Aphorisms" should, I think, have been accompanied by some warning how easy it is to understand even the wisest aphorisms too literally, and how essential it is for those who would profit by them to accommodate themselves to the mood of the thinker to whom the aphorism is due, and not to forget that a writer who is terse and sententious cannot afford to indicate where his words exceed or fall short of the truth on which his eye is fixed. Take, for example, one of the best of the aphorisms quoted by Mr. Morley,—Goethe's saying, in his play of *Tasso*,—" A talent moulds itself in stillness, but a character in the great current of the world." As applied to Tasso's strength and Tasso's weakness,—his poetic genius, which needed stillness for its growth, and his oversensitiveness, which made him shrink from contact with the world, instead of facing it and practising in it the self-control which was absolutely essential to save his personal career from wreck,—the saying is true enough. But treat it as a universal truth, and you see how little it is really worth. Of many of the stronger characters which have attracted the admiration of the world

28

we might almost say the reverse,—that their
talents had been moulded by the great current of
the world, and their characters formed in stillness.
Dr. Johnson's and Carlyle's wonderful talents for
conversation, for instance, were undoubtedly
moulded in the great current of the world; but I
suspect that the characters of both were moulded
in stillness, in the silent wrestling of their own
natures with their own inward temptations. No
one who reads Carlyle's story can doubt that his
character moulded itself most in the comparative
solitude of his early life in Edinburgh and at
Craigenputtock, and that some of his most brilliant
literary gifts, especially his graphic and humorous
vivacity, grew rapidly after his life in London, with
its comparative bustle and hurry, began. All
depends on what the deficiencies are which need
correcting. If they be deficiencies in the power to
deal with others, no doubt they will be best
supplied, if they can be supplied at all, in the great
current of the world. But if they be deficiencies in
self-conquest and self-knowledge, then to supply
such deficiencies it may need a period of solitary
conflict such as that out of which Wordsworth
emerged after his confusion at the issue of the
French Revolution had subsided, or that which
secured for Cardinal Newman opportunity for the
fermentation of his deepest religious principles,
during his voyage in the Mediterranean and his illness in Sicily in 1832-33. I believe that almost
as many characters of the higher order have been
moulded in stillness as in the crush of life, and that
almost as many talents of the higher order—debat-
ing talents, administrative talents, strategic talents,
for instance—have been moulded in the crush of life

as have been developed in stillness. It all depends
on what the character to be moulded is, and what
the talent. There are characters which never gain
their true significance till they have passed through
the fire of solitary conflict. And there are talents
which never come to light at all except in the
collisions of active life. Take, again, Vauvenargues'
saying which Mr. Morley so much admires,—
"Great thoughts come from the heart." Well,
that is true, and of the greatest significance, if it be
taken to mean only that men of noble intellects
who are deficient in large-heartedness will never
say things to stir man to the greatest depth ; but
then, it is equally true that men of the largest
hearts who have not got lucid and searching
intellects, are utterly incapable of saying them,—
nay, that if you compare the great thoughts of men
like Bacon, who was certainly deficient in what is
usually called "heart," with the thoughts of men
as good even as Fénélon (who was not at all
deficient in intellectual vision, though his heart was
clearly better than his head), few would doubt that
Bacon's aphorisms are likely to be remembered far
longer and more widely than Fénélon's. To speak
accurately, great thoughts are really born in the
head and not in the heart, though it is perfectly
true that the heads of men deficient in heart miss
something which would have made their greatest
thoughts greater still. You might almost as well
say that the power of steam is due to the fire alone,
and ignore the water whose expansion into vapour
is the immediate instrument through which the
energy works, as say that great thoughts come
from the heart, and not rather from the action
of the heart on the intellect by whose agency it

really effects its purpose. I rather wonder at Mr.
Morley's excessive admiration for Vauvenargues'
aphorism because, as it seems to me, Mr. Morley is
inclined to lay almost too much stress on the
sententious form of the saying, which is wholly due
to the mind, and to make too little of wise thoughts
which are not cast into a setting of happy and
epigrammatic words. For example, he dwells very
justly on the wisdom of Bacon's saying that " Being
without well-being is a curse, and the greater the
being, the greater the curse,"—a fine saying, of
which the epigrammatic chiselling is almost the
finest part, and of which it would be very difficult
to assert that it came from the heart at all. If it
came from anything deeper than the intellect, it
came from the conscience, and represented rather
the sad experience of a mighty nature's inward
discords, than the range of its sympathies or the
loftiness of its aspirations. Yet I doubt whether
any aphorism amongst all those referred to by Mr.
Morley is more accurately true without qualification
than this of Bacon's. Certainly it is far deeper and
truer than the rather clumsy and long-winded one
which Mr. Morley quotes from the close of the
fourth book of Goethe's *Tame Proverbs*. Indeed,
while Mr. Morley lays theoretically almost too
much stress on the epigrammatic form of the
aphorism,—and, of course, epigrammatic form is
essential to make it sparkle like a brilliant in the
memory,—he appears to accord almost too much
credit to Goethe's not unfrequently rather ill-cut
and clumsily set wisdom. For my part, I am
disposed to admire Goethe's proverbial sayings most
when they are put into the mouth of such a being
as Mephistopheles, and therefore polished so as to

express a certain scorn. And yet these are certainly not the great sayings " which come from the heart." Take, for instance, Mephistopheles' remark to the raw student on the procedure of professorial analysis, namely, that—

> He who would know and paint a living thing,
> Must first expel the spirit from its frame,
> Then all the broken bits together bring,—
> Though, wanting that, it is not quite the same.

That is true and fine, but not so terse as some one's aphorism (was it not Coleridge's) that analysis first kills what it would explain. Again, there is wonderful sagacity in Mephistopheles' sarcastic remark to the same student after he has made him feel an evil passion thrilling his blood and stirring him into excitement :—

> Grey, friend, is Theory,—true though Theory be,—
> And green the foliage of Life's golden tree.

These are hardly sayings which " come from the heart," and yet they are better, I think, than most of Goethe's proverbs. In fact, Mr. Morley is hardly justified in praising the aphorisms which come from the heart so much more than the aphorisms elaborated by a keen and active intellect, though I quite admit that when the intellect is equally broad and active, the great sayings which spring out of ardent sympathies are greater than those which spring only out of bitter personal experience. Mr. Morley quotes as one of the better class of aphorisms with which he illustrated his masterly speech, Lichtenberg's aphorism that

"Enthusiasts without capacity are the really dangerous people"; but was that one which came from the heart or the intellect? and does it not need great qualification before we can assent to its truth? I should have said that enthusiasts without capacity are absolutely harmless, but that the danger arises where you have enthusiasm endowed with great capacity for persuasion, but without great capacity for practical insight. I esteem as highly as Mr. Morley the aphorism as to the power of goodness, when it goes wrong, to stir up revolution, and the aphorism as to the folly of those wise men who allow themselves to be irritated by stupidity. But neither of these aphorisms seems to me to come from the heart. Here, nevertheless, is one on the same subject, of absolutely modern origin, which does come from the heart; and though it is not so finely cut as most of Mr. Morley's, I believe that it contains as much true wisdom as any of those that he has quoted:—"Why not feel as much sympathy for the dull as for the sickly? Do not the feeble in mind often make as gallant an effort to carry on the business of life under adverse circumstances as the feeble in body? Yet we pity the second and laugh at the first." That seems to me true wisdom, and the book from which it is taken— Miss Rickard's *Here and Hereafter* — is full of wisdom of a like kind, that only wants a certain epigrammatic form to make it a most memorable book. Yet probably this want of the epigrammatic form will prevent it from attaining all the popularity of other collections of aphorisms of very inferior calibre, just because the wisdom that "comes from the heart" makes comparatively

little impression on mankind, unless it is shaped
by wit into a keen and glittering gem. Aphorisms
to live for ever should be "winged words," and
something more; in addition to their wings, they
should have something of a sting.

THE USE OF PARADOX

THE "Paradox Club," to which Mr. Edward Garnett has just introduced us in an agreeable little book distinguished by a good deal of poetical feeling, appears to use the word "paradox" rather in the general sense of unnatural or extravagant, than in its more proper sense of that which administers a kind of slap in the face to conventional opinion, in order to make those who entertain the conventional opinion better understand, not necessarily that they are wrong, but certainly that they have forgotten how very far from plain-sailing it is to be right. The use of paradox is to awaken people to the various unsolved difficulties and evident shortcomings in judgments which seem to be conspicuous for their good sense, and which may, indeed, really be as near an approach to good sense as any judgment on the subject which could be embodied in anything like the same number of words, but which conceal half the obstacles in the way of holding the opinion adopted, and foreshorten all that they do not conceal. Thus, it is not a paradox to say, as one of the Paradox Club says, "In apprenticing a boy to the most humdrum business, we can guarante, his future, provided he is fairly dishonest"; ore

35

as another of the Club says, who maintains the superiority of woman to man, "The time is approaching when man will have the courage to sacrifice himself to his convictions, and refuse to drive a woman to the degradation of marrying her inferior." These are extravagant sayings, but they are not paradoxes. A paradox is a saying which, by its apparently flat contradiction of what is ordinarily taken to be true, forces us to think more deeply of the assumptions involved in that ordinary thought, as, for instance, the Greek paradox that "the half is often more than the whole." This saying brings vividly before the mind how much better it is to set other people fairly thinking for themselves on a great question, than to think it fully out for them, since in the former case you get their minds into activity, and give them a motive for keeping up that activity after your stimulus is removed; whereas if you round off the process for them and satisfy them, they probably relapse into inactivity almost as soon as they have followed you to the end. So, too, it was a paradox when Lessing said that if there were held out to him in one hand truth, and in the other the love of truth, and he might choose freely between the two, he would prefer the latter to the former,—a paradox which really outparadoxes paradox, because it is simply impossible for any one who with all his heart desires the truth, to be willing to rest in the condition of unsatisfied desire, and to forego the attainment of what he so profoundly yearns for. But though Lessing's was a paradox which exceeds all legitimate paradoxes, and, so to speak, gives itself the lie in the very moment of utterance, Lessing had, of course, a real meaning in it, and that meaning was that the *active* love of truth (which far from being satiated and chloroformed into indifference by the possession of truth, would only be stimulated to propagating the truth found in new fields and to the prosecution of new truth) is a far better thing than torpid and indolent acquiescence in true propositions, which, though it exercises a man's memory, need not stir a single new ripple of life in either his intellect or his heart. Hence, though Lessing's paradox exceeded the bounds of paradox, it answered the purpose of calling attention to the essential characteristic of the love of truth,—that it is not a wish to possess something that we can keep within ourselves, but a wish to be possessed by something greater and nobler than ourselves. In the same way Cardinal Newman was always fond of legitimate paradox,—though he kept his paradox well within the bounds which Lessing permitted it to pass,—as, for instance, when he said that the first condition for the capacity of true spiritual love was to be capable of true spiritual hate :—

> And wouldst thou reach, rash scholars mine,
> Love's high unruffled state ?
> Awake ! Thy easy dreams resign,
> First learn thee how to hate ;—
>
> Hatred of sin, and zeal, and fear,
> Lead up the holy hill ;
> Track them till Charity appear
> A self-denial still.
>
> Dim is the philosophic flame,
> By thought severe unfed :
> Book-lore ne'er served when trial came,
> Nor gifts, when faith was dead.

The paradox there which draws attention to the difference between the higher love and mere kindliness, or the wish to make every one more comfortable, asserts that the former implies all sorts of bitter self-denial, and often the special self-denial of making even those who are dearest very much the reverse of comfortable, and so it is a very happy illustration of what a paradox should be. Probably no man has ever been capable of the highest charity to whom that highest charity has not at times been a self-denial, as it must have been to St. Paul, when he first admitted the thought that those whom he had, with a good conscience, been persecuting for their desertion of orthodox Judaism, were perhaps more deeply possessed by the love of God than himself. St. Paul was indeed just an instance of what Dr. Newman meant by saying, that the power to hate truly what is evil must be involved in the power to love truly what is good, and must, indeed, usually precede the growth of the highest kind of love. There is a power to hate in all the noblest love, as there is a power to love in all the noblest hate, which prevents personal feeling of either kind from degenerating into "respect of persons,"—that is, into a passion which has regard to the person only, and not to the deeper spiritual quality which either dignifies or degrades the person. Thus, nothing shows more completely the deficiency in Shelley's apparently angelic power of love, than his deficiency of the power to hate what is hideous in those whom he supposed himself to love. His treatment of his friend Hogg, for instance, after Hogg's most disgraceful conduct towards his wife, betrays the elf-like quality of Shelley's character, which had not in it the highest capacity of love because it had not in it the highest capacity of hate.

But the freest use of paradox for the purpose of calling attention to the truth which conventional common sense misses through the automatic character of the habits of mind by which it lives, is to be found in some of the greatest of the inspired writings. Thus, Isaiah is one of the greatest masters of poetical paradox in the literature of the world; as, for example, when he enlarges on the blessings of affliction or the fertility which is engendered in the heart of barren desolation :—
"Sing, O barren, thou that didst not bear; break forth into singing, and cry aloud, thou that didst not travail with child : for more are the children of the desolate than the children of the married wife, saith the Lord." And, again, where has there been a nobler flight of imagination than in the passage in which the prophet calls upon those who have no money to buy and eat, to buy wine and milk "without money and without price"? No other language could have made so startling the contrast between the poverty of the blessings that are bought with human wealth, and the riches of those which are bought without it, though not without lavishing freely the treasures of the heart and soul. But the most fruitful use of paradox that was ever made is the use of it made by the Saviour himself in words that have probably pierced deeper than any other words in the Gospel,—" Verily, verily, I say unto you, Except a corn of wheat fall into the ground and die, it abideth alone : but if it die, it bringeth forth much fruit. He that loveth his life shall lose it; and he that hateth his life in this world shall keep it unto life eternal." That is

paradox, but paradox which opens the deepest meanings of life, instead of paradox which leads astray by the extravagance of false analogies.

The need for paradox is no doubt rooted deep in the very nature of the use we make of language. Just as everything that we do habitually, we come to do automatically, without being in any real sense conscious of what we do, or even of the purposes in the execution of which we first did it, so language is no sooner employed habitually than it comes to be used as a mere algebra,—to the meaning of which we pay no more attention than we pay to the particular sounds that go to make up the ringing of a bell which reminds us that certain daily duties have to be done. And there is no harm in this when the only object of the language is to remind us of the mechanical duties which we have to discharge; but, unfortunately, there is harm in it when the use to which we ought to turn our words is to remind us of the great realities of life, and when they fail to do so simply from the narcotic influence of habitual use. Then we need awakening anew to the old significance which lay beneath the words which have ceased to exert any magic over us; and nothing awakens the true meaning of language like paradox, which, while it appears to contradict the superficial sense attaching to the formulas of our daily life, really points to the hidden depth beneath them and the unseen height above, and restores to us the freshness and the wonder of the thoughts which had shrivelled with our constant manipulation of them till they seemed to have lost their sap. This function of paradox is the same which is ascribed to that divine life itself which makes all things new, and which the human

poet or creator humbly shares with the creative
power of God himself :—

> He found us when the age had bound
> Our souls in its benumbing round ;
> He spoke and loosed our hearts in tears.
> He laid us as we lay at birth
> On the cool flowery lap of earth,
> Smiles broke from us and we had ease ;
> The hills were round us, and the breeze
> Went o'er the sunlit fields again ;
> Our foreheads felt the wind and rain.
> Our youth returned ; for there was shed
> On spirits that had long been dead,
> Spirits dried up and closely furl'd,
> The freshness of the early world.

IS IRONY A FORM OF THE LUDICROUS?

IN the interesting paper on "The Theory of the Ludicrous" which Mr. Lilly contributes to the May number of the *Fortnightly Review*, he gives us twenty-one species of the genus "Ludicrous," as well as Schopenhauer's acute explanation of the essential character of the ludicrous, in which he concurs. According to Schopenhauer, if I understand him rightly,—like most German thinkers he is a little too technical to be perfectly lucid,—there is always something paradoxical in the ludicrous, and what causes laughter is the realising of the paradox in the same instant in which you also realise how truly from one point of view, and one only, those objects are related to each other which from every other point of view are essentially incongruous. For instance, when Hood says, in "Miss Kilmansegg and her Precious Leg," that Miss Kilmansegg was killed—

> By a golden weapon not oaken,
> In the morning they found her all alone
> Dead and bloody and cold as stone,
> For the leg, the golden leg was gone,
> And the golden bowl was broken,—

the essence of the ludicrous element in the passage is the contrast between the meaning of the word

"golden" as applied to the golden bowl, and the
same word as applied to a manufactured object like
the golden leg, although both, in a different sense,
were really precious.   And again, when Hood says
a little farther on—

> Gold, still gold, it haunted her yet,
> At the Golden Lion the inquest met,
> Its foreman a Carver and Gilder.
> And the jury debated from ten to three,
> And they brought it in as *felo de se*
> Because her own leg had killed her,—

Schopenhauer would regard the essence of the
ludicrous in that verse as the paradox of treating
the use of her golden leg as the instrument of her
murder, just as if she were quite as personally
responsible for what that lump of gold had effected
as she would have been if it had been an organic
part of her own body.   Well, that no doubt is a
perfectly true account of the essential element in
everything ludicrous.   To give another example of
the same incongruous mixture of likeness and
unlikeness—Dickens describes a London mother as
seizing on her naughty child, and that seizure as
being followed "by a rapid succession of sharp
sounds resembling applause," resulting in the discovery of the child on the coolest paving-stone of
the court, "weeping bitterly and loudly lamenting."
Here the ludicrous element in the passage is the
really close connection and yet striking contrast
between the sound of applause and the sound of a
particular kind of humiliating punishment applied
to a naughty child.   Schopenhauer's analysis of the
ludicrous is essentially sound, though he makes it
needlessly pedantic by his use of such words as

" concept " and "subsumption" in relation to so very simple and elementary a matter. To take a third and still simpler instance of the ludicrous, a man who was watching the motions of a herd of cows saw one of them running very fast down hill suddenly turn a complete somersault, and the startling contrast between the lumbering figure and the motion of the cow and the apparent agility of the feat, set him off into a fit of laughter from which he found it hard to recover—the clumsiness and the apparent agility were at once so inconsistent with each other and yet so closely united in the same physical act. In all these cases Schopenhauer's explanation of the essential character of the ludicrous applies strictly.

But is it not also essential to the ludicrousness of any paradox that the incongruity should be, or should at all events appear to be, real and not merely apparent ? I ask this question because Mr. Lilly includes "irony" among the species of the ludicrous ; whereas the higher irony—irony such as we sometimes find in Carlyle and sometimes in Swift, irony such as we find in Sophocles, irony such as we find in Elijah and Isaiah—seems to me not in any sense ludicrous, but in the highest sense sublime or even pathetic. Must it not be said that where the analogy which furnishes the principle of the likeness goes much deeper than the superficial paradox which furnishes the basis of the contrast,— and this is always the case in the higher irony,— the effect is not ludicrous at all, and may be even profoundly and overpoweringly solemn, like that stroke of the two-edged sword which divides asunder spirit and flesh ? When Elijah taunted the priests of Baal with the suggestion that their god was

probably on a journey, and that they would have
to shriek much louder to gain his attention to their
prayers, if indeed they could gain it at all, surely
the irony was not a species of the ludicrous, but a
species of the most sublime invective, as it proved
itself to be when it excited the priests of Baal to
self-torture in order that they might arrest their
god's attention.   To ensure any paradox containing
the essence of the ludicrous, the analogy must be
more apparent than real, and the paradox essentially
real and not merely apparent.   In all ludicrous
conceptions the incongruity is of the essence of the
situation, and the congruity is purely superficial.
It is the incongruity as brought out by the merely
superficial congruity which excites the laughter.
But in all the cases of piercing irony the real
resemblance is far deeper than the superficial
contrast.   Even when an idle boy translated
"Ignavia" "ignorance," and the master interposed,
"No, sir, but the *cause* of ignorance," the irony was
not a signal for laughter, but for serious reflection
in those who could at all appreciate its force ; and
that is but a very feeble illustration of the depth
to which irony often goes in cutting to the heart of
hearts.   Bishop Thirlwall, in his striking essay on
the irony of Sophocles, gives many illustrations of
the depth and poignancy of that attitude of mind ;
and I should say that in its higher phases it passes
quite out of the category of the ludicrous into a
region far beyond the play of the fancy or the
imagination, and may be said rather to draw blood
than to excite laughter.   May I not call it an instance of the very highest irony when our Lord
replies to the request of the sons of Zebedee, that
they might sit the one on His right hand and the

other on His left in His kingdom, "Ye know not
what ye ask.   Are ye able to drink of the cup
that I shall drink of, and to be baptized with the
baptism that I am baptized with?"   And when
they assure Him that they are, He goes on sadly:
"Ye shall drink indeed of my cup, and be baptized
with the baptism that I am baptized with: but to
sit on my right hand, and on my left, is not mine to
give, but it shall be given to them for whom it is
prepared of my Father."   No irony can be deeper
than that, and yet instead of exciting laughter it
goes far deeper than the source of tears.

No doubt there is a kind of bitter irony, such
irony as Heinrich Heine's, which is piercing irony,
and yet in some sense ludicrous, because while the
depth of the analogy between very closely related
ideas is undeniable, Heine manages to make the
superficial contrast so striking and emphatic that the
incongruity predominates for the moment over the
radical resemblance.   Matthew Arnold said of him
in some of his clumsiest, but also his most searching
verse:—

> The Spirit of the World
> Beholding the absurdity of men,
> Their vaunts, their feats,—let a sardonic smile
> For one short moment wander o'er his lips.
> *That smile was Heine!*   For its earthly hour
> The strange guest sparkled; now, 'tis pass'd away.

And that was true enough.   Heine's irony was the
keenest irony, and yet he rioted so in the mere sense
of the absurd, that he mixed absurdities with his
deepest and truest irony (as also did Swift), but
none the less, if you examine Heine's best irony,
you will find the absurdity adventitious and easily

removable; while the depth of the analogy on which he strikes is real and serious enough. For example, take the following given by Matthew Arnold as an example of Heine's indomitable ironic spirit:—

I have said he was not pre-eminently brave, but in the astonishing force of spirit with which he retained his activity of mind, even his gaiety, amid all his suffering, and went on composing with undiminished fire to the last, he was truly brave. Nothing could clog that aerial lightness. " Pouvez-vous siffler ? " his doctor asked him one day when he was almost at his last gasp ;—"siffler," as everyone knows, has the double meaning of to whistle and· to hiss :—" Helas ! non," was his whispered answer ; " pas même une comédie de M. Scribe ! " M. Scribe is, or was the favourite dramatist of the French Philistine.

The sarcasm at M. Scribe is very bitter and laughable, but Heine's attack upon himself as wishing to expend his very last breath in hissing a bad French play was sadder and more trenchant irony than any sarcasm on M. Scribe. Irony, as a rule, is not ludicrous. It is ludicrous only when it touches very trivial subjects. Its deeper stroke is not only serious, it is often profoundly tragic. Hence, though irony may be and often is a form of the ludicrous, it is only the lighter specimens of it which can be so treated. The deepest irony is not a provocative to laughter, for it often goes too deep for tears.

THE GENIUS OF DICKENS

WHILE all English-speaking peoples to whom the telegraph has carried the sad news of the death of Dickens are realising for the first time how vast a fund of enjoyment they owe to him, and how much happier than their fathers they have been in living in the time when Dickens gave a new province to English literature and new resources to English speech, it is the natural time to ask ourselves how we should all be mourning if, with the final vanishing of his figure from amongst us, it were inevitable for the innumerable crowd of Dickens's whimsical creations to be totally obliterated from our minds. Let any man seriously number the acquaintances, the continual right of personal intercourse with whom he would buy at the cost of renouncing for ever the acquaintance of Dickens's best creations, and he will soon become conscious of the greatness of the sacrifice which would be required of him. How many of our friends should we not give up before letting loose our hold on Mrs. Nickleby and the old gentleman who tossed vegetable marrows over her garden wall ? How many of our servants would receive warning before we consented to discharge " the Marchioness " from our memory, and forfeited for ever our vested rights in Sam Weller and Job Trotter ? How many

schoolmasters would retain their schools if parents
had to choose between their closing their doors and
the final breaking-up of Dr. Blimber's and his
successor in their minds? Where is the caller
whose cards we would not consent never to see
again, rather than lose the picture of the pack Mr.
Toots used to leave "for Mr. Dombey," "for Mrs.
Dombey," "for Miss Dombey"? Would not
London sacrifice fifty real boarding-houses without a
sigh, rather than lose its "Todger's"? And where
is the popular preacher, however large his tabernacle,
whom England would not surrender with resignation
rather than surrender the memory—fragrant, of
much rarer and more delightful odours than pine-
apple rum-and-water—of the immortal Shepherd?
Which of our thieves and housebreakers should we
not be inclined to pardon by acclamation rather than
sentence either Charley Bates or the Dodger to
intellectual transportation for life? Would not
even America—libelled America—part with many
an eminent candidate for the next Presidency rather
than lose its Pogram, or its Hominy, or its Jefferson
Brick? How long we might go on with such a list
of alternatives I dare not even try to calculate, but
I am certain that I am speaking well within the
mark when I say that there are at least a hundred
of Dickens's figures in every reading Englishman's
mind, no one of whom would he consent to lose to
keep the acquaintance of one-half of the living men
whom he would speak to with friendly greeting if he
met them in the streets. And if you add to the
definite loss of typical forms, the even greater
indefinite loss in the sense of humour which these
creatures have stimulated, or even generated, in
otherwise dull-minded, matter-of-fact Britons, the

debt of ever-accumulating mental wealth which we owe to the works of the great man who has just left us becomes immeasurable.

What was the secret—if it be possible in any brief way to describe the secret—of a genius so rich to overflowing in the creation of English types of humour ? Mainly it was, I think, due to three great literary gifts combined,—a sense of humour as delicate as Charles Lamb's, and much more inventive and active, which was at the basis of Dickens's genius, and by which he *sorted* his conceptions ; a power of observation so enormous that he could photograph almost everything he saw ; and, perhaps, partly as the result of these two powers in combination, but partly, it may be, of some others, a marvellous faculty of multiplying at will, and yet with an infinity of minute variety, new illustrations of any trait the type of which he had once mastered. Indeed, just as the great mystery of physiology is said to be how a single living cell multiplied itself into a tissue composed of an indefinite number of similar cells, so the great intellectual mystery of Dickens's fertile genius was his power of reduplicating a single humorous conception of character into an elaborate structure of strictly analogous conceptions. His greatest successes have always been gained on types of some complexity, such as that smart, impudent cockney, be it serving-boy, or serving-man, or adventurer, which is the basis of such characters as Bailey Junior's, Sam Weller's, Jingle's, and several others ; and his greatest failures have been made on attempts to convert individual peculiarities, like Mr. Jaggers' habit of biting his thumb, or Mr. Carker's of showing his teeth, into the keynote of a character.   But take which of his books you will, from the first to the one of which the publication had only just reached its third number at his death, and you will find the same secret of success and failure,—the former, the secret of success, inexhaustible power of illustrating an adequately conceived physical type of character, such as Mrs. Gamp, or Mr. Pecksniff, or Mr. Squeers, or either of the Wellers, or Mr. Winkle, or the Marchioness, or Miss Miggs, or Mr. Toots, or Mrs. Pipchin, or Noah Claypole, or Bradley Headstone, or Mr. Venus, —the latter, the secret of failure, a monotonous repetition of some trait too individual to admit of any adequate variety, and which consequently becomes the mere incarnation of a bodily habit or trick, such as the Fat Boy, and Joe Willett, and the brothers Cheeryble, and Cousin Feenix, and Mr. Jaggers, and "the Analytical Chemist," and a number of others. But whether a success or a failure, Mr. Dickens's characters are invariably structures raised by his humour on a single physical aspect. Sam Weller is always the smart or impudent cockney serving-man, — everything he says corresponds exactly with Mr. Dickens's first description of him as the sharp boots in the Borough inn, with a loose, red, neck-handkerchief round his neck, and an old white hat stuck awry on his head; Mrs. Gamp is always the snuffy old monthly nurse; the Marchioness always the keen-witted, stunted child-servant; Mr. Pecksniff always the candid hypocrite looking over a high wall of collar; and so on with all his characters. There is not, so far as I remember, a single successful character in all Dickens's works of which you could conceive more than one aspect. Mr. Swiveller is always roystering, good-natured and sentimental; Mr. Toots always nervous, good-natured, and idiotic; Dr. Blimber always pompous, patronising, and school-masterish; Miss Miggs always spiteful, vain, and cunning; Mr. Silas Wegg always sly, calculating, and quoting sentimental ballads; Mr. Venus always low-spirited, weak-eyed, and anatomical; and so forth. The great and unfailing wonder is how any novel-writer who gives so absolutely identical a tone to all the characters he conceives, manages to make them so full to over-flowing of fresh vitality and infinite humour. No one ever gets tired of Dick Swiveller, or Bailey Junior, or Mr. Pecksniff, or Mrs. Gamp, or old Mr. Weller, or Fanny Squeers, or Mr. Lillyvick, or Sawyer late Knockemorf, or Barnaby Rudge and his raven, or Simon Tappertit, or even of Jenny Wren. And it is marvellous that it should be so, for all these are always precisely consistent with the first glimpse we get of them; and with any genius less rich in variations on the same air than Dickens's we should be sick of them in no time.

But then no writer ever had the power which Dickens had of developing the same fundamental conception in so infinitely humorous a variety of form. Hunt through all Mrs. Gamp's monthly-nurse disquisition, and you will never find there a repetition,—excepting always in those great land-marks of the conception, the vast selfishness and self-admiration, the permanent desire to have the bottle left on "the chimley piece" for use "when so dispoged," and the mutual confidence between her and her mythical friend Mrs. Harris. With these necessary exceptions there is not one single repetition of a speech or a maxim. The central cell, as I may call it, of the character has multiplied itself a thousandfold without a single echo of an old idea. The marvel of Dickens is the exquisite ease, perfect physical consistency, and yet wonderful variety of paths by which he always makes his characters glide back into their leading trait. His greater characters are perfect labyrinths of novel autobiographical experience, all leading back to the same central cell. Mrs. Gamp, for instance, is barely introduced before she introduces also to the reader her great and original contrivance for praising herself, and intimating decently to all the world the various stipulations on which alone she agrees to "sick or monthly,"—that intimate friend whose sayings cannot be verified by direct reference to herself, because she is in reality only the reflex form of No. 1,—Mrs. Harris. "Mrs. Gamp," says this imaginary lady, as reported by Mrs. Gamp herself, "if ever there was a sober creetur to be got at eighteenpence a day for working-people and three-and-six for gentlefolks,— night-watching," said Mrs. Gamp with emphasis, "being an extra charge, you are that inwalable person." "Mrs. Harris," I says to her, "don't name the charge, *for if I could afford to lay all my fellow-creeturs out for nothink*, I would gladly do it, sech is the love I bears 'em." But this, we need hardly say, is a great humourist's creation *on a hint* from human life, and not human life itself. Any actual Mrs. Gamp no doubt might have invented sayings for actual friends of her own, but would never have indulged in the intellectual audacity of reproducing herself as her own best friend, and investing her with another name and a great variety of imaginary babies. And so, too, it is the great humourist, and not Mrs. Gamp, who answers so generously for her willingness "to lay all my fellow-creeturs out for

nothink, sech is the love I bears 'em." Note, too, the inexhaustible humour with which Dickens makes her slide back with the utmost naturalness and quite involuntarily into the provision for her own wants and the recollection of her own history, when she is apparently consulting for the comfort of others. She is making tea for Mrs. Jonas Chuzzlewit:—
" And quite a family it is to make tea for," said Mrs. Gamp, " and wot a happiness to do it! My good young woman," to the servant-girl, " p'raps somebody would like to try a new-laid egg or two not biled too hard. Likeways a few rounds of buttered toast, *first cuttin' off the crust, in consequence of tender teeth,* which Gamp himself, Mrs. Chuzzlewit, at one blow, being in liquor, struck out four, two single and two double, as was took by Mrs. Harris for a keepsake, and is carried in her pocket at the present hour, along with two cramp bones, a bit of ginger, and a grater, like a blessed infant's shoe, in tin, with a little heel to put the nutmeg in, as many times I've seen and said and used for caudle when required within the month."

The infinite number of avenues by which Mr. Dickens makes Mrs. Gamp, as Hegel would say, *return unto herself*, and the absolutely inexhaustible number of physical illustrations all of the monthly-nurse kind, by which she effects it, are the key-notes to his genius. Watch him with Mr. Pecksniff, or Bailey Junior, or old Weller the coachman,— a perfectly typical instance is his wonderful account of his second wife's death, " paying the last pike at a quarter past six," and of the condign punishment administered to Mr. Stiggins ; or watch him with Mr. Venus, or Mr. Honeythunder, or where you will, you will always note the same method, a central type out of which his mind creates all sorts of conceivable, and, to any one but himself, inconceivable, but always consistent, varieties, each and all of them full of the minutest knowledge of life, and therefore never wearying the reader. His power is like that of a moral kaleidoscope, all the various fragments of colour being supplied by actual experience, so that when you turn and turn it, and get ever new combinations, you never seem to get away from actual life, but always to be concerned with the most common-place of common-place realities. All the while, however, you are really running the changes on a single conception, but with so vast a power of illustration from the minutest experience, that you are deceived into thinking that you are dealing with a real being. Of course, no man ever really pretended to be so scrupulously candid as Mr. Pecksniff when he complained, " I have been struck this day with a walking-stick, *which I have every reason to believe* has knobs on it, on that delicate and exquisite portion of the human anatomy, the brain " ; nor was there ever any one so persistently desirous of finding disagreeable circumstances under which it would be a credit to be jolly, as Mark Tapley. This is the idealism of the author, idealism only disguised by the infinite resource of common physical detail with which he illustrates it. How little of a realist Dickens actually was in his creations of character may be seen whenever he attempts to deal with an ordinary man or woman, like Nicholas or Kate Nickleby, or again David Copperfield, who is to me quite as little real as Nicholas Nickleby, even though intended, as has always been said, for the author himself. Mortimer Lightwood and Eugene Wrayburn, in *Our Mutual Friend*, are deplorable failures, and the worthy minor Canon in *The Mystery of Edwin Drood* promised to be so too. The infinite multiplications of detailed illustrations of a single humorous type has always been Mr. Dickens's real secret of power. A realist as regards *human* nature he never was at all.

But it will be asked where, then, is the secret of Dickens's pathos, such pathos as that with which he describes little Paul Dombey's death, or Nancy's murder? Can that really come under such a rationale of his genius as I have given? In the first place, I do not believe that Dickens's pathos is by any means his strong side. He spoils his best touches by his heavy hand in harping on them. Even in the death of little Paul, a great deal too much is made of a very natural touch in itself,—the child's languid interest in the return of the golden ripple to the wall at sunset, and his fancy that he was floating with the river to the sea. Dickens is so obviously delighted with himself for this picturesque piece of sentiment, that he quite fondles his own conception. He used to give it even more of the same effect of high-strung sentimental melodrama, in reading or reciting it, than the written story itself contains. I well remember the mode in which he used to read, "The golden ripple on the wall came back again, and nothing else stirred in the room. The old, old fashion! The fashion that came in with our first garments, and will last unchanged till our race has run its course, and the wide firmament is rolled up like a scroll. The old, old fashion—Death! Oh, thank God, all who see it, for that older fashion yet of Immortality! And look upon us, angels of young children, with regards not quite estranged when the swift river bears us to the ocean." It was precisely the pathos of the Adelphi Theatre, and made the most painful impression of pathos feasting on itself. I more than doubt, then, whether Dickens can be called a great master of pathos at all. There is no true lyrical, no poetic touch about his pathos; it is, in the main, the overstrained pathos of melodrama. And that precisely agrees with my estimate of what he was greatest in. He could always abstract any single trait of human life, and collect round it all sorts of natural physical details. Just so, he describes the pity excited by little Paul's death, and frames his death-bed, as it were, in those gradual changes from light to shade, and shade to light, which take up so much of the perceptive power of a dying child. Of course, however, in all Dickens's attempts to describe, he describes with the intensity of genius. No one can fail to feel horror at the description of Sikes's feelings as he wanders about with his dog after the murder of Nancy. In the delineation of remorse he is, too, much nearer the truth of nature than in the delineation of grief. True grief needs the most delicate hand to delineate truly. A touch too much, and you perceive an affectation, and, therefore, miss the whole effect of bereavement. But remorse when it is genuine is one of the simplest of passions, and the most difficult to overpaint. Dickens, with his singular power of lavishing himself on one mood, has given some vivid pictures of this passion which deserve to live. Still this is the exception which proves the rule. He can delineate remorse for murder because there is so little limit to the feeling, so little danger of passing from the true to the falsetto tone. In general there is no delicate painting of emotion in Dickens. His love-passages are simply detestable.

By far his greatest success, here, is the mixture of profound love with worship which poor Smike feels from afar for the sister of his friend, because in that picture a certain amount of restraint was imposed on the somewhat vulgar tenderness in which his heroes and heroines otherwise delight. But this failure to depict any of the subtler emotions in their purest form, like his failure to depict single real character, as distinguished from his impersonation of a certain abstract type, surely confirms the impression that it is as a humourist, and as a humourist alone, that Dickens will be immortal. He drew one or two real moods of feeling with singular intensity, but fell into melodrama where delicacy of discrimination was requisite; but he could always accumulate round a single abstract type the most wonderful wealth of humorous illustration in the utmost detail, and it is his figures of this kind which will live for ever, not as men, but as impersonations. Molière's Tartuffe is poor and thin compared with Dickens's Pecksniff.

WHAT IS HUMOUR?

THE discussions, of which there have been some specimens in the *Spectator*, and many more elsewhere, as to the true characteristic of Charles Dickens's literary power, betray the usual difficulty in discriminating the true limits of humour and of its various subordinate species. I have even heard it denied by men of very acute and highly disciplined powers, that Dickens was in any sense a humourist of a high class; and when I have asked what then his genius really consisted in, I have been told that it lay in his wonderful command of ludicrous conceptions, but that the command of ludicrous conceptions is quite a distinct thing from true humour, which is founded in a knowledge of human nature; while a command of the ludicrous, such as Dickens displayed, may be based on little more than a strong feeling for all sorts of incongruities, and great fertility in inventing and varying them. I confess that such a distinction as this seems to me quite untenable, and that in any sense in which we can call Shakespeare one of the greatest of humourists, or Molière a great humourist, or Swift a great humourist, or Jane Austen or Thackeray great humourists, the genius of Dickens displayed

a humour richer and higher than the highest kind
attained by any of those, though some of them
were, of course, as far above Dickens in general
intellectual strength as Dickens was above Horace
Smith or Miss Burney.

I do not believe that there can be found any
definition of humour which will hold water for a
moment that will either draw a clear and impassable
line between wit and humour, or between humour
and any other subdivision of the faculty of the
ludicrous. All that keenly excites our sense of
incongruity comes in one way or other under the
same head, and it is the sense of the incongruous—
whether in that thinnest and most superficial shape
of puns or verbal tricks and artifices which form
the staple of our worst burlesques, or in the highest
of all forms in which the incongruity is brought
home to the very roots of human passion and
emotion—which constitutes the essence of every
witty, humorous, or ludicrous feat. When Pope,
parodying Sir John Denham's description of the
Thames in his poem on Cooper's Hill, likened
Welstead to a current of thin beer—

> So sweetly mawkish and so smoothly dull,
> Heady, not strong, and foaming though not full—

he gave what would be ordinarily called a tolerable
illustration of smartness in invective,—in other
words, of the lower order of satirical wit. The
pungency, such as it is, of such a couplet as this as
clearly consists in the various incongruities bound
up together, in the comparison between the beauties
of a flowing river and the muddy drippings of a
beer-barrel, or again, in the contrast between the

noble rapids of a full poetic genius and the frothy
eddies of a dull and vapid sentimentalism,—as does
Thackeray's fine stroke of humour when he makes
Becky, in the bitterest remorse for her own mis-
calculations, exclaim dolorously to Sir Pitt Crawley,
when he is on his knees begging her to become his
wife, "Oh, Sir Pitt, I'm married already ! " The
difference between the two cases is that the
incongruity which Thackeray delineates with his
usual swift and bitter strokes, is the incongruity of
the heart, the incongruity between the suggested
feeling of remorse and Becky's selfish self-reproach,
while the couplet in Pope contains nothing more
but a careful incongruity of metaphors and of
literary proportions. Burlesque, travesty, caricature, parody, satire, contemptuous parable of that
grim and saturnine kind in which Swift was so great
a master, and, finally, the humour rooted in the
deepest and most delicate sense of the inconsistencies of human motive and feeling, are all
varieties of the same genus, essays in incongruity
by minds more or less susceptible to the pleasant
shock caused by various shades of incongruity.
When Hamlet follows in imagination the noble dust
of Alexander till he finds it stopping a bunghole,
he is in precisely the mood of mind which gives
birth to humour ; and if it does not exactly touch
the springs of laughter, it is only because the contrasts between the humiliation of the flesh and the
triumphs of the spirit have in all ages been so
much the theme of meditation that we have ceased
to feel the incongruity as a *surprise*, which is an
absolute condition of the specific effect of either wit
or humour.

The difference so deeply felt between a wit and

a humourist consists only, I believe, in the greater
degree of sharp intellectual paradox on the one
hand, or of the paradox of personal and subjective
feeling on the other, which is at the basis of the
surprise. When Voltaire described taking medicine
as "putting drugs of which we know little into our
bodies of which we know less," the whole form of
the criticism was sharply intellectual, and involved
exceedingly little, if any, of that rapid gliding from
one personal and subjective phase of feeling to
another of an opposite kind to which it stands in
paradoxical contrast, which is of the essence of
humour. But when Coleridge, in his bitter attack
on somebody's porter, asserted that "dregs from
the bottom half-way up and froth from the top
half-way down constituted Perkins Entire," that
was a flash half-way between wit and humour. The
theoretical accuracy of the exposition, the satire
implied in the contrast between the spurious combination of dregs and froth and the word Entire
(*integer*), which expresses specifically wholeness and
soundness of essence, were all what we should call
wit ; but the ripple of personal feeling in passing
from the disgust of a thirsty man who has found
his porter all undrinkable, to so intellectual a form
of invective on it, is of the very essence of humour.
Again, Charles Lamb's tipsy delight when the
Cumberland stamp-distributor said that Shakespeare
was a very clever man, delight which he displayed
by lighting a bed-candle, dancing round him and
calling out, "Allow me to have a look at that
gentleman's organs," while Wordsworth, in utter
horror, tried to restrain him by reiterating, "Charles,
my dear Charles!" was pure humour. There
was hardly any intellectual operation involved

in the matter at all, only the rapid transition of Lamb's own personal feeling from sleepy indifference to the most vivid curiosity on hearing so silly a remark. Where any other man would simply have laughed, Lamb, in spite of his soporific brandy-and-water, was apparently stimulated into the most intense desire to explore the sources of such a moral enigma ; and the humour lies in his having realised the absurdity of the remark so much more vividly than he realised the conventional restraints imposed by social habits, that he could only ignore the latter altogether in his delight at finding a fine specimen of the literary idiot. So, again, Lamb's ready answer to the Highgate omnibus conductor, who put his head in to ask, "All full inside ? " when Lamb was half asleep in the corner,—" I really can't answer for the other ladies and gentlemen, but that last piece of pudding at Mrs. Gilman's did the business for me," was so humorous, not from the ready pun on the meaning of the conductor, but from the picture it presents to us of the interior mind of Charles Lamb, gravely assuming that the question was directed to the state of his stomach, and of the impulse of perfect candour which appeared to induce him to make this frank confession to the assembled company.

Now, applying this distinction between the tickling of the intellectual sense of incongruity involved in pure wit, and the ready transition from one condition of personal feeling to another almost inconceivable in close connection with it which is implied in humour, in the case of Mr. Dickens, I think I may fairly say that there was comparatively little of the wit, and a truly astounding amount of the humourist in him. Even his poorest successes, the successes in the way of parody and travesty with which he opened the *Pickwick Papers*, are feats of humour; for instance, "There sat the man who had traced to their source the mighty ponds of Hampstead, and enlightened the scientific world with his theory of tittlebats, as calm and unmoved as the silent waters of the one on a frosty day, or a solitary specimen of the other in the inmost recesses of an earthen jar,"—even this is humour, though humour of a comparatively poor kind. The contempt with which Dickens enters into the ostentatious rhetoric of charlatan science, the skill with which he chooses the illustrations most humiliating to it, and the high-sounding gravity with which he conducts his elaborate metaphors to a close, all transport you to the interior of his mind, and make you experience for yourself the slight moral shock with which you find the grandeur of the Parliamentary and the spurious scientific style of oratory undermined and toppling down into very closely allied nonsense. Just the same somewhat superficial but very lively humour pervades the whole of the admirable American parodies in *Martin Chuzzlewit*. When Mr. Putnam Smif writes "that every alligator basking in the slime is in himself an Epic self-contained," or Miss Codger dilates on the thrilling nature of the impressions on her feelings with which she finds herself introduced "to a Pogram by a Hominy," but asks herself why she calls them her feelings, or why impressed they are, or if impressed they are at all, "or if there really is, oh, gasping one! a Pogram or a Hominy or any active principle to which we give those titles," the humour surely consists in the exhibition of that close affinity between inflated intellectual ambition and positive idiocy,

which by happy and easy touches of exaggeration
the humourist renders so glaring. The humourist,
I believe, as distinguished from the wit, always
moves on the inner line of impulse and motive, always
identifies himself more or less with the secret springs
of paradox, always plays on the moral paradoxes of
the mind within ; while the wit occupies a critical
and external position, and makes his play with the
cross-purposes and antitheses he discovers in the field
of external thought or action. The most decisive note
of the former is the preference for speaking by the
very mouth of the person to be made ludicrous, of
the latter the preference for launching criticisms at
him from the outside.   Where humour and wit are
blended, as they so often are, the procedure is double,
as in the saying of Coleridge I have analysed
above ; there is, in the first place, a sharp intellectual paradox to excite amusement ; and then,
when we pass beneath it to the play of feeling and
motive in the mind of the wit, we find grotesque
contrasts of moral scenery which are more amusing
still, because they display humour as well as
wit.

And if Dickens may fairly be called a great
humourist in his moods of burlesque and travesty,
such as those in the early part of *Pickwick* and of
the American portion of *Martin Chuzzlewit*, he is
infinitely more so in those moods in which he
displays the plausibilities and falsehoods of human
nature through the mouths of his chief favourites,
his ideal vulgarities or impostures, Noah Claypole,
Mrs. Gamp, Mr. Pecksniff It will be asserted by
some that this is not true humour, because these
puppets of Dickens's are not real characters, because
they are only glorified abstractions of cowardice,

vanity, selfishness, and hypocrisy, and are free from all the inconsistencies of actual human nature. Doubtless they are not real men and women in the sense in which Shakespeare's characters, or Miss Austen's, or George Eliot's are real men and women. But I deny that this is in any way necessary for the purposes of a humourist. All that a humourist, as a humourist, can be expected to do, in order to attain the very perfection of humour, is to bring out perfectly the true moral absurdities and paradoxes in human nature; and this may be done as perfectly,—I believe more perfectly, so far as the humorous effect alone goes,—with a careful selection of moral qualities and a certain amount of subtle exaggeration of them, than it could be done with real men and women. Delightful as is the humour with which the birth-proud, purse-proud, and empty-headed Lady Catherine de Bourgh is painted in Miss Austen's *Pride and Prejudice*,—when she says, for instance, to the heroine, "I take no leave of you, Miss Bennet, *I send no compliments to your mother*, you deserve no such attention. I am most seriously displeased,"—the feat of humour as such is not enhanced by the fact that Lady Catherine throughout is always sketched as she might really have been—a narrow-minded, arrogant woman, so full of self-importance that she supposes any interruptions of the courtesies of life, on her part, will really be felt as severely as the withdrawal of an ambassador of a great State would be felt by the small State with which diplomatic relations were broken off. The humour of the conception, great as it is, is not at all the greater, I maintain, because the woman is truly painted and never overdrawn. Mr. Pecksniff is vastly overdrawn. No real hypocrite

42988

would ever be so ostentatiously hypocritical as he is.
Still, there is not less but more of real humour in that
exhibition of him,—as when he proposes to Martin
Chuzzlewit to surprise his dear girls, and accordingly begins to walk softly and on tiptoe over the
country though he was still a mile or two from
home; or when he gets tipsy, and tells Mrs. Todgers
of his late wife that "she was beautiful, Mrs.
Todgers—*she had a small property*,"—than in the
more delicate and real painting of Lady Catherine
de Bourgh's immeasurable self-importance.   The
humour does not consist in the reality of the whole
picture in either case, but in the shock of surprise
with which the grotesque blending of mean and
pretentious elements in human nature is in both
cases alike brought home to the reader.   Where this
shock is keenest and full of real moral paradox the
feat of humour is greatest.   And that this is often
greatest in cases where the humourist has left something *out* of nature, and perhaps exaggerated something else *in* it, in order to bring home his special
paradox more powerfully, seems to me past doubt.
Consider the wonderful humour with which the
enormous and immeasurable vanity of the last
person one would think likely to indulge vanity, a
snuffy, intemperate, monthly nurse, is brought out
in Mrs. Gamp.   The mixture of brutal selfishness
with that vanity is a much less subtle touch,
for that might be suggested by the professional
character of the woman.   But the inexhaustible
humour of the picture of Mrs. Gamp consists in
her vanity, and the subtleties of device to which
she has to resort in order to gratify it.   These
are the kind of conceptions which seem to me
to place Dickens at the very head of all English

humourists. His best figures are pure embodi-
ments of his humour,—not real characters at all,
but illustrations, conceived with boundless wealth
of conception, of the deepest moral incongruities of
the heart.

"JOHN INGLESANT" ON HUMOUR

MR. SHORTHOUSE, in the fine piece of English which he has contributed to *Macmillan's Magazine* on "The Humorous in Literature," has, as I understand him, tried to make out a case for the necessarily close connection between the source of laughter and the source of tears in all true humour. He holds, apparently, that "the condition of true humorous thought is individuality," and that you can never get close to the sources of any individuality without getting at the common source of what is ridiculous and what is pathetic, without a blending of that which stirs laughter and that which stirs tears. Now, I have no objection at all to the doctrine that *one* of the finest and highest kinds of humour does play on the involutions of these blending chords of bright and sad feelings, and awaken them in the closest connection, and therefore in the most vivid contrast. Undoubtedly, this is one of the highest kinds of humour, and I entirely agree with Mr. Shorthouse, that if Jean Paul Richter is to be taken as the type of perfect humour, it is in feats of humour of this particular kind that the perfect humour has manifested itself. But what I do not see my way to conceding is that true humour is limited to humour of this special kind, which I

understand to be the drift and tendency, though
not the express assertion of Mr. Shorthouse's essay.
He does not say that Dickens is no true humourist
because his pathos often rings false, but that is
what I should certainly gather as the general
meaning of his essay, which appears to insist on
"the tremulous change from the comic to the
pathetic," which is so perfectly distinctive of
Thackeray as well as of Paul Jean Richter, as the
most important of all the criteria of humour.   This
is where I cannot follow Mr. Shorthouse.   It seems
to me that this, though a criterion of one of the
noblest species of humour, is a criterion of one
species only.   Humour consists in all variations
played on the feelings by the subtle caprice of man,
and appears just as truly in Sydney Smith's grave
question to the doctor who ordered him " To take a
walk on an empty stomach "—" On whose ? "—as in
Thackeray's curious power of "tremulous change
from the comic to the pathetic."   It is the power
of suddenly and grotesquely varying the tone of
feeling struck, in which the humourist's skill
consists.   And that may be done as effectually
where neither of the chords of feeling brought into
sudden contrast is pathetic, as where one of them
is pathetic, and one comic.   Indeed, if I understand
Mr. Shorthouse's drift aright, it would shut out
England's greatest humourist, Dickens, from the
ranks of great humourists altogether.   The cases in
which Dickens's humour displays itself by suddenly
passing from the livelier to the sadder phases of
human things are comparatively very rare, and,
even when they occur, are not by any means the
best specimen of Dickens's humour.   His great
power was not, like Thackeray's, one of "tremulous

change" from the lively to the sad, but rather like
Shakespeare's, the power of throwing a strong light
on the mingled self-importance and emptiness of
men, till it seems as if your whole mind were lost
in amazement that emptiness can be so self-
important, and self-importance so empty. Shakespeare's Malvolio, his Polonius, his Dogberry, and
a hundred other portraits of that class, are surely
great feats of humour, whatever we may think of
Dickens's great creations,—which, to my mind, are
even greater feats of humour of the same general
type,—but they are not feats of humour of the
kind which Mr. Shorthouse selects as the most
characteristic of the quality; and, to tell the truth,
I doubt whether Shakespeare often does touch the
common source of laughter and tears after the
fashion which seems to Mr. Shorthouse the very
highest. Mr. Shorthouse speaks of the wonderful
humour in "Hamlet"; and, of course, strong
contrasts—like that, for instance, between the
grave-digger's coarse and jovial indifference to death,
and the grief felt for the hapless Ophelia—are the
sort of contrasts to which he alludes; but there is
no "tremulousness" in that transition; it is not
the gradual and finely shaded passing from one
feeling to the other, such as Mr. Shorthouse very
justly admires in Thackeray, in which Shakespeare
excels. On the contrary, he likes to introduce the
contrast in the sharpest possible form, to give us
Hamlet musing over the skull of Yorick, and
suggesting that the dust of Caesar may be used
eventually to stop a bunghole. If this sharply
drawn intellectual contrast between the smallness
and the greatness of human nature be what Mr.
Shorthouse means by the highest humour, I admit

that Shakespeare as a humourist comes up to the standard of Mr. Shorthouse. But I hold that these sharply drawn intellectual contrasts between the greatness and the littleness of life, such as Hamlet, for instance, so often indulges in, and such as Shakespeare still more often effects by bringing purely comical natures into close contact with grand natures, are not efforts of humour, properly so called at all, because they are all results of explicit intention— all intellectual contrasts—from which the capricious shimmer of humorous feeling is conspicuously absent. Mr. Shorthouse refers all Pope's and apparently most of Swift's achievements in this field to the sphere of wit, rather than of humour,— and quite rightly at least in the case of Pope,—I suppose because it is so evidently the spell of the intellect, and not of the feelings, by which these achievements are effected. But surely it is the spell of the intellect with which Hamlet works wonders when he muses over the skull of Yorick, or in the soliloquy, "What a piece of work is man!" And it is only by the device of referring everything of special individuality in man to his humour, that Mr. Shorthouse contrives to suggest that Hamlet's finest soliloquies are the soliloquies of a great humourist rather than the soliloquies of a great thinker. I should have preferred to say that Shakespeare as a humourist is seen not in such great creations as Hamlet, but in what are distinctly recognised as his comic characters; and that the kind of humour which Mr. Shorthouse most admires, though it is often found in Shakespeare, as, for instance, in the description of the death of Falstaff, is not particularly Shakespearian, — that that tremulous shimmer amongst subtly contrasted and

yet subtly allied feelings which was so wonderful
in Thackeray, is not by any means one of the most
characteristic moods of Shakespeare.

The difficulty of Mr. Shorthouse's theory of
humour—that it is coextensive with individuality,
and shows itself especially by commanding at once
the source of smiles and the source of tears—comes
out especially in the close of his essay, when he
tries to show that the Gospels, in touching the
deepest springs of human nature, must also give
examples of the deepest humour of which man is
capable. But the truth is, I think, that humour
is not coextensive with human nature, that it is
coextensive only with the unexpected and baffling
caprices of human feeling; and that where the
predominating feeling is all of one kind, and that
the kind which enhances to the highest degree the
importance of every word and act of human beings,
the element of humour is excluded, simply because
one of the terms of contrast is banished from the
field. In the Gospels, where God becomes man,
all that was small and insignificant in man seems
to vanish away beneath the glance of the incarnate
Divinity, and it is almost as impossible to find
room for those grotesque interlacings of opposite
feelings on which humour depends, as it is to find
room for the contrasts between light and shade
under the burning sun of an Arabian noon. Mr.
Shorthouse brings before us, in a passage of much
beauty, the parable of the Prodigal Son, appealing
to his readers whether, in its fine and unexpected
transitions from joy to sorrow, and from sorrow
back to joy, there is not all the reality of true
humour. It is not in the mere blending of joy
and sorrow—joy on one account, and sorrow on

another—that I should ever find an illustration of humour. When the humourist plays upon the blending chords of joy and sorrow, he does so in a manner to bewilder us, to confuse us as to whether we are glad or sorry at the same thing, to make us uncertain as to our real feeling, and disposed to confound the pathetic with the absurd. That is not in the least the way in which joy and sorrow are blended in the parable of the Prodigal Son. The joy is unmixed so far as the penitent Prodigal is concerned; the sorrow caused by the jealousy of the Elder Brother is unmixed also; but the two feelings are perfectly consistent, and by no means bewildering. The magic of the humourist consists in producing a certain bewilderment of feeling, in so rapidly changing from one current of feeling to another, that you do not recognise clearly the true significance of your own emotions; and of this there is no trace in the story of the Prodigal Son, nor, so far as I know, in the Gospels at all. One mighty chord vibrates too loud in the Gospels to be confounded with any other chord, and in this perfect absence of confusion of feeling the complete absence of humour from the Gospels is almost necessarily involved.

PATHOS

PATHOS in the truest sense is very much more often
felt than adequately expressed. The attempt to
express it too often defeats itself. Dickens, with
all his power, teaches us how impossible it is for
a writer who intends to be pathetic to succeed in
being so. The death of little Nell, and of Paul
Dombey, favourites as they are with the world at
large, have in them just that air of vigilant
scrutiny of the associations which rend the heart
most, that, to my mind at least, robs them of what
I mean by pathos in its truest sense,—that artless
cry of the dumb yet not despairing heart which
words so seldom render articulate and so often
utterly disguise. Perhaps the most perfect of the
earlier expressions of true pathos in literature is
the well-known parting of Hector and Andromache,
in the sixth book of the *Iliad*—a passage never
yet translated into English in anything like its true
beauty and simplicity. And the pathos there is
quite as much due to the relief given by the
natural diversion of the minds of both parents from
their miserable anticipations to the child's innocent
terror at Hector's helmet, as to the broken tenderness of the wife's dread and the prophetic gloom of
Hector's foreboding knowledge. I do not mean,

of course, that the cry of a dumb heart which is
absolutely despairing can never be adequately
given without something to attenuate the misery
of the cry; but only that when the passion is not
thus attenuated, it rises above the level of what
we call "pathos," and reaches that of tragedy.
In all cases of true pathos, though trouble pervades the scene, it does not overwhelm; it is held
in check by subdued feelings of a more grateful
and hopeful description, which soften the pain
and make the heart tremble with some undertone
of unexpected sweetness, even in the very keenest
vibration of its grief. Indeed, so true is this, that
I believe some of the most pathetic passages in
our literature are those in which the subdued
thankfulness or hope predominates over the pain,
instead of the pain over the hope. For example,
in the following exquisitely pathetic verses of
Hood's "On a Death-Bed," it is difficult to say
which of the two elements predominates, so completely is the equilibrium between the two waves
of feeling maintained :—

> We watched her breathing through the night,
>   Her breathing soft and low,
> As in her breast the wave of life
>   Kept heaving to and fro.
>
> So silently we seemed to speak,
>   So slowly moved about,
> As we had lent her half our powers
>   To eke her living out.
>
> Our very hopes belied our fears,
>   Our fears our hopes belied ;
> We thought her dying when she slept,
>   And sleeping when she died.

For when the morn came, dim and sad
    And chill with early showers,
Her quiet eyelids closed,—she had
    Another morn than ours.

In the truest examples of Sir Walter Scott's
pathos we sometimes find the passion of hope prevailing over that of anguish, as in Jeanie Deans's
plea to the Queen for her sister's life ; and sometimes
that of anguish prevailing over that of hope, as in
Mucklebackit's dreary grief for his son's death.   But
I cannot help thinking that the more moving scene
of the two—though both are moving in the highest
degree—is the one where the passion of hope
prevails over the passion of grief :—" My sister—my
puir sister Effie, still lives, though her days and
hours are numbered.   She still lives, and a word of
the King's mouth might restore her to a broken-
hearted auld man that never, in his daily and nightly
exercise, forgot to pray that his Majesty might be
blessed with a long and prosperous reign, and that
his throne, and the throne of his posterity, might be
established in righteousness.   O, Madam, if ever ye
kenn'd what it was to sorrow for and with a sinning
and a suffering creature, whose mind is sae tossed
that she can be neither ca'd fit to live or die, have
some compassion on our misery !   Save an honest
house from dishonour, and an unhappy girl, not
eighteen years of age, from an early and dreadful
death !   Alas ! it is not when we sleep soft and wake
merrily ourselves, that we think on other people's
sufferings.   Our hearts are waxed light within us
then, and we are for righting our ain wrangs and
fighting our ain battles.   But when the hour of
trouble comes to the mind as to the body—and

seldom may it visit your Leddyship—and when the
hour of Death comes, that comes to high and low—
long and late may it be yours—O, my Leddy, then
it isna what we hae dune for oursells, but what we
hae dune for others, that we think on maist
pleasantly.   And the thought that ye hae intervened
to spare the puir thing's life will be sweeter in that
hour, come when it may, than if a word of your
mouth could hang the hail Porteous mob at the tail
of ae tow."   It is the strong, plain, hopeful Scotch
sagacity in this speech, with its canny reverence for
station and rank, that makes the passion of tenderness for the sister and the father so much more
impressive, just as in old Mucklebackit's case, it is
the smothered fury with the old boat for having
been the unhappy instrument of his son's death,
that makes the vehement effort to patch and caulk
it for the next day's fishing so heartbreaking.   In
all cases of the higher pathos there must be
something that battles against the pain, as well as
some bitter cry of the pain in the heart.   Without
the former, the latter would be a situation, not of
pathos, but of despair.   Wherever there is true
pathos, there is the surging of a buoyant wave in
the heart breaking the force of the wave which
overwhelms it with dejection, and not unfrequently
even prevailing over it.   In the most pathetic
passage I know in our modern fiction, the passage
in which Lady Castlewood welcomes Henry Esmond
back to his home, after meeting him at the cathedral
service, the buoyancy of a thankful spirit more
than subdues the passion of a jealous and foreboding
heart :—" To-day, Harry, in the anthem, when they
sang it, ' When the Lord turned the captivity of
Zion, we were like them that dream,' I thought,

yes, like them that dream,—them that dream. And
then it went, 'They that sow in tears shall reap
in joy'; and 'He that goeth forth and weepeth,
shall doubtless come again with rejoicing, bringing
his sheaves with him'; I looked up from the book
and saw you. I was not surprised when I saw you.
I knew you would come, my dear, and saw the
golden sunshine round your head." She smiled an
almost wild smile as she looked up at him. The
moon was up by this time, glittering keen in the
frosty sky. He could see for the first time now
clearly, her sweet, careworn face. "Do you know
what day it is?" she continued; "it is the 29th
December, it is your birthday, But last year we
did not drink it,—no, no. My Lord was cold, and
my Harry was likely to die; and my brain was in
a fever; and we had no wine. But now, now you
are come again, bringing your sheaves with you, my
dear." She burst into a wild flood of weeping as
she spoke; she laughed and sobbed on the young
man's heart, crying out wildly, "Bringing your
sheaves with you, your sheaves with you."

I know no example of truer pathos, even in
poetry, than this passage; and in it, as in that most
pathetic of all the Psalms on which it dwells, the
strain of rapture overwhelms the strain of woe.
Even in the Psalm itself, as in the use here made of
it, the note of rapture is far from assured. Though
"the Lord had done great things for them already,"
whereof they were glad, there was still the necessity
for prayer, "Turn again our captivity, O Lord, as
the streams in the south." He that now goeth on his
way weeping had not yet "come again with joy,
bringing his sheaves with him," but it is only
promised that he shall do so. The exultation is

prophetic, the tears are actual; but the note of exultation prevails over the note of anguish, though not sufficiently to dry the falling tears. Surely in that picture we have the very highest form of pathos, the highest form because the note of triumph swells so high over the note of woe, without drowning, nay, without even attempting to silence it. The highest pathos is latent in the rapture into which suffering sometimes breaks when it discerns a glory in suffering which it had never found in unmixed delight.

KEATS

MR. SIDNEY COLVIN, in the charming study of Keats
with which he has just enriched Mr. John Morley's
series of "English Men of Letters," is anxious to
convince his readers that the genius of Keats held
in solution all those great qualities by which
Shakespeare's transcendent imagination was distinguished, and that if Keats had not died pre-
maturely at twenty-five, he would have shown that
he could follow with no unequal step in the great
master's track. I cannot say that I think this conjecture at all a probable conjecture. It is perfectly
certain that it can neither be confuted nor confirmed.
The law of genius, such as that of Keats, is far
beyond our gauging. The rainbow's colours have
been reduced to law, but the rainbow colours of the
human imagination have not been reduced to law ;
and there is, so far as we know, no analogy upon
which we could even venture to found any probable
inference as to the development of Keats's rich and
fiery fancy. If I were to hazard a conjecture at all
in regions so very far beyond the clear survey of
human reason, I would rather have said that a mind
so marked by early and tropical luxuriance as that
of Keats, was hardly likely to have yielded the

grandest fruits of intellectual strength. The childhood of genius has frequently presented us with a
foretaste of its maturer years, a foretaste which has
proved to be a better guide to the maturer forms of
that genius than to the intermediate forms which
arise under the magnetism of youth. The child
Goethe was in many respects more like the oracular
sage who conversed with Eckermann than the youth
who wrote the *Sorrows of Werther* and *Goetz of
Berlichingen.* The child Scott, who kept all his
schoolfellows on the stretch to hear the stories he
invented, was much more like the great novelist
than the young man who translated Bürger's
"Leonora," and related in verse the romantic
legend of his wizard ancestor. And Cardinal
Newman has told us how, in his own childhood,
there were strange auguries, which in his later
years he could hardly understand or even credit,
of the close of his career in the great Church of
which he is now a prince. But in Keats's childhood,
while we have evidence of the most fiery com-
bativeness and the most glowing generosity and
chivalry of heart, there appears to be no trace of
that largeness of undeveloped power which would
anticipate many-sided wisdom and an immense range
of human insight. On the contrary, great anima-
tion, considerable tumultuousness of feeling, and
sudden, almost abrupt impulsiveness, seem to have
been the chief characteristics of his childhood. We
should expect, I think, in the childhood of a
Shakespeare something of that sedateness and calm-
ness which belong to wisdom and humour even
when still in the germ. Keats's childhood seems to
have been almost as tumultuous as his youth ; and
yet in the childhood of many-sided wisdom there is

apt, I imagine, to be evidence of the slow preparation of Nature for a great intellectual birth.
However, all this, as I have said, is beyond the
field of anything but conjecture, though, if I were
to conjecture at all, my conjecture would not fall
in with Mr. Sidney Colvin's. Shakespeare, I think,
could never have lived to Keats's age without betraying more evidence of overflowing humour and
delight in rendering the various forms of human character than Keats ever displayed, for even Mr. Sidney
Colvin does not pretend that in " Otho the Great,"
or the fragment of " King Stephen," or the " Cap
and Bells," Keats betrayed anything like the faculty
which went to create "The two Gentlemen of Verona,"
or "The Merry Wives of Windsor," or "A Midsummer
Night's Dream." Very likely the last-mentioned play
is due to a period in Shakespeare's life which Keats
never lived to attain. And, of course, it might well
be that a genius which flowered so early and
luxuriantly as that of Keats, might have taken
longer to ripen into the higher phases of its power
than even Shakespeare's, which, so far as we know,
never produced anything so rich and perfect as
Keats's poems at the age at which Keats produced
them. Still, I cannot easily believe that a genius
which was so profuse and incomparable in one
field, could have given absolutely no indication of a
gigantic power like that of Shakespeare in another
and very different field, even before the age at
which Keats died. Was that almost hectic brilliance, that redundancy of fervent susceptibility and
vividness, quite compatible with the travail of a
mind in which so mighty an imagination as
Shakespeare's was slowly bringing its power to the
birth ? It is not usually the forest trees which

flower most brilliantly,—rather the creepers and the flowers and the shrubs. It is hard to imagine that so mighty a nature as Shakespeare's should have had so early and yet so wonderfully brilliant a flowering season as was given to the fancy of Keats.

But passing by Mr. Sidney Colvin's intellectual conjecture for what it is worth, I cannot deny that he has brought out for us with great clearness and beauty the distinctive traits of the genius which has immortalised the name of Keats. "I think poetry," said Keats, "should surprise by a fine excess"; and it would be impossible to express more exactly the surprise which Keats's poetry certainly gives us. There is "a fine excess," an excess which would revolt us if it were not so fine, a fineness which we should be very apt to miss if it were not the fineness of excess, in all the singular glory of Keats's happiest verse. Take the lines in "St. Agnes Eve," on the beauty of which Mr. Sidney Colvin dilates with so much enthusiasm—

> But to her heart her heart was voluble,
> Paining with eloquence her balmy side.

Surely Mr. Sidney Colvin is himself guilty of a fine excess when he says that the beauty of these lines "resides in truth only,"—for Madeline could never have thought of her own side as "balmy"; and it is the artifice and effort by which Keats unites artificially in one view the passion of the maiden with the passion of her lover, the volubility of Madeline's heart's love with the rapture of Porphryo's gaze, which are the special characteristics of that

couplet. It is the same with nearly every one of
Keats's most characteristic lines :—

> O for a beaker full of the warm South,
> Full of the true, the blushful Hippocrene,
> With beaded bubbles winking at the brim
> And purple stained mouth !

There is a fine excess in every phrase of that stanza,
most of all in the phrase by which Keats so
vividly describes the swift rising and vanishing of
the "beaded bubbles." And Keats's "fine excess"
is always spent on luxuriating in beauty, whether
sensuous or spiritual. Mr. Colvin tells us that
Keats's mother was a lively, impulsive woman,
"passionately fond of amusement, and supposed to
have hastened the birth of her eldest child by some
imprudence." If so, a considerable element in
that eldest child's nature, and the ardour with
which he, too, luxuriated in whatever seemed to
stimulate his vivid sensations and emotions, may
have been in great measure due to his having
inherited his mother's temperament. You see this
temperament which luxuriates in enjoyment, in the
enjoyment even of woe, everywhere in Keats, in
his letters as well as in his poems. In both alike
you see the man who in the "Ode to Melancholy"
could say :—

> Ay, in the very temple of Delight
> Veiled Melancholy has her sovran shrine,
> Though seen of none save him whose strenuous tongue
> Can burst Joy's grape against his palate fine ;
> His soul shall taste the sadness of her might,
> And be among her cloudy trophies hung.

A "fine excess," and a fine excess in the direction
of luxuriating in rare emotion, could surely never

have been more aptly expressed than in these lines.

The richness of Keats is, of course, anything but classical, as Mr. Sidney Colvin very justly observes, and yet it is a richness which suggests Greek feeling, not in the least from the form, but from the poet's equal passion for all beauty wherever beauty is to be found. Unlike the modern poets, Keats never dwells specially on those human affections which, in the romantic era, so much superseded the passion for mere beauty. Nothing can be less Greek than the vast profusion with which Keats pours out his sense of beauty; nothing can be less Greek than that taste for "excess," even though it be a "fine excess," with which he seeks to surprise us. I can hardly imagine anything less Greek, for instance, than this, which is so characteristic of Keats that any good critic, even though he might not recognise the lines individually, would cry out "Keats" at once :—

> Sudden a thought came like a full-blown rose,
> Flushing his brow, and in his pained heart
> Made purple riot.

Nothing can be less Greek than the famous aspiration "to cease upon the midnight with no pain," in the "Ode to the Nightingale." What was Greek about Keats was his profound love of beauty as beauty. What was the very reverse of Greek was that proneness to an artificially "fine excess" with which he piled up luxuriant details of beauty till you cease to be able to see the forest for the trees. There was something like inebriety in that tendency to push delight in beauty up to the swooning point to which Mr. Colvin calls attention. But say what we will in attenuation of his claims to admiration, Keats was "a priest to all time," if not of the wonder, at least of "the bloom of the world," which "we see with his eyes and are glad."

A POET'S LOVE-LETTERS

In days when the wishes of the "pious founder" are not regarded with any superstitious respect, it is, I suppose, natural that the wishes of the poetic letter-writer should be regarded with none at all. As far as one can judge from the intense and acute horror with which Keats evidently regarded the discussion of his love by a coterie of friends, the notion of confiding his love-letters to the general public, though it were more than fifty years after his death, would have been simply hateful to him. He had all the dread which every man of strong nature is sure to feel of any contact between purely personal, though very deep emotions, and the curious criticism of an indifferent world. Feelings, the only meaning of which is individual, ought to be reserved for those for whom they have a meaning. When thrown into a poetic or imaginative form, they are, of course, so far transformed by that process as to be made applicable to the feelings of a thousand different minds under similar circumstances. But while they remain in the form of passionate avowals from A to B, and are marked by all the individual detail which applies only to the circumstances of A and B, there is a certain amount of indelicacy in inviting the inspection of all the world, from which

88

Keats certainly, for his lifetime at all events, had the most sensitive shrinking. And though I do not say that the death of both parties, the fame of one of them, and the gulf of intervening time, do not diminish to some extent the unbecomingness of publishing this kind of correspondence, yet if I may trust the impression which it has produced upon my mind, there is still something decidedly unbecoming in doing this offence to Keats's feelings; and Mr. Forman would have judged better, I think, had he recommended the owners of these letters to give them to the flames. In proportion to our admiration for a man of genius, should be our wish to consult his wishes as to the disposal of his private concerns. And what can be a more private concern to any one than the fate of letters meant only for one person's eyes, and more or less liable to appear unseemly, eccentric, wanting in reticence, if brought under the eyes of any one else? Even the truest admirer of Keats will read these letters with a sense that they are prying into what he would have kept from them, if he could. And surely it is a very bad return to make to a man of genius for the delight he has given us, thus to avail ourselves of the permanence of records to which he would certainly have given, if he had been able, no longer existence than that of the two persons of whose tie to each other these letters formed some of the most important links. You might almost as fitly reproduce the actual lovers' talks and sighs of the present day for our posterity fifty years hence, by the help of the talking phonograph, as reproduce letters of this kind, which were evidently meant to perish with the relation which they recorded and modified. Yet who would dream of making love in the presence of a talking phonograph? Keats assuredly least of all. And we may be sure that if he could have procured paper which was bound to crumble into dust before the death of the lady to whom he wrote, such paper he would have procured.

I cannot say, then, that the reading of this little volume has given me anything like unmixed pleasure. I have felt all through that I was guilty of an intrusion, which, like all intrusions in such a region, Keats would have warmly resented. And I have felt, too, something besides this, and quite independent of the uncomfortable feeling of intrusion, that much in these letters which Keats could easily have justified, and would have justified, if he had been writing a poem or a play,—by the very simple expedient of making us see the object of his passion, as well as the glow of the subjective passion itself,—has an uncomfortably naked, unnatural effect here, where we have only his own side of the relation, and hardly even a single glance of the other side of it. To hear even a poet raving about his "swooning admiration" of a lady's beauty, while that lady's beauty is blank to us, or worse than a blank,—represented by a very ugly black silhouette of a lady with a high cap, an impossible waist, and a big nose,—is quite as painful in an artistic sense as it is in a moral sense, by giving us the feeling of being made party to a breach of personal confidence. I am aware that Miss Brawne indicated her impression that ultimately these records of Keats's passion might be published, but in so doing she only betrayed, I think, how imperfectly she understood or how little she respected Keats's horror of any revelation of the kind.

But though this little book is in both the ways
I have mentioned distasteful to me, it would be
false to say that it is without interest. It bears
the mark of Keats's genius in many of the letters,
and the marks of his individual character in almost
all. It is, for instance, most characteristic of
Keats to say that if the lady with whom he is so
deeply in love, should ever feel for a man at the
first sight what he did for her, he should not
quarrel with her, though he should hate himself,
but he "should burst, if the thing were not as
fine, as a man, as you are for a woman." So
passionate a love of beauty had Keats, that doubtless he was capable, even in such a trial as this,
of admitting to himself—at least if so it were—
that "the thing" was "as fine as a man" as his
fiancée was for a woman. Whether Keats himself,
however, would have felt less inclined "to burst"
after making that avowal to himself, than he
would have done if he had, in his æsthetic conscience, been compelled to deny this indignantly
in regard to "the thing," it is not easy to say.
Nor does he seem to have been actually tried to
this extent. Still, it is most characteristic of Keats,
that he should even have imagined himself likely
to suffer less if the lady of his choice were to fall
in love with "a thing" who was "as fine as a man
as she was as a woman," than he would have
suffered if she were to fall in love with a creature
of less excellence.

Again, the intense horror of "settling" in life
which Keats expresses, *i.e.* of falling into a limited
and conventional routine, is only less individually
characteristic of Keats, because it has certainly
haunted many another poet—Goethe, for instance

—quite as sharply.   Still, not only is it characteristic of the class of poets to which Keats belonged,
but the mode in which he gives expression to it
is highly characteristic of himself individually.   In
leaving Shanklin for Winchester he writes :—

You would delight very greatly in the walks about
here, the cliffs, woods, hills, sands, rocks, etc., about here.
They are, however, not so fine but I shall give them a
hearty good-bye to exchange them for my Cathedral.
Yet, again, I am not so tired of scenery as to hate
Switzerland.   We might spend a pleasant year at Berne
or Zurich—if it should please Venus to hear my " Beseech
thee to hear us, O Goddess."   And if she should hear,
God forbid we should what people call *settle*—turn into
a pond, a stagnant Lethe—a vile crescent, row, or buildings.
Better be imprudent movables than prudent fixtures.
Open my mouth at the street door like the lion's head
at Venice to receive hateful cards, letters, messages.   Go
out and wither at tea-parties ; freeze at dinners ; bake
at dances ; simmer at routs.   No, my love, trust yourself to me, and I will find you nobler amusement,
fortune favouring.

One of his great pleasures at Winchester was to
be the following :—"At Winchester I shall get your
letters more readily ; and it being a cathedral city,
I shall have a pleasure, always a great one to me
when near a cathedral, of reading them during
the service up and down the aisle."   Rather a
cynical, peripatetic pleasure, this, during service-
time, and one that can only have been taken not
very considerately for the worship of others.   But
in another letter Keats says, " My creed is Love,
and you are its only tenet," and that was, I
suppose, his excuse for reading its homilies in the

Cathedral, "during the service, up and down the aisle."

The most characteristic, however, of any of these letters, at least the most characteristic of those which are not so personal as to give us the sense of prying into his secrets in the perusal, is the last letter written from Winchester, in what Keats regarded as a hard literary mood, when his heart was surrounded with the *aes triplex* of imaginative prepossessions. In this letter he speaks of seeing the lady of his choice through a mist of other images and cares, and apologises throughout (with much tenderness) for the iron hardness of his thought and style :—

Winchester, August 17th. (*Postmark*, 16th August, 1819.)—My dear girl, what shall I say for myself ? I have been here four days and not yet written you—'tis true I have had many teasing letters of business to dismiss—and I have been in the claws, like a serpent in an eagle's, of the last act of our tragedy. This is no excuse ; I know it ; I do not presume to offer it. I have no right either to ask a speedy answer to let me know how lenient you are—I must remain some days in a Mist—I see you through a Mist ; as I daresay you do me by this time. Believe in the first Letters I wrote you : I assure you I felt as I wrote—I could not write so now. The thousand images I have had pass through my brain—my uneasy spirits—my unguessed fate—all spread as a veil between you and me. Remember I have had no idle leisure to brood over you—'tis well perhaps I have not. I could not have endured the throng of jealousies that used to haunt me before I had plunged so deeply into imaginary interests. I would fain, as my sails are set, sail on without an interruption for a Brace of Months longer—I am in complete cue— in the fever ; and shall in these four Months do an

immense deal. This Page as my eye skims over it I see
is excessively unloverlike and ungallant—I cannot help
it—I am no officer in yawning quarters; no Parson-
Romeo. My Mind is heap'd to the full; stuff'd like a
cricket-ball—if I strive to fill it more it would burst.
I know the generality of women would hate me for this;
that I should have so unsoften'd, so hard a Mind as to
forget them; forget the brightest realities for the dull
imaginations of my own Brain. But I conjure you to
give it a fair thinking; and ask yourself whether 'tis
not better to explain my feelings to you, than write
artificial Passion.—Besides, you would see through it.
It would be vain to strive to deceive you. 'Tis harsh,
harsh, I know it. My heart seems now made of iron—
I could not write a proper answer to an invitation to
Idalia. You are my Judge: my forehead is on the
ground. You seem offended at a little simple innocent
childish playfulness in my last. I did not seriously
mean to say that you were endeavouring to make me
keep my promise. I beg your pardon for it. 'Tis but
just your pride should take the alarm—*seriously.* You
say I may do as I please—I do not think with any conscience I can; my cash resources are for the present
stopp'd; I fear for some time. I spend no money, but
it increases my debts. I have all my life thought very
little of these matters—they seem not to belong to me.
It may be a proud sentence; but by Heaven I am as
entirely above all matters of interest as the Sun is above
the Earth—and though of my own money I should be
careless; of my Friends' I must be spare. You see how
I go on—like so many strokes of a hammer. I cannot
help it—I am impell'd, driven to it. I am not happy
enough for silken Phrases, and silver sentences. I can
no more use soothing words to you than if I were at
this moment engaged in a charge of Cavalry. Then you
will say I should not write at all.—Should I not?
This Winchester is a fine place; a beautiful cathedral
and many other ancient buildings in the environs. The

little coffin of a room at Shanklin is changed for a large room, where I can promenade at my pleasure—looks out on to a beautiful—blank side of a house. It is strange I should like it better than the view of the sea from our window at Shanklin. I began to hate the very posts there—the voice of the old Lady over the way was getting a great Plague. The Fisherman's face never altered any more than our black tea-pot, the knob, however was knock'd off to my little relief. I am getting a great dislike of the picturesque, and can only relish it over again by seeing you enjoy it. One of the pleasantest things I have seen lately was at Cowes. The Regent in his Yatch [1] (I think they spell it) was anchored opposite—a beautiful vessel—and all the Yatchs and boats on the coast were passing and repassing it, and circuiting and tacking about it in every direction. I never beheld anything so silent, light and graceful. As we pass'd over to Southampton, there was nearly an accident. There came by a Boat, well mann'd, with two naval officers at the stern. Our Bow-lines took the top of their little mast and snapped it off close by the board. Had the mast been a little stouter, they would have been upset. In so trifling an event, I could not help admiring our seamen,—neither officer nor man in the whole Boat moved a muscle,—they scarcely notic'd it even with words. Forgive me for this flint-worded Letter, and believe and see that I cannot think of you without some sort of energy though *mal a propos*. Even as I leave off, it seems to me that a few more moments' thought of you would uncrystallise and dissolve me. I must not give way to it—but turn to my writing again —if I fail, I shall die hard. O my love, your lips are growing sweet again to my fancy—I must forget them. Ever your affectionate KEATS.

[1] This word is of course left as found in the original letter; an editor who would spell it *yacht* would be guilty of representing Keats as thinking what he did not think.

That seems to me a letter most characteristic of Keats, well worth preserving, and not of the purely personal character of most of the correspondence. The idea throughout is that the writer's heart, while it is occupied with the world of poetry, "seems made of iron"; that the sentences of the letter he wrote while thus employed are like "strokes of a hammer"; that instead of writing soothing words, he is "engaged in a charge of cavalry"; and that all this hardness is due to his poetic preoccupations. That fancy of his is very characteristic of the depth of his poetic life. And still more the touching plea for what he calls his "flint-worded letter," namely, that it proves, at all events, that he cannot think of her to whom it is addressed "without some sort of energy,"—and the melting into genuine love in the last sentence, as his fancy conjures up once more her to whom he is writing, are curiously characteristic of a poet whose love of beauty was so strong, that it alone seemed to satisfy him like love of a person, and was his only equivalent for personal affection, and who evidently made even the lady of his choice jealous of her own beauty, since she seems to have feared, not perhaps untruly, that he loved her for her beauty, not for herself, and so fearing, was not able to elicit from Keats any positive contradiction.

The little volume is, indeed, full of Keats. And yet I would rather that it had been buried in the oblivion to which assuredly he himself would have consigned it.

SHELLEY AS PROPHET

IT is probably not fair to the Master of University College, Oxford, to accept the report in the *Times* of Thursday week as adequately representing what he said of the prophetic character of Shelley. I should be very sorry to deny that Shelley had a true discernment of the character of the sentiment which his own poetry did so much to mould and to inspire. There was plenty of true anticipation in him, if not of that which, in the higher sense, we are accustomed to call prophecy. His aspirations after universal beauty, his yearnings for diffused love and loveliness, his intolerance of a slow and patient providence, his eagerness to promote a rapture of humanity at large into a more vivid world, have unquestionably proved contagious in the highest degree. Vague as were his visions, no man has done more to thrill the world with the ardours of his own heart, with the insatiable cravings, and quick, fitful anguish of his own hopes and griefs. But I should decline entirely to declare with Dr. Bright that Shelley delivered either any affective rebuke to our pessimism, or any effective augury of good omen to the human race. If the noble concluding lines of "Prometheus Unbound" be relied on as proving that Shelley was really a prophet of the triumph of good over evil,

I should cite the concluding lines of "Hellas"—a later poem, and one that was not forced by the very nature of its subject to paint Shelley's conception of what such a triumph should be, if it ever came at all—to prove that the former passage was rather dramatic than prophetic, and that what Shelley really conceived as his own forecast of the future was something like an alternation of good and evil of which he did not venture to face the ultimate issue :—

> Saturn and Love their long repose
>   Shall burst, more bright and good
> Than all who fell, than One who rose,
>   Than many unsubdued :
> Not gold, not blood, their altar dowers,
> But votive tears and symbol flowers.
>
> Oh, cease !   Must hate and death return ?
>   Cease !   Must men kill and die ?
> Cease !   Drain not to its dregs the urn
>   Of bitter prophecy.
> The world is weary of the past,
> Oh, might it die or rest at last !

That seems to me much the nearest approach Shelley ever made to expressing his own view of the future of our world.   And clearly, he regarded that future as too full of bitterness to admit of anything like steady contemplation.   His eye shrank from the vision, and his voice could only utter a musical wail of plaintive dread.   Dr. Bright's conception of Shelley as prophesying "good things and not bad," as a prophet whom it is "cheerful" to encounter, seems to me exceedingly ill justified by anything which Shelley has written.   Indeed, even at the close

of "Prometheus Unbound," there is the same indication of a belief in the Eternal alternation of evil
and good ; though, as Shelley was writing expressly
on the unbinding of the divine friend of man, he is
more or less compelled to let the pæan of triumph
rise highest and be heard last in the scale :—

Gentleness, Virtue, Wisdom, and Endurance,
These are the seals of that most firm assurance
   Which bars the pit over Destruction's strength ;
And if, with infirm hand, Eternity,
Mother of many acts and hours, should free
   The serpent that would clasp her with his length,
These are the spells by which to reassume
An Empire o'er the disentangled doom.

Moreover, Shelley took care, in the notes with which
he accompanied "Hellas," his latest considerable
work, to let the world know distinctly not only
what he thought of the superiority of "Saturn and
Love"—the deities who represented "the imaginary
state of innocence and happiness," as he called it,
which preceded Christianity—to Christ, but of the
superiority of Christ himself to the Power which
sent Him into the world. Shelley was no prophet
who augured the victory of Christ from the infinite
power of Him who so loved the world, that He gave
His only begotten Son that the world through Him
might be saved. On the contrary, he affixed this
remarkable note to the verses in which he described
the temporary return of a golden age before that
fatal swinging-back of the pendulum which he saw
in vision, and which made him cry out in anguish :
"Oh, cease ! must hate and death return ?" Here
is Shelley's own comment on his last poetic prophecy,
a prophecy which certainly does not seem to me to

be a cheerful prophecy of "good things and not bad" :—

Saturn and Love were amongst the deities of a real or imaginary state of innocence and happiness. *All* those *who fell*, or the gods of Greece, Asia, and Egypt; the *One who rose*, or Jesus Christ, at whose appearance the idols of the world—the Pagan world—were amerced of their worship ; and *the many unsubdued*, or the monstrous objects of the idolatry of China, India, the Antarctic islands, and the native tribes of America, certainly have reigned over the understandings of men in conjunction or in succession, during periods in which all we know of evil has been in a state of portentous, and, until the revival of learning and the arts, perpetually increasing activity. The Grecian gods seem indeed to have been personally more innocent, although it cannot be said, that as far as temperance and chastity are concerned, they gave so edifying an example as their successor. The sublime human character of Jesus Christ was deformed by an imputed identification with a Power who tempted, betrayed, and punished the innocent beings who were called into existence by his sole will. And for the period of a thousand years, the spirit of this just, most just, wise, and benevolent of men, has been propitiated with myriads of hecatombs of those who approached the nearest to his innocence and wisdom, sacrificed under every aggravation of atrocity and variety of torture. The horrors of the Mexican, the Peruvian, and the Indian superstitions are well known.

Assuredly, that does not seem to me at all the comment of one who, if Dr. Bright is rightly reported, was to his mind a great prophet " of good things and not bad." Shelley seems to have held Christ to be one who stood in the same relation to the Ultimate Power behind the world as that in

which his own Prometheus stood to Zeus, who, as
Dr. Bright says, still, " in some degree reigned " " as
the emblem of what was false and conventional."
And holding such a creed as that, I can scarcely
understand how any Christian teacher could regard
it as a creed in any way better than the modern
fatalism and pessimism. Shelley's vision was the
vision of a swooning spirit which sometimes, indeed,
exhorted us

> To suffer woes which Hope thinks infinite ;
> To forgive wrongs darker than death or night ;
>   To defy Power, which seems omnipotent ;
> To love and bear ; to hope till Hope creates
> From its own wreck the thing it contemplates ;
>   Neither to change, nor falter, nor repent.

—but oftener sank back again into the nightmare
dream of a world that is " weary of the past," and
"yet cannot so much as find courage to believe that
it will either die or "rest" at last.

But though I should certainly deny to Shelley
the great claim which Dr. Bright makes for him as
the opponent of our modern pessimism, I should
maintain that he anticipated that etherealised form
of modern pessimism which melodiously bewails the
evil with which it has not the strength to combat.
Shelley had no belief at all in the evil within him,
and therefore he laid the evil without him at the
doors of the great Power to which the constitution
of the world is due. Christ, he thought, was
"deformed by an imputed identification with a
Power who tempted, betrayed, and punished the
innocent beings who were called into existence by
his sole will." He had no trust in the righteous
Will behind all our evil thoughts and passions, no

confidence in the Everlasting Arms, no loathing for those miserable cravings and failures which defeat in us all the promptings of divine grace. No wonder he thought the destiny of man a sort of shuttlecock which was to be driven constantly to and fro between good and evil, for good and evil were to him mere alternating sentiments, equally deep rooted in the foundations of the world, which ebbed and flowed like the tides. And in so believing, he certainly anticipated a good deal of the most characteristic features of the modern sentimentalism, while penetrating it with a savour of sweetness and beauty with which only a great poet could have managed to have pervaded it. The modern notion that all pain is a positive wrong inflicted on those who suffer it,—a wrong that ought to be remedied at any cost, though the cost itself at which alone it can be remedied is a new wrong,—is of the very essence of Shelley's gospel, if gospel it can be called. No doubt he held willing suffering to be the greatest of all healing influences; but then he thought the mere existence of willing suffering a great blot on the holiness of the Ultimate Power by which it is permitted. Martyrdom was to him the great redeeming power, but then it was also the great arraignment of the Creative Spirit. Shelley's mind vibrated between a passionate admiration of Him who could suffer to save others, and passionate resentment that suffering to save others should ever be needful at all. He never even admitted for a moment the idea of a suffering God, and therefore he never admitted for a moment the root-idea of the Christian revelation and of all true prophecy. The prevalent optimism and the prevalent pessimism of the present day are alike reflected in the music of

Shelley's wonderful Æolian harp.   He took a great
deal more credit than was deserved for the amiable
wishes of the human heart, for the well-being of the
human race ; and he felt a great deal less shame
than was deserved for the eager and imperious self-
will of the various spontaneous affections of human
nature.   His was an Antinomian worship of sweet
emotion, and he anticipated, therefore, that Antinomian worship of sweet emotion, that "passionate
tumult of a clinging hope," which is inspired neither
by reason nor by conscience, but only by a credulous
belief in the divinity of desire.   To my mind,
Shelley is no prophet in any true sense of the word.
What he is, Mr. Watson has told us in language
hardly less lovely, and much more chastened, than
his own :—

> And power is his, if nought besides,
> In that thin ether where he rides
> Above the roar of human tides
>   To ascend afar,
> Lost in a storm of light that hides
>   His dizzy car.
>
> Below the unhasting world toils on,
> And here and there are victories won,
> Some dragon slain, some justice done,
> While through the skies,
> A meteor rushing on the sun,
> He flares and dies.

WHAT IS A LYRIC?

WHEN Coleridge and Wordsworth published their first joint-volume of poems they called them "Lyrical Ballads," though I should hardly think one of the many fine poems it contained to be in any definite sense lyrical. Coleridge's "Ancient Mariner," with which it opens, is an imaginary narrative. And a predominantly narrative poem, however saturated with imagination it may be, can hardly be called "lyrical" without suggesting ideas which, in one way or another, put a certain strain on the term. Johnson defines lyric as "pertaining to a harp or to odes or poetry sung to a harp," and in his illustration of the use made of the word by the greater writers he gives striking passages from Milton and Dryden. Milton's is as follows :—

> All his trophies hung or acts enrolled
> In copious legend or sweet lyrick song.

Here the "copious legend" is certainly distinguished from the "sweet lyrick song"; and though, no doubt, as Scott's "Lay of the Last Minstrel" shows us, long narrative poems were often sung to the harp's accompaniment, it was not the story, not the *incident* it contained, that gave such narrative poems their name of lyrics, but rather their impassioned openings or their close, in which the poet rose to a loftier strain of emotion, and burst into such passages as those which excited the admiration of Pitt, in Scott's "Lay," as, for example :—

> Amid the strings his fingers strayed
> And an uncertain warbling made,
> And oft he shook his hoary head.
> But when he caught the measure wild,
> The old man raised his face, and smiled ;
> And lightened up his faded eye,
> With all a poet's ecstasy !
> In varying cadence, soft or strong,
> He swept the sounding chords along :
> The present scene, the future lot,
> His toils, his wants, were all forgot ;
> Cold diffidence, and age's frost,
> In the full tide of song were lost ;
> Each blank, in faithless memory void,
> The poet's glowing thought supplied ;
> And, while his harp responsive rung,
> 'Twas thus the Latest Minstrel sung.

That is lyrical, no doubt, in the truest sense, as is also such a passage as that in which Scott declared in another of his poems that the wretch "concentred all in self "—

> Living shall forfeit fair renown,
> And doubly dying shall go down
> To the vile dust from whence he sprung
> Unwept, unhonoured, and unsung.

It was not the versified narrative of the long ballads which gave them a right to the accompaniment of the harp, but just those bursts of impassioned feeling which best entitled them to be *sung* rather than recited. Coleridge's "Ancient Mariner," fine as it is, contains hardly any passage of that kind. And accordingly Coleridge, with a sure instinct, describes it as recited, and never ventures to think of it as sung. Indeed, there is not one poem in the original "Lyrical Ballads" which I could think of as specially adapted for song. The passage which Johnson selected from Dryden to illustrate the meaning of the word "lyric" is equally to the point for the purposes of definition:—"Somewhat of the purity of English, somewhat of more equal thoughts, somewhat of sweetness in the numbers; in one word, somewhat of a finer turn, and more lyrical verse, is yet wanting." There you have it. True lyrical verse needs "somewhat of a finer turn" than ordinary verse, or, as Matthew Arnold termed it, needs more of "the lyrical cry," that tone which comes from the heart and rings through the voice to the very hearts of those to whom it is addressed. Now Wordsworth, though he called his earliest poems "Lyrical Ballads," could hardly have called them by a less fitting name. They were neither in the truest sense ballads nor lyrics. Could either the one word or the other be more grossly misapplied than each was, for instance, to the stately and, no doubt, in a very true sense, impassioned lines written near Tintern Abbey with which the volume of lyrical ballads closed? Nor, indeed, is there a single poem in that volume which naturally suggests to the mind either the attitude of song, or that lyrical cry which lifts verse into the mood in which you feel the need of music to give it a fuller expression. Wordsworth's poems are full of magnificent recitative; but even in relation to what he calls ballads —with one exception, the "Song at the Feast of

Brougham Castle," which both begins and ends in
the true lyric strain—we hardly ever recognise in
Wordsworth the true lyrical poet. Oddly enough,
Mr. Ernest Rhys, who has just given us a volume
called *The Lyric Poems of William Wordsworth*,
does not include in it what seems to me the truest
lyric Wordsworth ever wrote :—

> From town to town, from tower to tower,
> The red rose is a gladsome flower.
> Her thirty years of winter past,
> The red rose is revived at last ;
> She lifts her head for endless spring,
> For everlasting blossoming :
> Both roses flourish, red and white :
> In love and sisterly delight
> The two that were at strife are blended,
> And all old troubles now are ended.—
> Joy ! joy to both ! but most to her
> Who is the flower of Lancaster !

That has the true lyrical cry in it, and so has the
magnificent close :—

> Now another day has come,
> Fitter hope, and nobler doom ;
> He hath thrown aside his crook,
> And hath buried deep his book ;
> Armour rusting in his halls
> On the blood of Clifford calls ;—
> "Quell the Scot," exclaims the lance,—
> Bear me to the heart of France,
> Is the longing of the shield—
> Tell thy name, thou trembling field ;
> Field of death, where'er thou be,
> Groan thou with our victory !

Happy day, and mighty hour,
When our Shepherd, in his power,
Mailed and horsed, with lance and sword,
To his ancestors restored
Like a re-appearing star,
Like a glory from afar,
First shall head the flock of war!

Here we have the true lyric fervour and the rapid
beat of the lyric pulse. Generally, Wordsworth's
thought is reflective, meditative, more or less long
drawn out even when most impassioned. I hardly
know one of his poems except the one I have just
quoted which beats with the quick throb of the
true lyric. No doubt, "Three Years she grew in
sun and shower" is a lyric, and so *perhaps* is "She
was a phantom of delight," though that is more
meditative. Again, the poem to the Cuckoo, "O
blithe New-comer! I have heard, I hear thee and
rejoice," is a lyric; but on the whole Wordsworth's
verse at its best has too much weight and grandeur
of thought in it for the movement of the true
lyric. And it seems to me doubtful if, sublime as
his best poetry is, he is in any characteristic sense
a lyrical poet at all.

I should define a true lyric as a poem expressive
chiefly of emotion which makes the hearer long for
music to help him to utter its very heart. Shelley
is perhaps the greatest lyrical poet of our century,
for though Byron wrote one glorious lyric, "The
Isles of Greece," he was much greater in satirical and
descriptive poetry than in true lyrics. But Shelley
breathed out the sweetest and the most exquisite
expressions of grief and love, and melancholy and
rapture, in language that seemed made for music,
which English literature possesses:—

When the lamp is shattered the light in the dust lies
    dead—
When the cloud is scattered the rainbow's glory is
    shed.
When the lute is broken, sweet tones are remembered
    not ;
When the lips have spoken, loved accents are soon
    forgot.

There you have what Matthew Arnold justly
called Shelley's "lovely wail." Or take the exquisite lines to the Skylark, or the lines written in
dejection at Naples, or the following :—

> I can give not what men call love,
>   But wilt thou accept not
> The worship the heart lifts above,
>   And the Heavens reject not.
>
> The desire of the moth for the star
>   Of the night for the morrow,
> The devotion to something afar
>   From the sphere of our sorrow.

Shelley could throw his soul into the breath of a
passionate emotion, and embody it in the most
musical words, and that is the essence of a true
lyric. But for lyrics of less passion and more
pathos, lyrics of what I may call restrained feeling,
of resisted regret, Tennyson was one of the greatest
of our poets. His delicate songs dignify even those
dramas in which he so often failed. And again,
such poems as "Break, break, break," or "Tears,
idle tears," or "Blow, bugle, blow, set the wild
echoes flying," are perfect and exquisite specimens
of the "sweet reasonableness" of his gentle emotions.
Indeed, even such poems as "The Brook" and

"The Queen of the May," though much inferior in their lyrical beauty, seem to demand music to bring out their true character, and to give the full thrill to the minor key which runs through them. In this respect Wordsworth and Tennyson were at opposite poles, Wordsworth being saturated with that impassioned meditative mood that runs naturally to blank verses or the metre of the sonnet, while Tennyson was always at his best in crystallising a transient emotion of sensitive ecstasy or pathetic yearning. The happiest types of a true lyric which we have had in this century from any poet since Tennyson left us, have been given us in Mr. Watson's verse, which not only seems at times to have been written to some vibrating chord of joy or grief in his own nature, but to cry aloud for an accompaniment as richly modulated as that of the harp or the organ to fill up the full measure of its meaning. A recent satirist has described Mr. Watson as, "Wordsworth and water." "Wordsworth and music," or a lyrical Wordsworth, would have been a truer description.

THE MYSTICAL SIDE OF GOOD SENSE

THERE is a very interesting paper in the new number of the *National Review* by Mr. John Hogben, on "The Mystical Side of Wordsworth." I should like to show that where Wordsworth is most mystical, good sense itself, as Englishmen usually understand it, is almost identical in its assumptions, though instead of setting out in full the path by which these assumptions are reached, good sense is apt to lead to a conclusion without paying much attention to the somewhat mystical reasoning by which these assumptions are established. At the opening of his paper, Mr. Hogben shows how much Wordsworth relied on the conclusions to which his own mind came in what may be called a kind of mental somnambulism, a mood in which the senses seemed to be laid asleep, while some higher faculty was all the surer and more penetrating in its judgments on account of that partial sleep of the perceptive powers. In the great lines written near Tintern Abbey, for instance, Wordsworth insists on "that blessed mood" in which,

> Even the motions of our human blood
> Almost suspended, we are laid asleep
> In body, and become a living soul.

111

It is, he tells us, not by a restlessly inquisite eye, but by "an eye made *quiet* by the power of harmony and the deep power of joy" that "we see into the life of things." So, too, he defends himself for sitting hour after hour on an old grey stone in apparent vacancy, on the ground that :—

> The eye it cannot choose but see,
>   We cannot bid the ear be still,
> Our bodies feel, where'er they be,
>   Against or with our will.

> Nor less I deem that there are powers
>   Which of themselves our minds impress ;
> That we can feed this mind of ours
>   By a wise passiveness.

Again, when he is most deeply stirred by anything he hears, as, for example, by the old leech-gatherer's account of his own patient endurance of hardship, Wordsworth finds the figure which has thus deeply impressed him becoming almost unreal, "like one that I had met with in a dream." In other words, Wordsworth's vision is, in his own belief, never thoroughly lucid till he is rapt by it far away from the ordinary alertness which is commonly called quickness of sense, and transported into a region in which he is alone with his thoughts, and all but unconscious of the momentary changes going on around him. Well, is not Wordsworth confirmed by the good sense, the better sense of the world, in this view of his, that we are apt to catch our truest and most really informing vision of the deeper aspects of things around us, in the *least* studied of

our glances, or even in the retrospect with which
we revert to what we have previously seen without
seeing it, as, for instance, when we are half falling
asleep at night, or when we are just awakening, and
the events of the previous day flash back upon us
a new light which they did not give out at the
time ? We may call it mysticism when we are
speaking of it as a poet's explicit teaching ; but we
do not call it mysticism, we call it good sense, when
we attach more importance to the sidelights cast
on any scene by a tranquil memory, than to the
view of it which we took during the first eager gaze
of a too anxious inquisition. Even the mere man
of the world is conscious that when he is " laid
asleep in body," he often becomes a much more
" living soul " for those things which he is most
desirous to discern truly ; that as his senses sink to
rest, he recalls errors of which he was unconscious
when he committed them, or expressions on the
countenances of his friends or rivals which till then
he had completely ignored. And if this be so in
relation to things essentially of this world, it is
certainly much more so as to those deeper springs
of motive and character which it takes a still deeper
peace of spirit to perceive. Every one who has any
insight at all, knows that the false notes he has
struck during his hours of work come back to him
most clearly when he is no longer absorbed in the
strain or passion of the moment,—when, indeed, he
is not even consciously reviewing the events of the
day, but when they revisit him involuntarily, with
a new significance and in new relations of which he
had no glimpse before. It is not till something
has happened to quiet the whole nature, or, in
Wordsworth's phrase, to subdue it with " the power

of harmony," that the real drift of that which, with an agitated and excited nature, we had no power to discern at all, is grasped. It is not the eye which *sees* ill, for it does see that which the mind does not always note till the scene recurs in memory; but it is the mind which interprets ill, because it is too much blinded by the heat and hurry of the moment to take all in. We need a wise "passiveness" to interpret truly what we see. But the good sense of the world is quite at one with Wordsworth on this point. It, too, says that what we remember when the rush of events is over is apt to be much truer than what we see while the rush of events lasts.

Take another of Wordsworth's apparently mystical inspirations. There is nothing on which he dwells with more delight than the power of the imagination to transmute the greatest apparent obstacles which it has to face into the very substance of its own visionary energy, so that instead of being arrested by difficulties, it is the difficulties which elicit and display its real vitality and power : —

> Within the soul, a faculty abides
> That, with interpositions that would hide
> And darken, so can deal that they become
> Contingencies of pomp, and serve to exalt
> Her native brightness. As the ample moon
> In the deep stillness of a summer even,
> Rising behind a thick and lofty grove,
> Burns like an unconsuming fire of light
> In the green trees ; and, kindling on all sides
> Their leafy umbrage, turns the dusky veil
> Into a substance glorious as her own,
> Yea, with her own incorporated, by power

> Capacious and serene :—like power abides
> In man's celestial spirit ; virtue thus
> Sets forth and magnifies herself ; thus feeds
> A calm, a beautiful, and silent fire
> From the incumbrances of mortal life,
> From error, disappointment, nay, from guilt,
> And sometimes, so relenting justice wills,
> From palpable oppressions of despair.

In like manner he dwells on :—

> Sorrow that is not sorrow, but delight,
> And miserable love that is not pain
> To hear of, for the glory that redounds
> Therefrom to human kind and what we are.

It is a subject on which Wordsworth is never tired
of insisting, that the imagination of man has in
itself a spring of joy so deep that it can transform
the most gloomy subjects with its own light, till
the gloomier they are intrinsically, the better they
serve to glorify the power of the mind by which
they are grasped and transformed.   That explains
why Wordsworth seized so eagerly on subjects
which all his contemporaries jeered at as unpoetical.
He sought to show that the power of imaginative
joy in him could make them all the more poetical
from their unpromising appearance.   In short, the
more impervious to light the substance on which
the imagination shed its rays, the more glorious the
transformation it effected by touching it with the
magic of its passion.   Well, is not the good sense
of the world completely at one with Wordsworth in
the result, though it does not dwell on the process
with the minute care with which he dwells on it ?
Does it not believe that it is difficulties which make

a man,—whether imaginative or otherwise,—who is
worth making at all? Does it not hold that the
most ennobling fate for a really great man is to
have all sorts of obstacles cast in his way that he
may surmount them, and by surmounting them
come to realise the deep-stored energy within, of
which otherwise he might never know the depth?
The better sense of the world takes little account of
a man who has had no difficulties, it takes much of
one who has had great difficulties and conquered
them, and more still of one who has sought out,
without the need for doing so, a difficult path that
leads to a great goal, and conquered the obstacles in
the way. No sound judge would trust a man whose
life had been plain sailing. We all know that the
nature which has not been early tested, and often
tested, is not to be trusted, that it is not tempered
as we like to see all good steel tempered before we
use it in a great conflict. Wordsworth's profound
belief that this power was in the mind before it
came out of it, and only waited to be brought out
by conflict, does not concern the world, which does
not busy itself with the source of the energy so long
as the energy is there and is proved. But as
profoundly as Wordsworth believed that conflict and
resistance were essential to bring to light the poet's
inborn power, so profoundly does the better sense
of the world believe that no man is really great who
has not found out for himself the best difficulties
to overcome, even if they did not challenge him to
overcome them.

Or, again, what can be more apparently mystical
than Wordsworth's belief that he could feel—
intuitively feel—the wholeness of the universe and
the greatness of that whole?—

I have felt
A presence that disturbs me with the joy
Of elevated thoughts ; a sense sublime
Of something far more deeply interfused
Whose dwelling is the light of setting suns,
And the round ocean, and the*living air,
And the blue sky, and in the mind of man ;
A motion and a spirit that impels
All thinking things, all objects of all thought,
And rolls through all things.

And yet is it not this very sense of the wholeness
of the universe, and especially of the essential
harmony of the whole universe with the most
sublime things in it, like "the light of setting suns,
and the round ocean, and the living air, and the
blue sky, and in the mind of man," which good
sense half unconsciously insists upon as one of the
first requisites of a large and sagacious nature ?
There is nothing good sense sooner takes offence at
than either want of a large sympathy and insight
into the world without, or on the other hand,
pessimism,—want of the former implying want of
feeling for the way in which one thing touches
another, and gets itself into true relations with it,
and the latter implying a disposition to interpret
the facts of life from the ugly and dark side of it,
instead of from the beautiful and bright side of it.
Either the one disposition or the other is offensive
to the really good sense of the world, which is
nevertheless all unconscious that in thus insisting
on a feeling for the whole, as distinct from a feeling
for insulated parts, and in insisting on interpreting
the whole by that which is greatest and most
beautiful, and not by that which is smallest and
most ugly, it is really insisting on a mystical view

of the universe, and especially on Wordsworth's mystical view of it,—the view which discerns a prevailing harmony in the whole, and which makes joy the keynote for explaining sorrow, and not sorrow the keynote for explaining joy.

WORDSWORTH THE MAN

In the exquisite little sketch which Mr. Myers has given of Wordsworth, in Mr. John Morley's series of "Men of Letters,"—as a piece of English at least, the gem, I venture to say, of the whole series,— the only thing which, in the perfect candour and singularly chastened truthfulness of the essay, I am disposed to think has been a little inadequately rendered, is the effect of personal force which Wordsworth produced upon all who were competent to understand him at all. Mr. Myers has told us what De Quincey had preconceived of Wordsworth, from a knowledge of his poetry,—namely, that he "prefigured the image of Wordsworth," to what he called his own "planet-struck eyes," as one before which his faculties would quail, as before " Elijah or St. Paul." But in his explanation how this profound homage to Wordsworth was possible on the part of such a master of the secrets of literature as De Quincey, Mr. Myers, though he dwells very justly and appropriately on Wordsworth's claim to be in a sense the poet of a new revelation, hardly attaches enough importance, I think, to the general intensity and rugged power of the man. He has not quoted the impression formed of Wordsworth by a much harder and less impressionable man than

119

De Quincey, and one not at all disposed to receive humbly Wordsworth's "revelation." Hazlitt, perhaps the most cynical critic who ever had an omnivorous appetite for what was good in literature, however unique its kind, early formed a very strong impression of Wordsworth's power, and has left a sketch of him as he was in his earliest poetic epoch, —that is, about the age of twenty-five years, for Wordsworth ripened late, and was hardly a poet at all till he was a mature man. "He answered in some degree," says Hazlitt, "to his friend's (Coleridge's) description of him, but was more gaunt and Don Quixote-like. He was quaintly dressed (according to the costume of that unconstrained period) in a brown fustian jacket and striped pantaloons. There was something of a roll or lounge in his gait, not unlike his own Peter Bell. There was a severe, worn pressure of thought about his temples, a fire in his eye (as if he saw something in objects more than the outward appearance), an intense, high, narrow forehead, a Roman nose, cheeks furrowed by strong purpose and feeling, a convulsive inclination to laughter about the mouth a good deal at variance with the solemn, stately expression of the rest of the face. Chantrey's bust wants the marking traits, but he was teased into making it regular and heavy. Haydon's head of him, introduced into the 'Entrance of Christ into Jerusalem,' is the most like the drooping weight of thought and expression. He sat down and talked very naturally and freely, with a mixture of clear, gushing accents in his voice, a deep, guttural intonation, and a strong mixture of the northern burr, like the crust on wine." That, coming from Hazlitt, describes a man of no ordinary power; for it must be remembered that Hazlitt was by no means a disciple of Wordsworth's, though he was a great admirer of his. He hated Wordsworth for having given up his first Radicalism. He referred all Wordsworth's finest poetry to his egotism, and asserted that Wordsworth's strength was virtually due to "excess of weakness." Nevertheless, when he was describing him as he had first seen him, Hazlitt was far too intelligent a critic to describe a man in whom weakness was the key to strength. On the contrary, he described the "severe worn pressure of thought about his temples," and the fire in his eye as of one who saw something in objects beyond their outward appearance. And everything we know of Wordsworth confirms this. His mother, who died when he was but eight years old, said that the only one of her children about whose future life she was anxious was William, and that he would be remarkable either for good or evil. And Wordsworth himself explains this by saying that he was of a "stiff, moody, and violent temper," and once as a child had gone into one of his grandfather's rooms to find a foil with which to destroy himself, because he thought he had been unjustly punished. When abroad at the time of the French Revolution, though not at all a perfect master of the French language, he seriously thought of offering himself as a Girondist leader, and was only prevented by his English friends stopping his allowance, so that he had to return home to find the means of living. Even after his return his mind long dwelt with the most brooding melancholy on the future of the Revolution, of which he had formed such passionate hopes. For months and even years he says that the French collapse haunted him so that his nights were full of horrible dreams. He dreamt of dungeons, massacres, and guillotines. He dreamt long speeches with which he was pleading before unjust tribunals on behalf of accused patriots. He dreamt of treachery, desertion, and that last sense of utter desolation, when the last strength ebbs even from the soul of the dreamer. After this he fell into the state in which nothing is credited without the most ample and formal demonstration, nothing held true unless it is warranted by the senses. But even at this time, moody and fitful as Wordsworth's life had been,—Mr. Myers says that even at a later period he might not unfairly have been taken for "a rough and somewhat stubborn young man, who in nearly thirty years of life had seemed alternately to idle without grace and to study without advantage,"—he was in no sense the mere egotist Hazlitt wanted to make of him. His sister compared her two brothers thus :—" Christopher is steady and sincere in his attachments, William has both these virtues in an eminent degree, and a sort of violence of affection, if I may so term it, which demonstrates itself into every moment of the day, when the objects of his affection are present with him, in a thousand almost imperceptible attentions to their wishes, in a sort of restless watchfulness which I know not how to describe, a tenderness that never sleeps, and at the same time a delicacy of manner as I have observed in few men." And this passionate tenderness he showed in many relations of life. When his brother, the captain of the East Indiaman, went down with his ship off the Bill of Portland, Wordsworth's grief and suffering were far beyond the measure of ordinary men. Mr. De Vere says that nearly forty years after Wordsworth had

lost two of his children, "he described the details of
their illnesses with an exactness and an impetuosity
of troubled excitement such as might have been
expected if the bereavement had taken place but a
few weeks before."

This is not the picture of an egotist.   Nor do I
suppose that any complaint would ever have been
made of Wordsworth's egotism if it had been
limited to that fitfulness, occasional gustiness, or
even moodiness of mind to which, in some form
or other, almost every great poet has been subject,
and which, in many cases at least, has contributed
rather to enhance than to diminish a poet's fame.
Wordsworth's picture of himself, quoted by Mr.
Myers, in the lines written in Thomson's "Castle of
Indolence," is not a picture which would ever have
made him unpopular :—

> Full many a time, upon a stormy night,
> His voice came to us from the neighbouring height,
> Oft did we see him driving full in view
> At mid-day when the sun was shining bright ;
> What ill was on him, what he had to do,
> A mighty wonder bred among our quiet crew.
>
> Ah ! piteous sight it was to see this Man
> When he came back to us a withered flower,—
> Or, like a sinful creature, pale and wan.
> Down would he sit ; and without strength or power
> Look at the common grass from hour to hour ;
> And oftentimes, how long I fear to say,
> Where apple trees in blossom made a bower,
> Retired in that sunshiny shade he lay ;
> And, like a naked Indian, slept himself away.
>
> Great wonder to our gentle tribe it was
> Whenever from our valley he withdrew ;

For happier soul no living creature has
Than he had, being here the long day through.
Some thought he was a lover, and did woo ;
Some thought far worse of him, and judged him wrong :
But Verse was what he had been wedded to ;
And his own mind did like a tempest strong
Come to him thus, and drove the weary wight along.

That is a perfectly true picture, no doubt, and
gives us a better conception of the hidden fire in
Wordsworth than anything else which his poems
contain. But it is not moodiness, still less is it
fire, which ever gains for a poet the reputation of
egotism, and Wordsworth certainly has gained that
reputation more than any great English poet who
ever lived. What has given Wordsworth the reputation of an egotist, and made that part of the world
which does not care for his poetry depreciate him as
a man, is the peculiarly inward turn which his mind
took, so that, instead of multiplying his points of
relation with the world at large, as a poetic temperament usually does multiply them, Wordsworth's
genius appeared rather to shut him up in himself,
and to separate him by the most separating medium
in the world,—a totally alien method of regarding
things from that of the wondering and observing
world. Other great poets have generally had a
much higher command than the rest of mankind of
those same feelings, and thoughts, and fancies, of
which all of us have some command. But it was
hardly so with Wordsworth. That he had the
deepest human sympathies and affections we have
seen, and that he had the keenest and most hungry
eye for all that was beautiful in Nature we know
too ; but his poetic mode of treating his own feelings,
whether those due to human beings or those due to

Nature, was altogether alien to the method of the mass of mankind. Instead of finding direct expression for the feeling, whatever it was, his inward genius led him to resist its immediate drift, to put it at a distance from him, to muse upon it, to see whether, if it were painful, more profit could not be made of it by enduring, submitting to, and reflecting upon the pain, than by expressing it; and if it were joyful, whether more could not be made of it by husbanding and deferring the joy, than by exhausting it. He was warned by some inward instinct always to restrain emotion, however strong and stormy, till he could find a peaceful and lucid reflection of it in the mirror of a quiet mind. His mind, like Michael's, was "keen, intense, and frugal," but his temperament was far, indeed, from cool. He told a friend that he had never written love poetry because he dared not, it would have been too passionate. The truth is that his nature and genius were averse to direct expression. They made him wait till he could gain a reflex image of feeling in the deep, cool wells of thought. And this habit of his was so strange to the world that it set the world against him; and when the world was set against him, he set himself, of course, against the world; and, being well aware of his own genius, became a little too much absorbed in its ideas, and a little too deaf to other ideas which were outside the interests of his life. Mr. Myers accounts for a good part of Wordsworth's stiffness by his unpopularity. "The sense of humour is apt to be the first grace which is lost under persecution; and much of Wordsworth's heaviness and stiff exposition of commonplaces is to be traced to a feeling which he could scarcely avoid, that all day long he had lifted up his voice to a perverse and gainsaying generation." But is that the true explanation? If Wordsworth had had humour, persecution would hardly have robbed him of the humour. I doubt much if he ever had any. He was a "prophet of Nature," and as a prophet of Nature he had, like the prophets of God, a certain rapture of his own which rendered him insensible to humour. As the countryside said of him, he went "booing about," that is, half chanting to himself the thoughts which Nature and God put into his heart, and had little or no room for that fine elasticity in passing from one mood to another which is of the essence of all humour. He was a man of high passion, though he never let the world see it except in the reflex form of rapturous meditation. He was a man of deep affections, though he forbade to joy and sorrow their most natural outlets. For he was, above all, a man of deep reserves, a man of "keen, intense, and frugal" nature, who had little part in the ordinary excitements and enjoyments of the world, and was therefore also one in whose excitements and enjoyments the world could find little beyond food for amazement.

MR. MORLEY ON WORDSWORTH

MR. MORLEY'S politics do not use him up or wear him out. He has seldom written anything fresher or more vigorous than the essay on Wordsworth which he has prefixed to Macmillan's new and admirable one-volume edition of the poet,—the only complete edition, as it alone contains "The Recluse," which is now published for the first time. Yet while I heartily admire this admirable introduction, which touches the true Wordsworth at so many points and with so much delicacy, I do not agree with what I understand to be Mr. Morley's view, that it is more as teacher and less as pure poet that Wordsworth is most admirable. For my part, wherever Wordsworth becomes didactic I find his poetry below par. I heartily agree with Matthew Arnold's commentary on the passages from Wordsworth which bald-headed and spectacled educationists pour forth from educational platforms, and almost found it in my heart to cheer the scornful satire with which Mr. Arnold entreated us to turn "from these bold, bad men" to the true Wordsworth. I will admit to Mr. Morley that "there are great tracts in Wordsworth which by no definition and on no terms can be called poetry." I will admit to him that "Wordsworth hardly knows how to be stern as Dante or Milton was stern; nor has he the note of plangent sadness which strikes the ear in men so morally inferior to him as Rousseau, Keats, Shelley, or Coleridge; nor has he the Olympian air with which Goethe delivered sage oracles." But I cannot admit—I strenuously deny—that "in purely poetic quality" Wordsworth is surpassed by men who were below him in weight or greatness. I should say that in genuine "poetic quality"—though it is genuine poetic quality of a somewhat unique and limited if infinitely lofty kind, and not one which includes either "depth and variety of colour," or "penetrating and subtle sweetness of music"—Wordsworth is not surpassed by any English poet who ever lived. It is true, I think, that wherever Wordsworth is greatest he lifts us into a world far above our own, and that wherever he is most lamentably dreary he tries so to lift us, and fails; but what I vehemently deny is that he succeeds in lifting us into that world above our own by virtue of his didactic impulse, which, indeed, he often tries upon us with no effect but that of repelling instead of exalting us. But in his proper field, I hold, that (as Mr. De Vere, himself no mean poet, has maintained in a very striking essay) Wordsworth's passion is passion of the most genuine kind,—indeed in my estimation far more exalted than the passion of Byron, or Shelley, or Keats, or Coleridge, or even Burns. But then, its proper field is a field which hardly any poet but himself knows how to enter at all; it introduces us to a sort of fourth dimension in the poetic world, to a previously untravelled region of poetry where Wordsworth lives almost

alone, and nearly every other poet is simply
nowhere. Poems like the "Ode to Duty," the
"Lines Written near Tintern Abbey," "The
Cuckoo," "The Daffodils," "I wandered lonely as
a cloud," "The Affliction of Margaret," and at
least fifty others, seem to me to have genuine
"poetic quality" of a sort in which Wordsworth
has not only no rival, but hardly even a companion.
Perhaps there is a piece or two among Henry
Vaughan's beautiful poems in which I might say
that he indicates poetic quality of the same high
kind. But where is the highest passion to be
found, if it is not to be found in poems such as
these of Wordsworth,—passion in its highest and
truest sense, in the sense in which it indicates a
true rapture, because it means that the poet is
carried off his feet by a spirit which at once takes
possession of him and exalts him? Shelley's poetry
often expresses the same sense of rapture, but in
a much lower region, for while we feel that
Shelley is taken possession of by some exquisitely
musical passion of sorrow or desire, the rapture
does not exalt him, as it exalts Wordsworth, into
a sphere far purer and loftier than his own. Every
one knows the "Ode to Duty," and every one who
is not so definitely hostile to Wordsworth as to be
unable to enter into it at all, is struck by it; and
for my part, I doubt whether there is any rapture
expressed in our language quite so exalting as the
rapture of the last stanza but one :—

> Stern Lawgiver! yet thou dost wear
> The Godhead's most benignant grace;
> Nor know we anything so fair
> As is the smile upon thy face:

> Flowers laugh before thee on their beds
> And fragrance in thy footing treads ;
> Thou dost preserve the stars from wrong ;
> And the most ancient heavens, through Thee, are
>   fresh and strong.

It is quite true that in Wordsworth's highest strain there is always the note of "volition and self-government," but that indicates the theme rather than the poetic force or movement. You see that Wordsworth prepared himself for his highest work by offering a strong resistance to the impulses which solicited him, instead of yielding to them as Shelley would have done; but so far he had not even touched the mood of poetry; he had only prepared himself for inspiration by a sort of spiritual initiation of his own. For he well knew that the Muse was most accessible to him in this mood, and that when he had prepared himself by strenuous effort to receive her, she was most likely to lift him to her highest heaven. But it was not the ascetic preparation of heart and will which involved any element of rapture; it was only that without this ascetic preparation the rapture never came, or never came in its noblest and loftiest form. If he waited in vain, then he wrote the sort of verse which Mr. Arnold's "bold, bad men" love to pour forth from platforms. But often, at least, he did not wait in vain, and then Wordsworth was able to express, as no other English poet has ever been able to express, what Mr. Bagehot so finely described as "the lonely rapture of lonely minds." For though that rapture is in Wordsworth a consequence of volition, it is by no means true that when it comes it usually contains in even such a "direct appeal to will and conduct" as does

the "Ode to Duty." Take the exquisite poems
on "Yarrow Unvisited," "The Solitary Reaper,"
"Three years she grew in sun and shower," among
scores of the same kind, and you will not find a
line in any of them which the "bold, bad men"
would care to quote, or which would answer the
purpose of any one who wanted to make "a direct
appeal to will and conduct." How would it answer
their purpose to proclaim to the world the existence
of a boy among the woods and islands of Winander
of whom it might be truly said that—

> with fingers interwoven, both hands
> Pressed closely palm to palm, and to his mouth
> Uplifted, he, as through an instrument,
> Blew mimic hootings to the silent owls
> That they might answer him. And they would shout
> Across the watery vale, and shout again,
> Responsive to his call, with quivering peals
> And long halloos, and screams and echoes loud,
> Redoubled and redoubled ; concourse wild
> Of jocund din ! And when there came a pause
> Of silence such as baffled his best skill ;
> Then sometimes in that silence, while he hung
> Listening, a gentle shock of mild surprise
> Has carried far into his heart the voice
> Of mountain torrents ; or the visible scene
> Would enter unawares into his mind
> With all its solemn imagery, its rocks,
> Its woods, and that uncertain heaven received
> Into the bosom of the steady lake.

What "appeal to will and conduct" could be extracted from that? The "bold, bad men" would
probably say that this was a "bold, bad boy," who
ought to have been studying the rudiments of
political economy or sociology, instead of blowing

"mimic hootings to the silent owls that they might answer him"; and yet, though there is no vestige of an "appeal to will and conduct" in these lines, there is ample evidence in them that they are the offspring of volition and self-government, so far as this, that they flow from a mood born of Wordsworth's "steady resistance to the ebb and flow of ordinary desires and regrets." The "shock of mild surprise" that "carried far into his heart the voice of mountain torrents," was a shock of rapture sprung from that vigilant and eager solitude in which the boy severed himself from Nature, in order that he might watch the incoming to his mind of "the voice of mountain torrents," and surprise the solemn imagery that had entered it "unawares," and had yet taken more definite shape within it than even in "the bosom of the steady lake." Or take such a characteristic passage as that in the third book of "The Excursion," where the Solitary, after the loss of his child and wife, describes how—

By pain of heart—now checked—and now impelled—
The intellectual power through words and things
Went sounding on, a dim and perilous way.

Here, again, there is nothing that Mr. Arnold's "bold, bad men" would quote, except as a warning; but no poet except Wordsworth could have written these three lines. They, too, are the offspring of a mood of volition and self-control; but the grandeur of them is no product of the loom of volition and self-control; it is due to a rapture of solitude which no voluntary power possesses the spell to summon up. Wordsworth had watched his own heart, now checking, now impelling his intellect, as the latter cast the leads into the deep soundings of human hope

and dread, of human endeavour and failure; and
the result was these noble lines, which shadow forth
the intellectual history of many a soul that has been
shipwrecked and yet has ultimately reached "the
haven where it would be"; and of many a soul,
too, that has been shipwrecked without ultimately
reaching that desired haven.   Yet passages such as
those that have been quoted, and poems such as
those that have been named, could have sprung from
the genius of no English poet but Wordsworth, and
could not have sprung from even his mind, in spite
of all its careful sweeping and garnishing, had not
a spirit and a passion descended upon him for which
that sweeping and garnishing were a mere invocation.
Mr. Morley finely says that Wordsworth could not
command that "note of plangent sadness" which
strikes the ear in men morally his inferiors in every
way.   And that is true, for "plangent sadness" is
the sadness conveyed by the idle lapping of the
wave, and Wordsworth, even if he sat on "an old
grey stone" and seemed to dream his time away,
was one who brought with him a heart "that
watches and receives"—that watched hungrily and
received gratefully.   But though there was no
perfect note of "plangent sadness" in Wordsworth,
there was a note of far rarer and higher kind, a
triumphant sadness which steadily faces the worst
sufferings of humanity, and wins from them a more
exalted hope.   If he paints, as he often does, "dim
sadness and blind thoughts I knew not nor could
name," if he can tell us—

> I thought of Chatterton, the marvellous boy,
>   The sleepless soul that perished in his pride;
> Of him who walked in glory and in joy,
>   Following his plough upon the mountain side:

> By our own spirits are we deified ;
> We Poets in our youth begin in gladness,
> But therefore come in the end despondency
>   and madness—

it is not to depict the lapping of any wave of sadness
on his heart, but to show how he can triumph over
it, and elicit the sense of human grandeur even from
the most desolate of human fates.   I cannot at all
agree with Mr. Morley that Wordsworth "had not
rooted in him the sense of Fate, of the inexorable
sequences of things, of the terrible chain that so
often binds an awful end to some slight and trivial
beginning."   What does he say to such lines as these?

> Amid the groves, under the shadowy hills,
> The generations are prepared ; the pangs,
> The internal pangs are ready,—the dread strife
> Of poor humanity's afflicted will.

But with this sense of fate Wordsworth had a conviction that in man there is something intended to
defy fate, and to wring even from "the inexorable
sequences of things," even from "the terrible chain
that so often binds the awful end to some light
and trivial beginning," a strength greater than the
strength of fate, which fate cannot crush.   Wordsworth had convinced himself that even where fate
oppresses, it oppresses to show—

> that consolation springs
> From sources deeper far than deepest pain ;

and he carried about with him the passionate
exaltation of that conviction.

DOROTHY WORDSWORTH'S SCOTCH
JOURNAL

EVERYTHING fresh we learn of Wordsworth deepens
the impression of that hardy, imaginative simplicity
which is the chief characteristic of his genius. This
is one great charm of his sister's diary of the
Highland tour of 1803. Miss Wordsworth, who
cherished every incident connected with the origin
of one of his poems, puts down in this journal, not
for public perusal, but for the wife who stays behind
with her child, the modest story of their adventures,
and yet not a word of it from beginning to end
betrays the conscious seeker after æsthetic feelings,
or suggests the attendant nymph sharing something
of the glow of a poet's inspiration. There is a
remarkable self-restraint, not to say fortitude, in
the manner in which the constantly recurring bad
weather, and not unfrequently severe discomforts
of the journey are described, as though nothing
better were to be expected. There is not a trace
of the feeling that there was any sort of merit in
the ideal object of the travellers' search, or any
prerogative belonging to a poet who is injuriously
treated by the buffets to which ordinary men are
liable. The journal is as simple and natural as if
there were no poetic reputation either to gain or to

keep up. When any touch of poetry marks the journal, it is as plain that it comes there through the natural ardour of the writer's own—not even her brother's—feelings, as it is that when you might conventionally have expected it, it is often not to be found. Miss Wordsworth writes generally with extreme literalness of the incidents of travel, though, of course, as one whose expectations are on the stretch for the beauties of which she has heard so much. Her brother and Coleridge figure not in the least as poets, but simply as fellow-travellers who share her fatigues and enjoyments, and who frequently help her to discern what is most memorable. Anything less like the style of a "sentimental journey," of a pilgrimage made in order to experience exalted feelings, it is impossible to imagine. Moreover, there is no effort in Miss Wordsworth's diary to look at things with her brother's eyes. She keeps her own eager, lively eyes on everything, and even when she gets hold of a scene which profoundly strikes her, she does not attempt to Wordsworthise upon it, but just defines her own impressions, and there leaves it. A being of completer simplicity than Dorothy Wordsworth I should think it not easy to find again. Principal Shairp, in his very interesting preface, gives us De Quincey's graphic account of her wild bright eyes and abrupt reserve of manner thus :—

Her face was of Egyptian brown ; rarely in a woman of English birth had I seen a more determinate gipsy tan. Her eyes were not as soft as Mrs. Wordsworth's, nor were they fierce or bold ; but they were wild, and startling, and hurried in their motion. Her manner was warm, and even ardent ; her sensibility seemed constitutionally deep; and some subtle fire of impassioned intellect apparently burned within her, which—being alternately pushed forward into a conspicuous expression by the irresistible instincts of her temperament, and then immediately checked in obedience to the decorum of her sex and age and her maidenly condition—gave to her whole demeanour, and to her conversation, an air of embarrassment, and even of self-conflict, that was almost distressing to witness. Even her very utterance and enunciation often suffered in point of clearness and steadiness, from the agitation of her excessive organic sensibility. At times the self-counteraction and self-baffling of her feelings caused her even to stammer. But the greatest deductions from Miss Wordsworth's attractions, and from the exceeding interest which surrounded her, in right of her character, of her history, and of the relation which she fulfilled towards her brother, were the glancing quickness of her motions, and other circumstances in her deportment (such as her stooping attitude when walking), which gave an ungraceful character to her appearance when out of doors.

But though this bright, eager manner penetrates many portions of her diary, there is no trace in it of the embarrassment or conflict of feeling of which De Quincey speaks, and which may very possibly have been more or less provoked by his own critical glances. What one notes in it is the delicacy of her appreciation of all the human interests of the scenes visited, a considerable power of artless intensity in describing any scene, whether grand or simple, which struck her imagination,— and was oftener simple than grand,—and a certain ardent nimbleness in her manner of looking at things, which reminds one very often of the few sets of verses by her published amongst her brother's poems. One is especially often reminded in this journal of that charming little child's poem by Miss Wordsworth, beginning—

What way does the wind come ? Which way does he go ?
He rides over the water, and over the snow,
Through wood and through vale, and o'er rocky height,
Which the goat cannot scale, takes his sounding flight.

The *full* brightness of that gay and breezy little poem is to be found less frequently than one could wish in the diary of this rather gloomy-weathered tour ; but one is very often struck with the pleasure which Miss Wordsworth feels in tracing, just as in that poem, the effect of an influence of which she cannot tell the whence or the whither, and the extreme enjoyment with which she takes note of anything like a godsend. Take this, for instance :—

The woman of the house was very kind : whenever we asked her for anything it seemed a fresh pleasure to her that she had it for us ; she always answered with a sort of softening-down of the Scotch exclamation, "Hoot ! Ho ! yes, ye'll get that," and hied to her cupboard in the spence. We were amused with the phrase, "Ye'll get that," in the Highlands, which appeared to us as if it came from a perpetual feeling of the difficulty with which most things are procured . . . We asked for sugar, butter, barley-bread, and milk, and with a smile and a stare more of kindness than wonder, she replied, "Ye'll get that," bringing each article separately . . . We caroused our cups of coffee, laughing like children at the strange atmosphere in which we were : the smoke came in gusts, and spread along the walls and above our heads in the chimney, where the hens were roosting, like light clouds in the sky. We laughed and laughed again, in spite of the smarting of our eyes, yet had a quieter pleasure in observing the beauty of the beams and rafters gleaming between the clouds of smoke. They had been crusted over and varnished by many winters, till, where the fire-light fell upon them, they were as glossy as black rocks on a sunny day cased in ice. When we had eaten our supper we sat about half an hour, and I think I never had felt so deeply the blessing of a hospitable welcome and a warm fire . . . The walls of the whole house were of stone unplastered. It consisted of three apartments,— the cow-house at one end, the kitchen or house in the middle, and the spence at the other end. The rooms were divided, not up to the rigging, but only to the beginning of the roof, so that there was a free passage for light and smoke from one end of the house to the other. I went to bed some time before the family. The door was shut between us, and they had a bright fire, which I could not see; but the light it sent up among the varnished rafters and beams, which crossed each other in almost as intricate and fantastic a manner as I have seen the underboughs of a large beech-tree withered by the depth of the shade above, produced the most beautiful effect that can be conceived. It was like what I should suppose an underground cave or temple to be, with a dripping or moist roof, and the moonlight entering in upon it by some means or other, and yet the colours were more like melted gems. I lay looking up till the light of the fire faded away, and the man and his wife and child had crept into their bed at the other end of the room. I did not sleep much, but passed a comfort-able night, for my bed, though hard, was warm and clean: the unusualness of my situation prevented me from sleeping. I could hear the waves beat against the shore of the lake; a little "syke" close to the door made a much louder noise; and when I sate up in my bed I could see the lake through an open window-place at the bed's head. Add to this, it rained all night. I was less occupied by the remembrance of the Trossachs, beautiful as they were, than the vision of the Highland hut, which I could not get out of my head. I thought of the Fairyland of Spenser, and what I had read in romance at other times, and then, what a feast it would be for a London panto-mime-maker, could he but transplant it to Drury Lane, with all its beautiful colours!

Evidently the indications of poverty of resource in the Highland woman's larder, the triumph with which she identified anything asked for, as amongst the very small category of things obtainable in her house, made the little meal all the more delightful to Miss Wordsworth, who felt a poetry in the surprises of nature and life, which she could not so much feel in the habitual order thereof. This seems to have been the secret also of her delight in the flying shadows crossing the rafters as she lay in bed in the Highland hut, listening to the plash of the waves of Loch Katrine, and yet thinking more of the novelty and picturesqueness of her own position, in one compartment of a hut shared with her by a cow and the Highland ferryman and his family. Indeed, as every one has noticed who has hitherto criticised this diary, Miss Wordsworth is always more alive to the human touches in the midst of natural beauty than even to the natural beauty itself. On Loch Lomond she singles out a little bark-hut on a lonely island as an object of special interest, and they get the boatman to land at the bark-hut that they may enjoy its beauty the more. Again, how a single desolate figure makes the whole scene seem desolate to her, and how her words immediately shiver, as it were, in sympathy with the loneliness she feels!—

Came to a bark-hut by the shores, and sate for some

time under the shelter of it. While we were here a poor woman with a little child by her side begged a penny of me, and asked where she could "find quarters in the village." She was a travelling beggar, a native of Scotland, had often "heard of that water," but was never there before. This woman's appearance, while the wind was rustling about us, and the waves breaking at our feet, was very melancholy ; the waters looked wide, the hills many, and dark, and far off—no house but at Luss. I thought what a dreary waste must this lake be to such poor creatures, struggling with fatigue and poverty and unknown ways !

What a tone of sympathetic dreariness there is in the words, "the waters looked wide, the hills many, and dark, and far off," when they come in as the mere shadow of the poor woman's desolation. Again, observe her delight when the solitude of Loch Awe is broken by the sudden appearance of a vessel on it :—

After we had wound for some time through the valley, having met neither foot-traveller, horse, nor cart, we started at the sight of a single vessel, just as it turned round the point of a hill, coming into the reach of the valley where we were. She floated steadily through the middle of the water, with one large sail spread out full swollen by the breeze, that blew her right towards us. I cannot express what romantic images this vessel brought along with her—how much more beautiful the mountains appeared, the lake how much more graceful. There was one man on board, who sate at the helm, and he, having no companion, made the boat look more silent than if we could not have seen him. I had almost said the ship, for on that narrow water it appeared as large as the ships which I have watched sailing out of a harbour of the sea.

Of course, the chief interest of this journal will be usually regarded as its accounts of the few incidents which were the germs of some of Wordsworth's most striking poems,—that, for instance, which suggested the lines to a Highland girl at Inversneyde, upon Loch Lomond, and that which gave rise to the lines, "What, you are stepping Westward?" In both instances we see something more than the mere occasion, indeed, the true germ of the poetic conception which makes the poem, in Miss Wordsworth's own thought. In both cases we find it easy to conceive that Wordsworth's fine tribute to his sister,—

> She gave me eyes, she gave me ears,
> And humble cares and delicate fears,
> A heart the fountain of sweet tears,
> And love and thought and joy,

was literally true; for in both cases the starting-point of the poem, its very mood and tone of feeling, is supplied by the sister, though all the brooding power of the brother was needed to make so much out of so little. Take the first case as an example. This is Miss Wordsworth's account of the Highland girl to whom her brother's poem was, but not till after many weeks, written :—

I think I never heard the English language sound more sweetly than from the mouth of the elder of these girls, while she stood at the gate answering our inquiries, her face flushed with the rain : her pronunciation was clear and distinct : without difficulty, yet slow, like that of a foreign speech . . . She moved with unusual activity, which was chastened very delicately by a certain hesitation in her looks when she spoke, being unable to understand us but imperfectly.

And here is the fine passage into which Wordsworth expanded his sister's thought :—

> Thou wear'st upon thy forehead clear
> The freedom of a Mountaineer :
> A face with gladness overspread !
> Soft smiles, by human kindness bred !
> And seemliness complete, that sways
> Thy courtesies, about thee plays;
> With no restraint, but such as springs
> From quick and eager visitings
> Of thoughts that lie beyond the reach
> Of thy few words of English speech :
> A bondage sweetly brook'd, a strife
> That gives thy gestures grace and life !
> So have I, not unmoved in mind,
> Seen birds of tempest-loving kind—
> Thus beating up against the wind.

Noble as the passage is, and especially its concluding image, Miss Wordsworth's description conveys a far more distinct definition than this does of the real manner portrayed, when she speaks of the girl's want of knowledge of English as " very delicately chastening " her activity by the hesitation of bearing and modesty of speech it produced. Wordsworth's phrase,

> A bondage sweetly brook'd, a strife
> That gives thy gestures grace and life,

is more deeply charged with meditation ; but the "delicately chastened" activity conveys better the exact idea of the feminine modesty with which the Highland lass deprecated her own power to choose her words correctly, than the grander range of the poet's language.

SIR WALTER SCOTT

MR. BALFOUR said well in the Chapter House of Westminster Abbey, that happy as was Sir Walter Scott's style in so painting his large canvases as to give us an adequate conception of the most striking scenes of a long past, it was not mainly in his style, but in the matter of his inimitable stories, that he has surpassed all the other writers of English romance. It is true enough that Scott represented, and represented as no other writer has ever represented, the reaction against the abstract doctrines of the eighteenth century, and substituted for them the concrete and rich detail of which his imagination was so full. But by that very capacity for combining all the glow and colour of a picturesque past with the concrete historic figures and vivacity of detail in which that past life attained its greatest dignity and interest, Scott deviated from the earlier conception of romance and mingled with it the criticism of a broad sagacity and the business insight of a shrewd realist. Sir Walter hardly ever takes us into a dull world, but nevertheless never into an unreal or abstract world. His history is, as Mr. Balfour said, often inaccurate ; indeed, it was usually made intentionally so, that he might give a more concentrated picture of that which struck his own imagination most powerfully. His inaccuracy was almost always of a kind which gave the impression of the truth far better than the most painstaking accuracy ever could have given it. Indeed, so far as I differ from Mr. Balfour at all, it would be in doubting whether Scott did depend so much on the opportuneness of his gifts for the special temper of the world in which he lived, as Mr. Balfour suggests. It may well be that the genius of some men is so great that they really *create* the demand for what they can bestow. And of these Sir Walter Scott seems to me one of the most conspicuous. There is something so large and simple in his genius that his readers hardly think of themselves as readers of mere romance. The peasants are drawn as vividly as the kings, and the kings as the peasants. His readers are admitted to the very heart of reality, even when the romantic touch is most vigorous.

Scott never gives you the sense of confining his interest to his story. There is always a lifelike background, a sense of the largeness and complexity of human life, of its business, and of its manifold enterprises clashing against each other, which takes you out of the narrow interests of passion and mere adventure. In *Kenilworth* we have Queen Elizabeth playing off her nobles against each other as only a great Queen could do it; in *The Fortunes of Nigel* the fussy and timid James consoles himself for his own conscious weakness by displaying gleams of shrewdness even when he is cowering before his own courtiers; in *The Heart of Midlothian* a canny Scotch nobleman avails himself of Queen Caroline's deep sense of what was in the larger sense expedient because it was just,

and just because it was expedient, to obtain a
pardon for the sister of the heroine; in *Ivanhoe*
a most picturesque contrast is drawn between the
crafty dealings of the great order of the Templars
and the heavy Saxon nobles with their clumsy
strength and dull straightforwardness; in *Old
Mortality* the mind is fixed on the contest between
the stern Puritan fanatics and the military cold-
bloodedness of Claverhouse and his soldiers; in
Anne of Geierstein, the heart-broken pride of
Margaret of Anjou dying in the midst of King
René's vain and shallow and tinselled court is
painted with singular force.   Everywhere in Scott's
stories you see a large background depicting the
real affairs of the world, and you feel as if you were
moving amidst the bewildering paradoxes of human
nature on a large scale, and not on the narrow stage
of mere adventure or romance.   Nor is it in the
field of the greater historic exploits alone that
you feel the touch of a vivid realism.   Not only is
Louis XI. pictured in all his courage and craft
and superstition, overfinessing his own hand in his
eagerness to master the mad rages of his powerful
vassal, Charles the Bold, but in the very same story
we have the most lively picture of the singular
combination of cold treachery and tenacious
gratitude in the tribes of gipsies who were just then
spreading over Europe; and, again, the rashness and
shrewdness of those great Flemish burghers who,
with all their keenness for commercial gain, were so
arrogant and heady as to risk all their wealth on
the fortunes of an unequal contest with the great
military power of Burgundy, in credulous reliance
on the secret promises of a wily French King who
never hesitated to sacrifice an ally when he failed to

mature his crafty schemes, is set before us with equal power. Again, what could be more striking than Scott's intimacy with all the details of the life of the poor, when he paints the toil and griefs of the poor fishermen and fishwomen on the coast of Fife, or the dumb fidelity of the Saxon serf, or the struggles in the heart of the father of Jeanie and Effie Deans, when he has to choose between love for his daughter and fidelity to his religion ; or the humours of the Scotch vagrant, Edie Ochiltree, or the didactic conceit and selfish unscrupulousness of the Pharisaic gardener, Andrew Fairservice ? Scott is as much at home with the serving-men as he is with the Queens and Kings with whom his imagination delighted to busy itself. Everywhere you see large glimpses of the real world through the spacious windows of his glowing mind and memory. He is as familiar with the kitchen of the palace as he is with its Court. The Earl of Murray's menials are as powerfully suggested as his grim counsellors and jealous rivals, and James I.'s cook is almost as necessary a figure in the picture of his Court at Westminster as is Buckingham or Prince Charles. This it is which makes Scott's romances so much more fascinating than ordinary novels. They fill you with the sense of the greatness and complexity of the world, and yet they never weary you with those long digressions with which the more ambitious writers of romance try to fill in the background of their story. Compare Scott's stories, for instance, with Bulwer's *Last Days of Pompeii*, or *Last of the Barons*, and you see immediately the vast superiority of the former in mingling the realities of life with the glow of passion and the charm of pageant.

Of course it is quite true that Scott is not always at his best. Walking ladies and gentlemen, like Rowena in *Ivanhoe*, or Isabella Wardour in *The Antiquary*, glide through his pages and hardly leave a trace on the memory. The humour of his "Introductions," as well as of the tags to which his oddities are addicted, is often overweighted, is often heavy. I weary of his Jedediah Cleishbottom, and even of Lady Margaret Bellenden in her castle of Tillietudlem. Nor are his semi-supernatural personages like Meg Merrilies and Magdalen Graeme as impressive as they ought to be. But yet he has a great genius for that touch of madness which makes both his daft Scotch boys, and his pictures of genuine mental excitement, like that of Madge Wildfire, so effective. There was a harebrained element in Scott that when it really took possession of him was full of eeriness, all the more that his great breadth of sober sense threw it out with singularly vivid force. There is nothing more powerful than his picture of Mary Stuart's mind in *The Abbot* when it gets unhinged in recalling the tragedies of her earlier life; or than the scenes in the *Bride of Lammermoor*, where Lucy Ashton's anguish turns her brain. Even in his own life, in the journal which he kept of his private dreads and sufferings, one sees traces of the fire of that great imagination when it carried him beyond the control of his cool and lucid judgment. Without that strain of wildness in Scott which showed itself in such despair as the motto which he wrote when he first realised the failing of his genius, in *Count Robert of Paris*, we should never have had the greatest of all our imaginative writers excepting only Shakespeare :—

The storm increases—'tis no sunny shower
Fostered in the moist breast of March or April,
Or such as parched Summer cools his lip with ;
Heaven's windows are flung wide ; the inmost deeps
Call, in hoarse greetings, one upon another ;
On comes the flood in all its foaming horrors,
And where's the dike shall stop it ?

There, and in the burst of chivalrous feeling that
suggested the verse,—

> Sound, sound the Clarion, fill the fife,
> To all the sensual world proclaim
> One crowded hour of glorious life
> Is worth a world without a name,—

we have the touch of fire that electrified into living
and moving forms all the massive contents of that
great mind,—and that went far towards shattering
his earthly happiness while it secured his everlasting
fame.

THE JOURNAL OF SIR WALTER SCOTT

THIS is such a book as the world has not often seen. No doubt the most impressive portions of it are not new, for Mr. Lockhart quoted freely from it in the most delightful of all biographies. But to have it without the omissions then made, and to have it in a single whole, is as different from having it as a mere factor in a fascinating biography, as to have the whole web of a skilful weaver is different from having a great composite structure into which parts of that web have been skilfully incorporated. These two impressive volumes contain one of the most effective pictures of a really strong man, painted as only that man himself could have painted it, which the English language contains. It is true tragedy without the idealising background generally given to tragedy, the story of a great intellectual and moral struggle ending in defeat, but in defeat in which there is absolutely no personal failure, no conscious yielding of a single inch of ground, no concession to weakness, no self-deception, no shrinking from the truth, no despondency, and no ostentation of pretended indifference. Everywhere you see the same large, clear insight, the same large, genial nature, the same indomitable resolution, the same sober suffering, the same calm fortitude, the same frank

150

determination to face the worst and to do the best. It is rarely, indeed, that so sunny a nature as Scott's is seen in such dark eclipse without a great deal more bitterness or collapse than Scott ever betrays. And yet, though the heart of religion is in Scott, you cannot say that his Journal shows what can be called a spiritual nature.   He feels keenly the duty of submission to God's will in his misfortunes, but he does not dwell on it, he submits in the darkness, as it were, but without at all realising that to implant the disposition to subdue his heart to the right frame of feeling was perhaps the very object of the sufferings with which he copes so manfully. The whole force of his large nature is thrown at once into the struggle to *do* what is honourable and right, and the effort to feel rightly is almost lost sight of in the effort to brace all his nature to high action. How little of the conscious spiritual life there is in him, I see when the sense of worldly honour bursts out so strongly in his resolve to fight a duel about his *Life of Napoleon* rather than submit to the disgrace, as he held it, of not standing to his colours on behalf of his country.   No man who had thought first and most of his spiritual life would have done that ; but Scott had the highest kind of natural goodness rather than of the supernatural, and that is precisely what makes the vivid light which this Journal throws on his inner life so profoundly interesting.   You see the grandeur of the man's whole make and character,—the large sympathy with all suffering, the magnanimity, the habit of endurance, the slight scorn for his own sensitiveness, and yet the frank and hearty desire not to suffer, to have an end of his sufferings, which bespeaks the true man of the world, though a high-minded and

noble man of the world. It is the semi-Christian
stoicism in Scott which makes the inner life of this
Journal so fascinating, and at times so grand a spectacle. Fortunately, for the reader, the Journal opens
a day or two—though only a day or two—before
the anxieties as to the coming crash of his fortunes
begin. The first entry is the 20th of November
1825, the first note of the approaching storm appears
on the 22nd, and on the 25th Sir Walter records his
firm resolve to economise, but within a few days the
whole pressure of the approaching catastrophe is felt,
and on January 16, 1826, the crash came. The
illness and death of his wife followed in the same
spring, and then for three or four years Scott went
labouring on in the interest of his creditors, using
his great imagination as long as it would work
through his enfeebled physical organisation, to restore what he owed, to retrieve the spendthrift
prodigality of his earlier years, and to reconcile
himself to himself, so far as he could do so after his
large, clear sense had fairly recognised how deeply
his rather harebrained passion for land and position
had involved him in responsibilities for other men
whose speculative tendencies he could not control,
and who were quite unfit to control their own.

Let us take first what the Journal shows in
abundance,—the large, sunny good sense that was
the background of Sir Walter Scott's great imagination. What could be happier than this criticism
on the sanguineness of the Whig mind ?

November 25 : — Read Jeffrey's neat and well-
intended address to the mechanics upon their combinations. Will it do good ? Umph ! It takes only the
hand of a Liliputian to light a fire, but would require

the diuretic powers of Gulliver to extinguish it. The Whigs will live and die in the heresy that the world is ruled by little pamphlets and speeches, and that if you can sufficiently demonstrate that a line of conduct is most consistent with men's interest, you have therefore and thereby demonstrated that they will at length, after a few speeches on the subject, adopt it of course. In this case we would have (no) need of laws or churches, for I am sure there is no difficulty in proving that moral, regular, and steady habits conduce to men's best interest, and that vice is not sin merely, but folly. But of these men each has passions and prejudices, the gratification of which he prefers, not only to the general weal, but to that of himself as an individual. Under the action of these wayward impulses a man drinks to-day though he is sure of starving to-morrow. He murders to-morrow though he is sure to be hanged on Wednesday. And people are so slow to believe that which makes against their own predominant passions, that mechanics will combine to raise the price for one week, though they destroy the manufacture for ever.

That is almost as nearly true of our too sanguine reformers to-day as it was sixty years since. Then, as to his genial stoicism, take this little entry a few days later, when his daughter and Lockhart are leaving Scotland for London, Lockhart being about to take up the editing of the *Quarterly Review* :—

December 5 :—This morning Lockhart and Sophia left us early and without leave-taking ; when I rose at eight o'clock they were *gone*. This was very right. I hate red eyes and blowing of noses. *Agere et pati Romanum est.* Of all schools commend me to the Stoics. We cannot indeed overcome our affections, nor ought we if we could, but we may repress them within due bounds, and avoid coaxing them to make fools of those who should be their masters. I have lost some of the comforts to which I chiefly looked for enjoyment. Well, I must make the more of such as remain—God bless them. And so "I will unto my holy work again," which at present is the description of that *heilige Kleeblatt*, that worshipful triumvirate, Danton, Robespierre, and Marat.

Again, take this living sketch (written in the middle of his own anxieties) of Henry Mackenzie, the author of *The Man of Feeling* :—

December 6 :—A rare thing this literature, or love of fame or notoriety which accompanies it. Here is Mr. H(enry) M(ackenzie) on the very brink of human dissolution, as actively anxious about it as if the curtain must not soon be closed on that and everything else. He calls me his literary confessor ; and I am sure I am glad to return the kindnesses which he showed me long since in George Square. No man is less known from his writings. We would suppose a retired, modest, somewhat affected man, with a white handkerchief and a sigh ready for every sentiment. No such thing : H. M. is as alert as a contracting tailor's needle in every sort of business—a politician and a sportsman—shoots and fishes in a sort even to this day—and is the life of the company with anecdote and fun. Sometimes, his daughter tells me, he is in low spirits at home, but really I never see anything of it in society.

I give these passages to show the wise and sagacious background of the mind by which the long four years' struggle of imaginative power, with accumulating physical and moral troubles, was maintained. Now let me illustrate the temper of the same mind under the first heavy shock of

impending ruin. Mr. Douglas has enriched this
edition of the Journal with extracts from Mr.
Skene's reminiscences of Scott, which greatly add
to the impressiveness of the Journal. And I shall
illustrate the remarks in the Journal of January
the 23rd, 1826 (just a week after the crash), by
Mr. Skene's account of his walk with Sir Walter
on the same day :—

January 23 :— Slept ill, not having been abroad
these eight days—*splendida bilis.* Then a dead sleep in
the morning, and when the awakening comes, a strong
feeling how well I could dispense with it for once and
for ever. This passes away, however, as better and more
dutiful thoughts arise in my mind. I know not if my
imagination has flagged : probably it has ; but at least
my powers of labour have not diminished during the
last melancholy week. On Monday and Tuesday my
exertions were suspended. Since Wednesday inclusive
I have written thirty - eight of my close manuscript
pages, of which seventy make a volume of the usual
Novel size. Wrote till 12 A.M., finishing half of what
I call a good day's work—ten pages of print, or rather
twelve. Then walked in Princes Street pleasure grounds
with good Samaritan James Skene, the only one among
my numerous friends who can properly be termed
amicus curarum mearum, others being too busy or too
gay, and several being estranged by habit.

To this passage the following note is appended :—
" On the morning of this day Sir Walter wrote
the following note to his friend :—

Dear Skene—If you are disposed for a walk in your
gardens any time this morning, I would gladly accom-
pany you for an hour, since keeping the house so long
begins rather to hurt me, and you, who supported the

other day the weight of my body, are perhaps best disposed to endure the gloom of my mind.—Yours ever,

W. S

CASTLE STREET, *January* 23.

I will call when you please : all hours after twelve are the same to me."

On his return from this walk, Mr. Skene wrote out his recollections of the conversation that had taken place :—

Of his power to rebuild his shattered fortunes, Scott said, "But woe's me, I much mistrust my vigour, for the best of my energies are already expended.   You have seen, my dear Skene, the Roman coursers urged to their speed by a loaded spur attached to their backs to whet the rusty metal of their age—ay ! it is a leaden spur indeed, and it goads hard."   I added, "But what do you think, Scott, of the bits of flaming paper that are pasted on the flanks of the poor jades ? If we could but stick certain small documents on your back, and set fire to them, I think you might submit for a time to the pricking of the spur."   He laughed and said, "Ay ! Ay !—these weary bills if they were but as the thing that is not—come, cheer me up with an account of the Roman Carnival."   And, accordingly, with my endeavour to do so, he seemed as much interested as if nothing had happened to discompose the usual tenor of his mind, but still our conversation ever and anon dropt back into the same subject, in the course of which he said to me, "Do you know, I experience a sort of determined pleasure in confronting the very worst aspect of this sudden reverse,—in standing, as it were, in the breach that has overthrown my fortunes, and saying, Here I stand, at least an honest man.   And God knows, if I have enemies, this I may at least with truth say, that I have never wittingly given cause of

enmity in the whole course of my life, for even the
burnings of political hate seemed to find nothing in my
nature to feed the flame.   I am not conscious of having
borne a grudge towards any man, and at this moment
of my overthrow, so help me God, I wish well and feel
kindly to every one.   And if I thought that any of my
works contained a sentence hurtful to any one's feelings,
I would burn it.   I think even my novels (for he did
not disown any of them) are free from that blame."   He
had been led to make this protestation from my having
remarked to him the singularly general feeling of good-
will and sympathy towards him which every one was
anxious to testify upon the present occasion.   The
sentiments of resignation and of cheerful acquiescence
in the dispensation of the Almighty which he expressed
were those of a Christian thankful for the blessings left,
and willing, without ostentation, to do his best.   It was
really beautiful to see the workings of a strong and
upright mind under the first lash of adversity calmly
reposing upon the consolation afforded by his own
integrity and manful purposes.   " Lately," he said, " you
saw me under the apprehension of the decay of my
mental faculties, and I confess that I was under mortal
fear when I found myself writing one word for another,
and misspelling every word ; but that wore off, and was
perhaps occasioned by the effects of the medicine I had
been taking ; but have I not reason to be thankful that
that misfortune did not assail me ?   Ay ! few have
more reason to feel grateful to the Disposer of all events
than I have.—*Mr. Skene's Reminiscences.*

That comparison of Scott's, of his later imaginative career,—in which, by the way, he wrote
Woodstock, The Fair Maid of Perth, and *Anne of
Geierstein,* as well as a great portion of the *Life
of Napoleon,* and a multitude of smaller literary
papers, besides discharging all his duties as Clerk

in the Courts of Law,—to the efforts of the Roman
coursers driven forth free from the control of any
rider, but pricked on by spurs which jangled constantly against their sides, seems to me a singularly
fine and appropriate one, which really helps me to
conceive and understand the labours of the last
and greatest four years of his literary life,—
greatest, of course, not imaginatively, but morally.
Even during the composition and printing of his
first real failure,—*Count Robert of Paris*,—the first
book in which signs of the ruin of the great
imagination became distinctly visible, Scott seems
to me almost greater and nobler than he had ever
been before. The power of his glorious imagination was gone, but the mighty and sober will
which struggled on even under the overwhelming
burden of a conscious sense of decay, was more
impressive in defeat than it had been even in
victory. Scott would hardly have been persuaded
that in many respects this private journal was his
greatest work,—and of course, imaginatively speaking, it is far from his greatest work,—but it is
certainly the work which is more likely to subdue
other minds, struggling with much less, but to their
lesser power perhaps relátively equal burdens, to
that spirit of deep resignation and grave resolve
with which Scott met some of the greatest trials
man can have to bear, than anything which he had
written in the heyday of poetic inspiration and of
dazzling imaginative triumphs. This book is one
of the greatest gifts which our English literature
has ever received.

SIR WALTER SCOTT'S POEMS

THERE is but one fault to find with this admirable and complete edition of Sir Walter Scott's Poems,— which appears in two forms, one with broad margins on large paper, which makes its physique as perfect as that of any book can be, and one of a somewhat smaller, though not an inconveniently small, size. Its great merit is that it contains all the poetical mottoes prefixed by Scott to the chapters of his various novels, as well as all his contributions to the *Border Minstrelsy*, and also a brief, adequate, and very discriminating memoir by the editor, whose criticism is always wise and generous. The fault is, that while all the poems are carefully dated, they are not—apparently for some insufficient reason connected with the convenience of the printer—arranged in chronological order. "The Lady of the Lake" precedes "Marmion," which it ought to follow, and "The Bridal of Triermain," which ought to succeed "Rokeby" and to precede "The Lord of the Isles," is printed last of the long poems. This is almost as much a subject for regret as it would be, in a history of British poetry, to place Scott before Burns, or Wordsworth before Cowper. We understand Scott's genius better if we read "The Lady of the Lake" after "Marmion,"

and "The Lord of the Isles" better if it concludes
the series of the longer poems. But that is the only
fault to be found with a singularly perfect and
attractive edition of Scott's Poems. Mr. Dennis's
Memoir, moreover, displays excellent taste and
judgment, though I wish he had given us a little
more of his own fine criticism on Scott as a poet
than in his editorial modesty he has thought fit.
Sir Walter knew a good deal of the nature of his
own genius. Mr. Dennis quotes his remark: "If
there be anything good about my poetry or prose
either, it is a hurried frankness of composition
which pleases soldiers, sailors, and young people
of bold, active disposition." And Mr. Dennis adds,
very justly, that this "hurried frankness of composition" has often a special charm for people of
a very opposite temperament, — that it had, for
instance, a special attraction for Cardinal Newman,
who confessed that, while he admitted the unquestionable superiority of Wordsworth, Sir Walter's
verse gave him greater pleasure. When Scott
spoke of the principal charm of his style consisting
in the "hurried frankness" of his composition he
was thinking, no doubt, of his battle-pieces, which
certainly seemed to rush along with all the passion
of a charge of horse as in the Battle of Flodden
Field, the combat between James and Roderick
Dhu, or the splendid ballad concerning the revenge
taken on the Regent Murray in "Cadyow Castle."
But, except in the battle scenes, I venture to doubt
whether the occasional hurry of Scott's thought—
perhaps there might be a slight hurry in the mere
words, in the mere *expression* of the thought, even
where the mood is most tranquil and leisurely—
does display to us his poetry at its best.   Pitt, who

lived to read and admire profoundly "The Lay of
the Last Minstrel," picked out the picture of the
old harper's self-distrust and hesitation, and then
of his rising courage as he perceives the sympathy
of his audience, and feels once more the glow of
rapture with which the eager gaze of fair and
admiring listeners fills him, for special admiration;
and certainly there is no "hurry" in that exquisite
and delicately-shaded delineation of the ebb and
flow of a Minstrel's ardour :—

> And then, he said, he would full fain
> He could recall an ancient strain,
> He never thought to sing again.
> It was not framed for village churls,
> But for high dames and mighty earls ;
> He had played it to King Charles the Good
> When he kept court in Holyrood ;
> And much he wished, yet feared, to try
> The long forgotten melody.
> Amid the strings his fingers strayed
> And an uncertain warbling made,
> And oft he shook his hoary head.
> And when he caught the measure wild,
> The old man raised his face, and smiled ;
> And lightened up his faded eye
> With all a poet's ecstasy !
> In varying cadence, soft or strong,
> He swept the sounding chords along :
> The present scene, the future lot,
> His toils, his wants, were all forgot :
> Cold diffidence, and age's frost,
> In the full tide of song were lost ;
> Each blank, in faithless memory void,
> The poet's glowing thought supplied ;
> And while his harp responsive rung,
> 'Twas thus the Latest Minstrel sung.

There is no "hurry" in the thought there, rather
the poet lingers gently on the theme, though he
deals with it with the simplicity and frankness of
an unstudied ease.   Perhaps it is true that the
short lines and entire absence of elaboration bespeak
there, as in almost all his poetry, a certain indifference to the *mode* of saying what he had to say; but
at least there is no impatience to have done with
the theme.   He dwells upon his thought with a
happy pathos of detail that expresses anything but
the rush of battle.   When Mr. Dennis says, in his
preface to "Marmion," "For his master on the
battlefield we must go back to Homer," I am not
at all sure that the exception should have been
made.   Homer is much more than Scott's master in
beauty, in clearness of vision, in brilliancy of touch,
in wideness of comprehension, in harmony of treatment, but as to his battle-scenes, I doubt their
conveying half the sense of rapture in war which is
conveyed in the battle-scenes of the rugged northern
minstrel.   In his descriptions of conflict he is far
more eager, more anxious to show whither the conflict tends, than Homer himself.   The fever of the
strife gets into his blood.   But Scott is not all
battle-scenes.   And when his mind is dwelling on
some fresh and beautiful aspect of human life or
external nature, he is often at his very best.   Then,
though his style gives us all the sense of careless
and buoyant frankness, the thought often dwells
with a loving and tranquil delight on what his
vision shows him.   Take, for instance, the various
exquisite introductions to the different cantos of
"Marmion," the passages in which he recalls with
so much rapture the scenery that he had loved
as a child, or as a youth.   Every one knows

the delightful picture of Smailholme Tower, and
the

> Barren scene, and wild,
> Where naked cliffs were rudely piled ;
> But ever and anon between
> Lay velvet tufts of loveliest green ;
> And well the lonely infant knew
> Recesses where the wallflower grew,
> And honeysuckle loved to crawl
> Up the low crag and ruin'd wall.

There is certainly no hurry in the thought of
that tender and delightful picture, though the
wording there, as everywhere, seems to have something of the swiftness and carelessness of the
mountain stream.   But let us take a somewhat less
well-known passage, that in which his memory
recalls his summer wanderings with Mr. Skene :—

> To thee, perchance, this rambling strain
> Recalls our summer walks again ;
> When, doing nought,—and, to speak true,
> Not anxious to find aught to do,—
> The wild unbounded hills we ranged,
> While oft our talk its topic changed,
> And, desultory as our way,
> Ranged, unconfined, from grave to gay.
> Even when it flagged, as oft will chance,
> No effort made to break its trance,
> We could right pleasantly pursue
> Our sports in social silence too ;
> Thou gravely labouring to portray
> The blighted oak's fantastic spray ;
> I spelling o'er, with much delight,
> The legend of that antique knight,
> Tirante by name, ycleped the White.

At either's feet a trusty squire,
" Pandour " and " Camp " with eyes of fire,
Jealous, each other's motions viewed,
And scarce suppressed their ancient feud.
The laverock whistled from the cloud ;
The stream was lively, but not loud ;
From the white thorn the May-flower shed
Its dewy fragrance round our head :
Not Ariel lived more merrily
Under the blossomed bough, than we.

That is the picture of a mind that loved to muse,
though it did not dwell on the words in which it
shaped its musings with the fastidious delight of
Keats or Tennyson. Whatever hurry there is there
is mere hurry of speech ; the thought lingers so wist-
fully, that it seems to grudge the omission of any
detail which would recall the scene more perfectly.

Again, though there is eagerness of expression,
how tender and dreamy is the delight which lingers
over the description of the heroine in "The Lady
of the Lake" :—

The maiden paused, as if again
She thought to catch the distant strain.
With head upraised, and look intent,
And eye and ear attentive bent,
And locks flung back, and lips apart,
Like monument of Grecian art,
In listening mood, she seemed to stand,
The guardian Naiad of the strand.
And ne'er did Grecian chisel trace
A Nymph, a Naiad, or a Grace,
Of finer form, or lovelier face !
What though the sun, with ardent frown,
Had slightly tinged her cheek with brown,—
-The sportive toil, which, short and light,
Had dyed her glowing hue so bright,

Served too in hastier swell to show
Short glimpses of a breast of snow :
What though no rule of courtly grace
To measured mood had trained her pace,—
A foot more light, a step more true,
Ne'er from the heath-flower dashed the dew ;
E'en the slight harebell raised its head,
Elastic from her airy tread :
What though upon her speech there hung
The accents of the mountain tongue,—
Those silver sounds, so soft, so dear,
The list'ner held his breath to hear !

There, again, if there is little or no sense of the
fastidious and dainty delight with which the artist
in words selects and shades and softens the colours
with which to convey his picture, there is at least
ample evidence of the rapture with which Scott
dwells upon his theme,—nay, that he was hardly
able to tear himself away from it. Indeed, the
extract tells very imperfectly what the poem itself
proceeds to delineate with innumerable touches. It
is only in the *expression* of Scott's feeling that there
is a certain carelessness, as if the poet somewhat
despaired of conveying it by speech at all, and
passed from one trait to another in impatience of
his own imperfect utterances.

There was, however, at the heart of Scott's
poetry not only this unstudied frankness of utterance, but a passionate sympathy with all masculine
emotion which gives buoyancy and grandeur to his
studies of love, wrath, and revenge. It is not
simply the poet who is great—it is the *man* whom
the poet only half delineates. What can be more
descriptive of a suppressed element in Scott's own
nature than the haughty and vindictive passion in

the noble ballad on the assassination of the Regent
Murray ?—

> Sternly he spoke—" 'Tis sweet to hear
>   In good greenwood the bugle blown,
> But sweeter to Revenge's ear,
>   To drink a tyrant's dying groan.
>
> Your slaughtered quarry proudly trode,
>   At dawning morn, o'er dale and down,
> But prouder base-born Murray rode
>   Through old Linlithgow's crowded town.
>
> From the wild Border's humbled side,
>   In haughty triumph marched he,
> While Knox relaxed his bigot pride,
>   And smiled, the traitorous pomp to see.
>
> But can stern Power, with all his vaunt,
>   Or Pomp, with all her courtly glare,
> The settled heart of Vengeance daunt,
>   Or change the purpose of Despair ?"

And again, how passionate is Scott's reverence
for the past—the main secret, no doubt, of Cardinal
Newman's great delight in him. How stately, for
instance, is the image by which he tries to persuade
his readers that the obsolete poetry of Thomas the
Rhymer of Ercildoune was far superior to the
bards of his own degenerate century :—

> In numbers high, the witching tale
>   The prophet poured along ;
> No after bard might e'er avail
>   Those numbers to prolong.
>
> Yet fragments of the lofty strain
>   Float down the tide of years,
> As, buoyant on the stormy main,
>   A parted wreck appears.

All that was left of Thomas the Rhymer was a "parted wreck" indeed; but it was the imagination of the modern poet which gave it its majestic impressiveness, much more than any trace of grandeur in the broken fragments which survived.

THE CHARM OF MISS AUSTEN

MR. GOLDWIN SMITH has added another to the not inconsiderable roll of eminent men who have found their delight in Miss Austen. His little book upon her just published by Walter Scott in the series on "Great Writers," edited by Professor Eric S. Robertson, is certainly a fascinating book to those who already know her and love her well; and I have little doubt that it will prove also a fascinating book to those who have still to make her acquaintance. Every one knows how enthusiastically her six novels were admired by Sir Walter Scott, by Sydney Smith, by Lord Macaulay, by George Eliot, by Walter Bagehot, and almost all the finest judges of delicate literary workmanship. Mr. Goldwin Smith proves himself to be one of the finest of these judges of delicate literary workmanship, though I protest against his view that Sir Walter Elliot's empty family pride and Lady Catherine de Bourgh's ill-bred insolence of station are overdone. That only means, I take it, that they would be less natural and credible now than they were in Miss Austen's time, which is true; but it is equally true that a good many other social features of that day, —for example, Mr. Collins's clerical servility, and Mrs. Jennings's unashamed vulgarity,—would be less

natural and credible now than in Miss Austen's time.
But, on the whole, Mr. Goldwin Smith is as fine
a critic of Miss Austen's slight imperfections as he
is of her manifold perfections. He is more trust-
worthy, for instance, than Lord Macaulay, for he
rightly denies to Miss Austen's men anything like
the exquisite truth and finish which he finds in her
women. Admirable as are many of her pictures of
men, there are not a few very vaguely and in-
distinctly outlined,—Edward Ferrars, for example,
and Edmund Bertram. The chief interest in this
fresh delineation of Miss Austen's wonderful literary
power is the light it throws on the question of her
secret charm for the few and her want of charm for
the many,—for it cannot be denied that for a very
considerable number of remarkably able men, Miss
Austen wields no spell at all, though for those over
whom she does wield a spell, she wields a spell of
quite curious force. I believe that the secret both
of her great charm for those whom she does charm,
and of her complete failure to fascinate a large class
of able men, is in the fineness—and, indeed, I may
say, the reduced scale—of her exquisite pictures.
It is not everybody who can appreciate the miniature;
it is not everybody who can see life at all through
a minifying instead of a magnifying medium. On
the other hand, to those who can, there is a peculiar
attraction in such life. You can get a glimpse of
what it was in Sir Walter Scott's remark : "The
big bow-wow strain I can do myself, like any one
now going; but the exquisite touch which renders
ordinary commonplace things and characters interesting from the truth of the description and the
sentiment, is denied to me." That just hits the
mark where it makes Scott disparage his own "big

bow-wow strain,"—in other words, the deep passions and eager ambitions which really filled his own imagination,—but it misses the mark when he supposes himself unable to touch off the truth and sentiment of commonplace situations, for no one could do it better than Scott, where the truth and sentiment of commonplace things was of a plain masculine type, like the interest of Jeanie Deans in her home, in her cows, and her dairy, or of Dinmont in his farm, or of the canny keeper, Neale Blane, in keeping well with Covenanters and Royalists alike. But what Scott really meant that he could not do, and that Jane Austen could do, was so to epitomise and yet delineate pride and meanness, and vulgarity and selfishness, and the like, as to give in one and the same sentence a glimpse of the reality and yet of the amusingness of life, to reduce its scale while really multiplying its humours. No one does this like Miss Austen. Sir Walter Scott and Fielding, and Dickens and Thackeray, and George Eliot all need considerable space for their pictures; and when you have got them, even the least literary eye can see that the scale of drawing is by no means harmonious throughout; that some passions are life-size, and others hastily indicated by a line here and a line there; that some characters are slightly exaggerated, and others hardly made visible at all; and that while the imagination is roused and exalted by some scenes, there are others which, though necessary to the story, are not additions to its charm. But with Miss Austen this is hardly ever so. No drawing so delicate and yet so artistic has been seen in English literature. It is a selection of all that is most superficially interesting in human life, of all that is most easily appreciated without going very

deep, and an exclusion of all that it takes real
wear and tear of spirit to enter thoroughly into.
That was what made its singular charm to men like
Sir Walter Scott and Sydney Smith, and Lord
Macaulay and Mr. Goldwin Smith, who have wanted
rest and entertainment when they turn to fiction,
rather than new labour. And that is what renders
Miss Austen caviare to the great majority of men,
who want, not rest and entertainment, but new
excitement, new stimulus. "What should I do,"
says Miss Austen to a contemporary, "with your
strong, vigorous sketches, full of variety and glow?
How could I possibly join them on to the little bit
(two inches wide) of ivory on which I work with so
fine a brush as produces little effect after much
labour?" In that minute scale and high finish we
have the secret, in my opinion, both of the delight
which is felt in Miss Austen by the few and the
indifference felt for her by the many. In order to
work upon that little bit of ivory with any effect,
she had to select only what could be given without
broad or strong touches; she had to select just
what interested and amused herself; and that was
not either the most substantial or the most tragic,
or the most impressive or the most representative
parts of human life; but was just what chiefly excited the interest of a lively and humorous woman
who lived her life amongst the rural gentry of the
southern counties in the time of the great war at the
beginning of the century. It was hardly possible
to find a finer sieve, a more effective strainer for
artistic material than such a mind as this, and the
result was something exquisitely interesting and
attractive to those who liked the fastidious selection
of social elements which such a mind instinctively

made for itself, and intolerably uninteresting and unattractive to those who loved to brood over the larger enterprises, the deeper passions, the weightier responsibilities, the more massive interests at which Miss Austen hardly glanced except to convince herself that she must leave them to the care of others. The many statesmen and thinkers, and the many humorous women who love Miss Austen's books, love them because they find in them a social world like enough to the real world to be for the time eagerly lived in, and yet one relieved of the bitterest elements and infinitely more entertaining than the real world, a world which rivets the attention without wearying it, and makes life appear far less dreary and burdensome, though also far less laborious, eager, and anxious than it really is.   This is the true charm of Miss Austen to those who love her, and the true source of indifference to those who do not. The former want a lively social picture in which they will be constantly amused and interested, and never required to attempt any great stretch of their powers of sympathy and imagination, one in contemplating which they can constantly laugh at the pompous self-importance of some men, and the frank selfishness of others, without grappling too closely with any of the great problems of duty or any of the great mysteries and paradoxes of faith.   The anti-Austenites, on the other hand, want something very different in literature from this.   The lively superficies of life is nothing to them in a mere literary mirror ; they like to study it at the original sources among the smiles and frowns and flying shafts of actual society.   When they take the trouble to read a book at all, they want something that excites and awakens them, that makes a kind of impression, which even the most lively society could not provide, but which they might remember in their dreams. Miss Austen's fine feminine sieve sifts away all that has most interest for such men, and leaves nothing but the aroma of society without the actual interest of personal relations. The delicate touches which the miniature preserves are interesting enough to men of this kind, if they see them in living eyes and on living lips, but when they are registered only in the fine strokes of the literary miniature they do not affect them. They expect literature to reveal something beyond even the best and most delicately sifted experiences of ordinary life; they expect it either to stir them to the very depths and electrify them, or to present them with some new mass of facts not otherwise attainable; and the delicate literary miniature painting answers neither purpose. But for those who like nothing better than to live by imagination alone among just such figures as would bore them if they were in the flesh, but only delight them in the delicately conceived field of a refined and vivid artist's canvas, Miss Austen's novels are the most perfectly amusing in the world. There is absolutely no *strain* in them, nothing but the lightest tracing of the characteristic vanities, self-deceptions, follies, and weaknesses, as well as shrewdnesses and wit of human life, so delineated as to make them all alike, seem even less important than they really are; and yet they secure all, and more than all, the charms of society to those who do not care to be themselves actors in the society they observe. If the Lady of Shalott had had Miss Austen's pictures before her, she would perhaps have been satisfied without plunging into the stream of real life; for no magic mirror ever reflected so much of it that amuses, and so little that heats and excites the soul to thirst after, and taste the reality. In Miss Austen's world we are content to live as mere observers, while most of the great novelists of Europe succeed in agitating the heart and stimulating the instincts which lead to passion or action.

GEORGE ELIOT

ENGLAND has suddenly lost the greatest writer among Englishwomen of this or any other age. There can be no doubt that George Eliot touched the highest point which, in a woman, has been reached in our literature,—that the genius of Mrs. Browning, for instance, though it certainly surpasses George Eliot's in lyrical sweetness, cannot even be compared with hers in general strength and force. The remarkable thing about George Eliot's genius is, that though there is nothing at all unfeminine in it, if we except a certain touch of scientific pedantry which is not pedantry in *motive*, but due only to a rather awkward manipulation of somewhat unfeminine learning,—its greatest qualities are not in the least the qualities in which women have usually surpassed men, but rather the qualities in which, till George Eliot's time, women had always been notably deficient. Largeness of mind, largeness of conception, was her first characteristic, as regards both matters of reason and matters of imagination. She had far more than many great men's power of conceiving the case of an opponent, and something approaching to Shakespeare's power of imagining the scenery of minds quite opposite in type to her own. There was nothing swift, lively, shallow, or flippant about her; and yet she could draw swift, lively, shallow, and flippant people with admirable skill and vivacity; as, for example, Mrs. Poyser, Mrs. Cadwallader, and many more. Her own nature was evidently sedate and rather slow-moving, with a touch of Miltonic stateliness in it, and a love of elaboration at times even injurious to her genius. Yet no characters she ever drew were more powerfully drawn than those at the very opposite pole to her own, for example, Hetty's childish, empty self-indulgence, Tito's smooth and gliding voluptuousness passing into treachery, Rosamond's tender susceptibility and heartless vanity. She herself was painstaking, even beyond the point up to which genius is truly defined as the power of taking pains. She often took too much pains. Her greatest stories lose in force by their too wide reflectiveness, and especially by an engrafted mood of artificial reflectiveness not suitable to her genius. She grew up under Thackeray's spell, and it is clear that Thackeray's satirical vein had too much influence over her from first to last, but especially in some of those earlier tales into which she threw a greater power of passion, than any which she had to spare for the two great efforts of the last ten years. *Adam Bede*, which might otherwise be the greatest of all English novels,—many, no doubt, really think it so,— is gravely injured by those heavy satirical asides to the reader in which you recognise the influence exerted over her mind by the genius of Thackeray,—asides, however, which are by no means in keeping with the large, placid, and careful drawing of her own magnificent, and on the whole tranquil, rural cartoons. I, at least, never take up these earlier stories—*Silas Marner* excepted—without a certain sense of irritation at the discrepancy between the strong, rich, and free drawing of the life they contain, and the somewhat falsetto tone of many of the light reflections interspersed. George Eliot had no command of Thackeray's literary stiletto, and her substitute for it is unwieldy. Even in the "Scenes from Clerical Life" this jars upon us. For example, this sentence in "Janet's Repentance": "When a man is happy enough to win the affections of a sweet girl, who can soothe his cares with crochet, and respond to all his most cherished ideas with braided urn-rugs and chair-covers in German wool, he has at least a guarantee of domestic comfort, whatever trials may await him out of doors," does not please an ear accustomed to the happy bitterness of Thackeray's caustic irony. It is heavy, not to say elephantine; and this heavy raillery rather increases upon George Eliot in *Adam Bede* and the *Mill on the Floss*. One is annoyed to have so great a painter of the largest human life turning aside to warn us that, "when Tityrus and Meliboeus happen to be on the same farm, they are not sentimentally polite to each other"; or that a High-Church curate, considered abstractedly, "is nothing more than a sleek, bimanous animal, in a white neckcloth, with views more or less Anglican, and furtively addicted to the flute." These sarcasms are not good in themselves, and still less are they good in their connection, where they spoil a most catholic-minded and marvellous picture. George Eliot's literary judgment was not equal to her reason and her imagination, and she took a great deal too much pains with the discursive parts of her books.

Imaginatively, I hardly recognise any defect in this great painter, except that there is too little movement in her stories; they wholly want dash, and sometimes want even a steady current. No novelist has combined so much power of painting external life on a board canvas with so wonderful an insight into the life of the soul. Her English butchers, farriers, auctioneers, and parish clerks are at least as vigorously drawn as Sir Walter Scott's bailies, peasants, serving-men, and beggars; while her pictures of the inward conflicts, whether of strong or of feeble natures, are far more powerful than any which Sir Walter Scott ever attempted. Such a contrast as that between Hetty and Dinah, such a picture as that of Mr. Casaubon's mental and moral limitation and confusion, such a study as that of Gwendolen's moral suffering under the torture administered by Grandcourt, was as much beyond the sphere of Sir Walter Scott, as his historical pictures of Louis XI., Mary Stuart, Balfour of Burley, Claverhouse, or James I., are beyond the sphere of George Eliot. On the only occasion on which George Eliot attempted anything of the nature of historical portraiture,—in *Romola*,—the purely imaginative part of the story is far more powerful than the historical. The ideas of the time when the revival of learning took place had quite possessed themselves of George Eliot's mind, and had stirred her into a wonderful imaginative effort. But her conceptions of the purely imagined figures —of Bardo, of Baldassarre, and of Tito—are far greater than her study of Savonarola. The genius for historical portraiture, for gathering up into a single focus the hints of chroniclers and historians, is something distinct from that of mere creation, and demands, apparently, a subtler mixture of interpreting with creating power, than most great creators possess. Even Sir Walter Scott failed with Napoleon, where he had not free movement enough, and the wealth of historical material shackled and overpowered the life of his imagination. It would not be true to say that George Eliot failed in like fashion with Savonarola. No doubt her picture of the great Italian reformer is fine, and up to a certain point effective. But in looking back on the story Savonarola fades away from the scene. It is Bardo, the old enthusiast for the Greek learning, or the fitfully vindictive gleam of Baldassarre's ebbing intellect as flashes of his old power return to him, or the supple Greek's crafty ambition, which stands out in one's memory, while the devout and passionate Dominican is all but forgotten.

No one can deny that the moral tone of George Eliot's books—*Felix Holt* being, perhaps, a doubtful exception—is of the noblest and purest kind, nor that the tone of feeling which prevails in them goes far in advance even of their direct moral teaching. I should say, for instance, that in regard to marriage, the spirit of George Eliot's books conveys an almost sacramental conception of its binding sacredness, though, unfortunately, of course, her career did much to weaken the authority of the teaching implied in her books. But the total effect of her books is altogether ennobling, though the profoundly sceptical reflections with which they are penetrated may counteract, to some extent, the tonic effect of the high moral feeling with which they are coloured. Before or after most of the noblest scenes, we come to thoughts in which it is almost as impossible for the feelings delineated to live any intense or hopeful life, as it is for human lungs to breathe in the vacuum of an air-pump. After she has breathed a noble spirit into a great scene, she too often proceeds to exhaust the air which is the very life-breath of great actions, so that the reflective element in her books undermines the ground beneath the feet of her noblest characters. In *Adam Bede* she eventually justifies her hero's secularistic coldness of nature, and makes you feel that Dinah was an enthusiast who could not justify what she taught. In "Janet's Repentance," again, she expresses in a few sentences the relief with which the mind turns away from the search for convictions calculated to urge the mind to a life of beneficent self-sacrifice, to those acts of self-sacrifice themselves :—

No wonder the sick-room and the lazaretto have so often been a refuge from the tossings of intellectual doubt—a place of repose for the worn and wounded spirit. Here is a duty about which all creeds and all philosophies are at one ; here, at least, the conscience will not be dogged by doubt, the benign impulse will not be checked by adverse theory ; here you may begin to act, without settling one preliminary question. To moisten the sufferer's parched lips through the long night-watches, to bear up the drooping head, to lift the helpless limbs, to divine the want that can find no utterance beyond the feeble motion of the hand or beseeching glance of the eye—these are offices that demand no self-questionings, no casuistry, no assent to propositions, no weighing of consequences. Within the four walls, where the stir and the glare of the world are shut out, and every voice is subdued, where a human being lies prostrate, thrown on the tender mercies of his fellow, the moral relation of man to man is reduced to its utmost clearness and simplicity ; bigotry cannot confuse it, theory cannot pervert it, passion awed into quiescence can neither pollute nor perturb it. As we bend over the sick-bed all the forces of our nature rush towards the channels of pity, of patience, and of

love, and sweep down the miserable choking drift of
our quarrels, our debates, our would-be wisdom, and
our clamorous, selfish desires. This blessing of serene
freedom from the importunities of opinion lies in all
simple, direct acts of mercy, and is one source of that
sweet calm which is often felt by the watcher in the
sick-room, even when the duties there are of a hard and
terrible kind.

There speaks the true George Eliot, and we may
clearly say of her that in fiction it is her great aim,
while illustrating what she believes to be the true
facts and laws of human life, to find a fit stage for
ideal feelings nobler than any which seem to her to
be legitimately bred by these facts and laws. But
she too often finds herself compelled to injure her
own finest moral effects by the sceptical atmosphere
with which she permeates them. She makes the
high-hearted heroine of her *Mill on the Floss* all
but yield to the physiological attraction of a poor
sort of man of science. She makes the enthusiastic
Dorothea in *Middlemarch* decline upon a poor
creature like Ladislaw, who has earned her regard
chiefly by being the object of Mr. Casaubon's
jealousy. She takes religious patriotism for the
subject of her last great novel, but is at some pains
to show that her hero may be religious without any
belief in God, and patriotic without any but an
ideal country. This reflective vacuum, which she
pumps out behind all noble action, gives to the
workings of her great imagination a general effect
of supreme melancholy.

I should rank George Eliot second only in her
own proper field—which is not the field of satire,
Thackeray's field—to Sir Walter Scott, and second
to him only because her imagination, though it

penetrates far deeper, had neither the same splendid
vigour of movement, nor the same bright serenity
of tone.   Her stories are, on the whole, richer than
Fielding's, as well as far nobler, and vastly less
artificial than Richardson's.   They cover so much
larger a breadth and deeper a depth of life than
Miss Austen's, that though they are not perhaps so
exquisitely finished, they belong to an altogether
higher kind of world.   They are stronger, freer,
and less Rembrandt-like than Miss Brontë's, and are
not mere photographs of social man like Trollope's.
They are patient and powerful studies of individual
human beings, in an appropriate setting of social
manners, from that of the dumbest provincial life
to that of life of the highest self-knowledge.   And
yet the reflections by which they are pervaded,
subtle and often wise as they are, to some extent
injure the art of the pictures by their satiric tone,
or if they do not do that, take superfluous pains to
warn you, and how very doubtful and insecure is
the spiritual footing on which the highest excellence
plants its tread.

   And this, too, is still more the fault of her poems,
which in spite of an almost Miltonic stateliness,
reflect too much the monotonous cadences of her
own musical but over-regulated voice.   The poems
want inspiration, and the speculative melancholy,
which only slightly injured her prose, predominates
fatally in her verse.   Throughout her poems she is
always plumbing the deep waters for an anchorage
and reporting "no soundings."   The finest of her
poems, "The Legend of Jubal," tries to affirm,
indeed, that death, the loss of all conscious existence,
is a sort of moral gain—as though the loss of self
were the loss of selfishness, which it not only is

not, but never could be, since selfishness can only be morally extinguished in a living self,—but the lesson is so obviously a moral gloss put on the face of a bad business, that there, at least, no anchorage is found. And in "The Spanish Gypsy" the speculative despair is even worse, while the failure of the imaginative portraiture is more conspicuous, because the portraiture itself is more ambitious. It will be by her seven or eight great fictions that George Eliot will live, not by her poems, and still less by her essays. But all these, one perhaps excepted, will long continue to be counted the greatest achievements of an Englishwoman's, and perhaps even of any woman's, brain.

THE IDEALISM OF GEORGE ELIOT AND MR. TENNYSON

A WEEK in which we have had additions (*Middle-march* and "The Last Tournament") to the permanent literature of England from both George Eliot and Mr. Tennyson,—indisputably the greatest literary artists of our own day, for however Mr. Browning may rival or surpass them in the field of imaginative thought and delineation, he cannot for a moment compare with them as mere artist,—seems to afford a natural occasion for comparing the merits of their similar but very divergent idealistic power and influence. Utterly different as they are in general effect,—so different that some would regard any comparison between them as unmeaning,—there are enough points of likeness in the nature of their genius, and the subject-matter of their speculative faculty, to make the comparison one of very considerable interest, not without some definite results. The great superficial difference between the faculties of these two great writers I should say is this,— that while, of the two, George Eliot has far the wider range of perception, and therefore much richer materials for the dramatic delineation of character at her command, her feeling for individuality seldom rouses the poetic faculty within her,—

184

which seems, indeed, to awaken rather in the attempt
to *escape from* the limits of concrete detail into
lofty generalisation,—while the Poet-Laureate, on
the other hand, is always drawn into the concrete
by the mere law of his poetic instinct, and is even
tempted by that instinct to crowd and overload his
pictures with the abundance of individual touches.
But George Eliot is never so far from the detail of
actual life in her poetry.   "The Spanish Gypsy"
might be said to be a poem on the influence of race
on temperament, in which the only defect, though
it was a great one, was that the pictures of individual temperament were so limited to what was
needed by the generalisation in her mind, that they
never took any living form on her canvas.   Again,
"The Legend of Jubal" was a mere song in praise
of Death, a eulogy on the fear of Death as a good
which drives men into useful and noble work.   And
"Armgart" was a meditation on the craving of the
artistic temperament for fame, and on the far higher
nobility of the self-sacrifice which works for others
without any such stimulus.   But in all these alike,
while there were plenty of sonorous and often
almost Miltonic apophthegms, there was a curious
and remarkable want of that dramatic clearness and
definition, by the vividness of which George Eliot's
genius has chiefly gained the admiration of the
world.   Verse and its harmonies seem to wrap in
mist the wonderful realism of her imagination, to
snatch her away from the region of actual perception into the region of large theoretic survey.   With
the Poet-Laureate, on the contrary, rhythm and
often rhyme seem essential even to his highest
realism,—even to such pictures as those of the two
Northern Farmers, who are described with a power

that seems for a moment to bring his province close
to that of the best scenes in George Eliot's most
perfect novels. The rhythm and music, which for
George Eliot drop a soft cloud over the moral detail
of life, and fill her soul with the principles she has
generalised from its study, rather than with the
minutiæ of its scenery, seem to help our great poet
to individualise still more sharply the visions which
pass before his imagination till they stand out with
the colour and solidity of actual life. And this
great difference probably arises from another, which
is curiously illustrated in the new contributions of
both these great writers. Both are great moral
idealists in the sense of believing intensely in a
moral ideal far above our actual life, from which
it ought to take its shape and colour ; but while
George Eliot is a pure idealist,—believing, apparently, that this ideal exists only in the mind of
man, and is rather mocked than enforced on us by
"the Supreme Power which has fashioned" our
natures,—Mr. Tennyson is most confident that he
is a realist in the midst of his highest idealism,
always seeming to be compelled by that higher
idealism to depict the broken music and maimed
purposes of human life more faithfully than ever.
Thus George Eliot's new book is intended, if I may
judge by what she terms its prelude, and the drift
of her first part, to illustrate the utter moral
failures into which high ideal purposes are apt to
lead women. After referring to St. Theresa, and
the success which a certain coherence in the social
faith and order of her day enabled her to achieve
in working out her high ideal, she adds that since
then "many Theresas have been born who found for
themselves no epic life wherein there was a constant

unfolding of far-resonant action,—perhaps only a
life of mistakes, the offspring of a certain spiritual
grandeur ill-matched with the meanness of opportunity ; perhaps a tragic failure which found no
poet, and sank unwept into oblivion." And she
adds, " Some have felt that their blundering lives
are due to the inconvenient indefiniteness with
which the Supreme Power has fashioned the natures
of women." Thus her new story is intended to
paint the misery of the moral chaos into which the
highest ideal yearnings naturally lead and plunge
her heroine. The Poet-Laureate, on the other
hand, touches the same subject, but differently.
His Arthurian poem of many parts is an elaborate
picture of a great moral failure to subdue earthly
circumstance to the highest will, but of a great
moral failure in which there is more glory than in
most success. In this last grand division of the
poem, the poor court fool who is, amongst all the
faithless, the only faithful found, who alone clings
sobbing to Arthur's feet when the king returns to
find Guinevere fled, and who, to the questioning of
the king as to who it is that clings to him in the
gloom, " sends up an answer sobbing,—"

> I am thy fool,
> And I shall never make thee smile again !

—this poor little jester, Dagonet, I say, while he
appears to affirm, is used really to refute this
teaching of George Eliot's that circumstance is so
hostile as often to foil and overwhelm most the
characters which are most worthy of an aureole
of glory. " Swine ? " he says, in answer to Sir
Tristram's contemptuous reproach,—

Swine ? I have wallowed, I have washed,—the world
Is flesh and shadow—I have had my day.
The dirty nurse Experience in her kind
Hath foul'd me,—as I wallowed, then I washed.
I have had my day and my philosophies,—
And thank the Lord I am King Arthur's fool.

Yet he who bears this strong testimony to the
soiling influence of the world, is also he who most
retains the faith in the "Harp of Arthur up in
Heaven," who most believes in the constellations of
which he says,—

It makes a silent music up in Heaven,
And I and Arthur and the angels hear ;

and who grieves the most when the spiritual order
which Arthur had established in his kingdom is
rent asunder, and the king finds himself the centre
only of a ruin, his purpose a failure, and even his
courage almost a wreck.   There is nothing finer in
English poetry in its way—that way which George
Eliot so finely describes as "an unfolding of far-
resonant action"—than Mr. Tennyson's picture, not
of the success, but of the ruin of a great ideal.
And yet it is exactly in the ruin—even in such
elements of the ruin as Lancelot's and Guinevere's
sin, where you cannot pretend that the idealism of
the soul is preserved unstained—that the poet
brings out most powerfully his faith in the divine
life which seems to have been so signally quenched.
That earthly circumstance clashes with the higher
purposes of men so as to foil their noblest designs,
is as clear to the great poet as to the great novelist;
but while the latter appears to find therein the
proof of the indifference of "the Supreme Power"

which fashions human nature to our failure or
success, the former seems to find in it only con-
firmation of his faith in that divine purpose which
shatters our hopes only to purify and enlarge them.

But to come back to the point from which I
started, the essential contrast between the great
poet and the great novelist of our day as artists
consists in this, that while both connect together
their works with a pure ideal thread on which they
string their great pictures, while both see clearly
that the ideal thread is not, and never can be, a
thread of even predominant joy, while both discern
and delineate the power of this high ideal temperament to blind the eyes of those who possess it to
the dull material realities of life, Mr. Tennyson,
nevertheless, uniformly gives it a victorious and
triumphant euthanasia in spite of all seeming failure,
while George Eliot almost as uniformly quenches
her ideal light in gloom.   A curiously blind critic
in the last number of the *Quarterly Review*, who
seems to me to enter as little into the Byron whom
it was his object to exalt, as into the Tennyson
whom it was his object to depreciate, remarks, with
that accurately-aimed infelicity with which blind
criticism does now and then manage to distinguish
its groping course, that there is no sort of wholeness
in Tennyson's "Idylls of the King,"—that the poet
"seems to have picked out a legend here and there,
as he wanted one for a subject, without regarding
its connection with the rest."   Now the power of
this great series of poems consists entirely in the
absolute unity of the imaginative centre to be traced
in every piece from first to last,—in the continuous
grandeur of that great earthly illusion by which
Arthur founds an empire on foundations far too

lofty to last, sees, without seeing, it slowly crumbling away beneath his touch from the very moment it appears to have gained its victory, dimly apprehends that he has in some sense injured his followers by the very loftiness of his requirements,—the grandeur of the vows which blight those by whom they are broken,—and survives the ruin of all his hopes with only a faithful fool to bewail their destruction. The king is so blinded by his own great dream that to some his career seems all illusion, and the saying,

Of bygone Merlin, " Where is he who knows ?
From the great deep to the great deep he goes,'

appears to such as these an adequate epitaph upon it. Yet no one who reads the series as a whole can help feeling the sense of triumph in the close, when Sir Gawaine's ghost goes shrieking down the wind, " And hollow, hollow, hollow, all delight," and Arthur passes to his isle of rest. The illusion that blinds the king is the illusion of infinite light—far more real than the world to which it blinds him. With George Eliot, on the other hand, the same idealism and illusion—not a whit less noble in their moral source—always come to some sad ending and partial or total quenching. The finer nature in Dinah suffers eclipse under the secular shadow of Adam Bede. Romola fails and fades in a melancholy twilight. The Spanish Gypsy succumbs to a part too hard for her. Jubal is extinguished with his song, and told to be grateful for extinction. Armgart loses all her fire and hope as she takes home her lesson of self-sacrifice ; and here, in this new work of our author's,—which is, I am sure, going to be a great one,—we are pretty plainly told

in the preface (why does she call it a "prelude"?)
that the heroine is to be the victim of her own
idealism, and to founder on the rocks of uncongenial
circumstance. That the sister of little feeling is to
see her way easily, and the sister of deep feeling to
stray far into the wilderness, I do not [complain.
All true realism teaches us that so it continually is.
But that we are to trace the history of a "foundress
of nothing, whose loving heart-beats and sobs after
an unattained goodness tremble off and are dispersed
among hindrances," seems to me the fiat not so much
of realism as of that deficiency in the faculties of
insight which only the stimulus of faith can supply.
The true idealism of life undoubtedly often leads to
failure and grief and outward ruin immeasurable;
but only infidelity to it, selfish recoil from it, leads
to that quenching and exhaustion of spirit in which
the finest characters of George Eliot's works are so
often allowed to flicker out their lives.

NEWMAN AND TENNYSON

The unveiling of Cardinal Newman's statue on Wednesday at the Oratory of St. Philip Neri was an event which I cannot help looking on as the consequence of a national mistake. Newman was no doubt a Roman Catholic, and a deserter from the Anglican communion, but he was a great Englishman before he was either, and perhaps more distinctively a great Oxonian than anything else. Oxford ought to have claimed him instead of rejecting him, as unluckily she did. His genius was full of the very essence of Oxford's great motto, "*Deus illuminatio mea*," and his manner was the embodiment of that "sweetness and light" which has characterised so many of the best Oxford teachers, till it has often been called the Oxford manner. The Roman Catholics saw this and generously offered the statue of their great thinker to Oxford; but Oxford was too shy of the Roman Catholic faith—though it was the faith of Oxford itself in an age when the University was more of a European than of an English institution—to accept the offer, and has thereby lost the memorial of one of the greatest and most impressive figures amongst her sons. The late Poet-Laureate, whose most characteristic aim in life was by no means

far removed from Cardinal Newman's, seeing that
both these great men confronted the deepest doubt
boldly, and yet in a spirit eager to show that faith
is deeper and truer than doubt, has said with something of paradox :—

> There is more faith in honest doubt,
> Believe me, than in half the creeds.

But though Newman would hardly have said that,
for he did not love paradox, and perhaps would
have been more disposed to say, what is also true,
"There is more doubt in shrinking faith, believe
me, than in half the heresies," there never was a
religious thinker, certainly a great ecclesiastic, who
expressed more powerfully and more candidly the
great doubts with which he grappled, or who
taught his friends to face them with a calmer and a
clearer glance.   Mr. Wilfrid Ward, who has done
so much to promote the knowledge of the great
Cardinal's writings,—with a complete belief in his
hero's ultimate solution of those doubts which I
have never been able to share,—has quite lately
published in a paper in the *New Review* (July
1896) a study of Tennyson, which seems to me to
demonstrate how much and how deep a sympathy
there was between the most characteristic aim of
Tennyson as a religious thinker and that of the
Oxford leader who ended his days as a Cardinal
of the Church of Rome.   And though Cardinal
Newman's name is never mentioned, so far as I
remember, in Mr. Wilfrid Ward's article, I am
very glad to avail myself of its drift to illustrate
my contention that there was quite enough of
parallelism between the religious aims of these

two very different men, with their two widely different manners, to show how ill Oxford understood her own characteristic aims, when she practically declined to recognise Newman except as a deserter from her fold. Newman, no doubt, was a far more earnest believer in the dogmas of Christianity than Tennyson, who never succeeded in reconciling himself wholly to the Christian creeds, profoundly as he revered and loved the person of Christ. But I do not scruple to say that his method was the same as Newman's, though he could not go so far as Newman went in accepting the intellectual form in which historical Christianity had embodied itself in the creeds of the Church. Mr. Wilfrid Ward's paper has been talked of as if it were an unauthorised revelation of private confidences between Tennyson and himself. Nothing can be more ridiculous than such a statement, and I doubt whether those who think so have carefully read what they so describe. It is, I venture to say, a lucid exhibition of thoughts written all over the most definitely religious of Lord Tennyson's poems, and though, with the exception of "The Two Voices," they are by no means amongst his greatest poems, they are certainly amongst the writings which most definitely express the aims dearest to Tennyson's heart, and bring him nearer to the great Tractarian leader, as regards his inmost thoughts, than I could ever have expected men so different and so widely severed in their origin and their walk in life to come.

What was certainly common to the dearest objects of Newman and Tennyson is—that while they both believed that faith is deeper than doubt, they both endeavoured to confront doubt with the

steadiest and most intrepid gaze, and held that
the more frankly we meet and measure it, even
when it seems to threaten us with utter disaster,
the more surely shall we ultimately triumph over,
not indeed all our doubts, but all those which
would leave us without any helm in the storm,
and without any compass by which to steer. Let
me trace the principles which seem to be common
to Newman and Tennyson in dealing with the
fundamental incredulities of the human intellect.
In the first place, there is perfect agreement on the
point that the sense of duty is the deepest root of
faith. Cardinal Newman, naturally enough, put
this with more point and effectiveness than the
Poet-Laureate, though both of them put it clearly
and definitely enough. Newman is never tired
of pressing the point that the spirit of obedience
to duty is the beginning of all true religion. He
held that even the most heretical parents should
find their children obedient, and that in that early
obedience the first step would be taken towards a
truer faith. He makes his hero in *Loss and
Gain* rebuke a friend for saying, "I can't believe
this or that," and declare that, if only he could
find any one with proper authority to say, "This
is true," then he "*ought* to believe it," and not to
say that he cannot believe it simply because it is
beyond the power of the human intellect to comprehend. Tennyson took the same line of thought
in dealing with doubt. He regarded the instinct
of the conscience as the root of faith. "His
method," says Mr. Wilfrid Ward, "consisted in
the presentation of two opposing veins of thought—
of questioning and doubt on the one hand, and
of instinctive assurance on the other. Each line

of thought is given its weight. The instinctive
assurance is not set aside in consequence of the
speculative doubt, nor is it allowed to check
the doubt in its critical function. Doubt and
questioning may lead to the discovery that some
instinctive beliefs are based on mere prejudice. Yet
there are instincts which bear in them signs of
authority,—as the inner voice appealed to in 'the
Ancient Sage,'—and the fact is recognised that
doubt and questioning may be morbid and a consequence of intellectual defect. In 'The Two
Voices' these two elements are formally expressed."
And Mr. Wilfrid Ward quotes the poet's own
definition of his aim :—

> As far as might be, to carve out
> Free space for every human doubt,
> That the whole mind might orb about.
>
> To search thro' all I felt or saw
> The springs of life, the depths of awe,
> And read the law within the law.

I do not suppose that Cardinal Newman ever
desired to provide fresh space "for every human
doubt," for which he thought that there was ample
space already in our restless intelligence, as we
know it. But he undoubtedly desired greatly
"to reach the law within the law," and there he
and Tennyson were working on common ground.
Moreover, as his University lectures show, he
wholly disapproved any attempt to *stifle* doubt as
distinct from the effort to confront it fairly with
the deeper facts of life.

Again, look at the profound sympathy between
the view of the late Poet-Laureate and the view of

Cardinal Newman on the subject of the limited and closely hedged-in free-will of man. Mr. Wilfrid Ward reports Lord Tennyson as saying, "Man is free, but only free in certain narrow limits. His character and his acquired habits limit his freedom. They are like the cage of a bird. The bird can hop at will from one perch to another, and to the floor of the cage, but not beyond its bars." And so, too, Cardinal Newman, though on this point more of an idealist than Tennyson, insisted on the narrow verge of human liberty, and even ventured to satirise the disposition to glory only in the possession of a liberty which we do not know how to use. Liberty, he insisted, is only valuable to those who can find the highest guidance for its exercise, and is even injurious to those who are satisfied with the mere possession of it, and regard the mode in which it is to be exercised as something more or less irrelevant to the joy of being at liberty to go wrong. He could not endure the jauntiness with which men riot in the idle possession of one of the most responsible of gifts. Those, he declared, who say to themselves, "I am examining, I am scrutinising, I am free to choose or reject, I am exercising the right of private judgment," are about as wise as the person who ostentatiously exults in his grief for a friend, and says, "I am weeping, I am overcome and agonised for the second or third time, I am resolved to weep," and of such a one I should certainly say that his grief was not profound. And so the sense of liberty cannot be serious in a man who is content to make a great fuss over it, and not to take that anxious care to exercise it rightly which alone shows his real value for it. To Newman liberty of choice was a "dread" gift :—

> Son of immortal seed, high-destined Man !
> Know thy dread gift,—a creature, yet a cause :
> Each mind is its own centre, and it draws
> Home to itself, and moulds in its thought's span
> All outward things, the vassals of its will,
> Aided by Heaven, by earth unthwarted still.

That is written in the noblest style of Tennyson's verse, but it was published before Tennyson had produced anything in that high strain.

Of course the most important and remarkable of the analogies between Newman and Tennyson was the very deep conviction shared by both of the absolute certainty of the relation of God to the soul of man. Newman tells in his *Apologia* that "from a very early age" he had "rested in the thought of two, and two only, supreme and luminously self-evident beings, myself and my Creator," and that conviction may be regarded as the very root of all he had to say in this world, however wide-spreading may have been its leaves and branches. It was nearly the same with Tennyson. Let us hear Mr. Wilfrid Ward's account of the manner in which Lord Tennyson, almost at the last, read to him the "De Profundis" as his deepest profession of faith :—

He raised his eyes from the book at the seventh line and looked for a moment at his hearer with an indescribable expression of awe before he uttered the word "spirit:—Out of the deep—Spirit—out of the deep." When he had finished the second greeting he was trembling much. Then he read the prayer—a prayer, he had told me, of self-prostration before the Infinite. I think he intended it as a contrast with the analytical and reflective character of the rest. It is an outpouring

of the simplest and most intense self-abandonment to the
Creator, an acknowledgment, when all has been thought
and said with such insight and beauty, that our best
thoughts and words are as nothing in the Great Presence
—in a sense parallel to the breaking off in the ode to
the Duke of Wellington :—

> Speak no more of his renown,
> Lay your earthly fancies down.

That is Tennyson, and what says Cardinal Newman
in his " De Profundis " :—

> Take me away, and in the lowest deep
>   There let me be,
> And there in hope the lone night-watches keep,
>   Told out for me.
> There, motionless and happy in my pain,
>   Lone, not forlorn,—
> There will I sing my sad perpetual strain,
>   Until the morn,
> There will I sing, and soothe my stricken breast,
>   Which ne'er can cease
> To throb, and pine, and languish, till possest
>   Of its Sole Peace.

Surely there we see a singular depth of ultimate
sympathy between the almost Puritan poet, whose
face, with its haggard and even moody lines, has
spoken the deepest spiritual truth to this generation
of the English people, and the great Cardinal whom
Oxford disowned, because he had in some sense
disowned Oxford when he left the University he
loved so tenderly in the fashion which he himself
had foreshadowed long before, when he described
himself as " a pilgrim pale with Paul's sad girdle

bound." Surely Newman, Roman Catholic though he was, should have been claimed for England as Tennyson was claimed for England. Of course he was not nearly so great a poet, but perhaps he was even greater as a man.

THOMAS CARLYLE

For many years before his death last Saturday, Mr. Carlyle had been to England what his great hero, Goethe, long was to Germany—the aged seer whose personal judgments on men and things were everywhere sought after, and eagerly chronicled and retailed. Yet it was hardly for the same reason. In Goethe's old age the ripeness of his critical judgment, and the catholicity, not to say even the facility, of his literary taste, induced a sort of confidence that he would judge calmly, and judge genially, anything, whether in life or literature, that was not extravagant. Mr. Carlyle was resorted to for a very different reason. The Chelsea shrine, as was well known, gave out only one sort of oracles, and that sort was graphic and humorous denunciation of all conventional falsehoods and pretentiousness, or what was presumed to be conventional falsehood and pretentiousness; and, consequently, recourse was had to that shrine only when some trenchant saying was wanted that might help in the sweeping away of some new formula of the sentimentalists, or of the panegyrists of worn-out symbols. His almost extravagant admiration for Goethe notwithstanding, Carlyle in his greatness was ever more disposed to sympathise with the great organs of destructive than with those of constructive force. He sympathised with Cromwell for what he destroyed, with Frederick in great measure for what he destroyed, with Mirabeau and Danton for what they destroyed, and even with Goethe in large degree for the negative tendencies of thought and criticism. With the constructive tendencies of the past he could often deeply sympathise,—as he showed in *Past and Present*,—but with those of the present, hardly ever. If I were asked what his genius did for English thought and literature, I should say that it did chiefly the work of a sort of spiritual volcano,—showed us the perennial fire subversive of worn-out creeds which lies concealed in vast stores beneath the surface of society, and the thinness of the crust which alone separates us from that pit of Tophet, as he would himself have called it. And yet, in spite of himself, he always strove to sympathise with positive work. His teaching was incessant that the reconstruction of society was a far greater work than the destruction of the worn-out shell which usually preceded it, only, unfortunately, in his own time, there was hardly any species of reconstructive effort which could gain his acquiescence, much less his approval. He despised all the more positive, political, and philanthropic tendencies of his time; felt little interest in scientific discoveries; concerned himself not at all about its art; scorned its economical teaching, and rejected the modern religious instructors with even more emphatic contumely than the "dreary professors of a dismal science." To Carlyle the world was out of joint, and his only receipt for setting it right—the restoration of "the beneficent whip" for its idlers, rogues, and vagabonds—was never seriously listened to by thinking men. Consequently, all that he achieved was achieved in the world of thought and imagination. He did succeed in making men realise, as they never realised before, into what fermenting chaos of passion human society is constantly in danger of dissolving, when either injustice or insincerity—what Mr. Carlyle called a " sham "—is in the ascendant, and rules by virtue of mere convention or habit. He did succeed in making men realise the wonderful paradox of all social order and discipline, in depicting to us the weakness and the hysterical character of much that is called patriotic and humane impulse, in making us see that justice and strength and a certain heroism of courage are all necessary for the original organisation of a stable society ; and that much sensibility in the body corporate, so far from making this organisation easier, is apt to make it both more difficult and more unstable. Carlyle's greatest power was the wonderful imaginative genius which enabled him to lift the veil from the strange mixture of convention, passion, need, want, capacity, and incompetence called human society, and makes us understand by what a thread order often hangs, and how rare is the sort of genius to restore it when once it goes to pieces. No one ever performed this great service for the world as Carlyle has performed it in almost all his works—notably in *The French Revolution* and *Sartor Resartus*, and this alone is enough to entitle him to a very high place among the immortals of literature.

And he had all the gifts for this great task, especially that marvellous insight into the social power of symbols which made him always maintain that fantasy was the organ of divinity. He has often been called a prophet, and though I have too little sympathy with his personal conception of good and evil so to class him,—though religious seer as he was, he was in no sense Christ-like,—he certainly had to the full the prophet's insight into the power of parable and type, and the prophet's eye for the forces which move society and inspire multitudes with contagious enthusiasm, whether for good or ill. He fell short of a prophet in this, that his main interest, after all, was rather in the graphic and picturesque interpretation of social phenomena than in any overwhelming desire to change them for the better, warmly as that desire was often expressed, and sincerely, no doubt, as it was entertained. Still, Carlyle's main literary motive-power was not a moral passion but a humorous wonder. He was always taking to pieces, in his own mind's eye, the marvellous structure of human society, and bewildering himself with the problem of how it could be put together again. Even in studying personal character, what he cared for principally was this :— for men who could not sway the great spiritual tides of human loyalty and trust, he had—with the curious exception of Goethe—no very real reverence. His true heroes were all men who could make multitudes follow them as the moon makes the sea follow her,—either by spiritual magnetism, or by trust, or by genuine practical capacity. To him imagination was the true organ of divinity, because, as he saw at a glance, it was by the imagination that men are most easily both governed and beguiled. His story of the French Revolution is a series of studies in the way men are beguiled and governed by their imagination, and no more wonderful book of its kind has ever been written in this world, though I should be sorry to have to estimate accurately how much of his picture is true vision, and how much the misleading guesswork of a highly-imaginative dreamer.

It is in some respects curious that Carlyle has connected his name so effectually as he has done with the denunciation of shams. For I am far from thinking that the passionate love of truth in its simplicity was at all his chief characteristic. In the first place, his style is too self-conscious for that of sheer, self-forgetting love of truth. No man of first-rate simplicity — and first-rate simplicity is, I imagine, one of the conditions of a first-rate love of truth — would express commonplace ideas in so roundabout a fashion as he; would say, for instance, in recommending Emerson to the reading public, "The words of such a man, — what words he thinks fit to speak, are worth attending to"; or would describe a kind and gracious woman as "a gentle, excellent, female soul," as he does in his *Life of Sterling*. There is a straining for effect in the details of Carlyle's style which is not the characteristic of an overpowering and perfectly simple love of truth. Nor was that the ruling intellectual principle of Carlyle's mind. What he meant by hatred of shams, exposure of unveracities, defiance to the "Everlasting No," affirmation of the "Everlasting Yea," and the like, was not so much the love of truth as the love of divine force, — the love of that which had genuine strength and effective character in it, the denunciation of imbecilities, the scorn for the dwindled life of mere conventionality or precedent, the contempt for extinct figments, not so much because they were figments as because they

were extinct, and would no longer bear the strain
put upon them by human passion. You can see
this in the scorn which Carlyle pours upon "thin"
men,—his meagre reverence for "thin-lipped, constitutional Hampden," for instance, and his contempt
for such men as the Edgeworth described in John
Sterling's life, whom he more than despises, not for
the least grain of insincerity, but for deficiency in
quantity of nature, and especially such nature as
moves in society. Greatly as Carlyle despised
"cant," he seems to have meant by cant, not so
much principles which a man does not personally
accept, but repeats by rote on the authority of
others, as principles which have ceased, in his
estimation, to exert a living influence on society,
whether heartily accepted by the individual or not.
Thus, in his life of Sterling, he indulges in long
pages of vituperation against Sterling for taking to
the Church,—not that he believed Sterling to be
insincere in doing so, but because what Carlyle
called the "Hebrew old clothes" were to his mind
worn out, and he would not admit that any one
of lucid mind could honestly fail to see that so
it was.

Carlyle, in short, has been the interpreter to
his country, not so much of the "veracities" or
"verities" of life, as of the moral and social spells
and symbols which, for evil or for good, have
exercised a great imaginative influence over the
social organism of large bodies of men, and either
awed them into sober and earnest work, or stimulated them into delirious and anarchic excitement.
He has been the greatest painter who ever lived of
the interior life of man, especially of such life as
spreads to the multitude, not perhaps exactly as it

really is, but rather as it represented itself to one who looked upon it as the symbol of some infinite mind of which it embodied a temporary phase. I doubt if Carlyle ever really interpreted any human being's career—Cromwell's or Fredrick's or Coleridge's—as justly and fully as many men of less genius might have interpreted it. For this was not, after all, his chief interest. His interest seems to me always to have been in figuring the human mind as representing some flying colour or type of the Infinite Mind at work behind the Universe, and so presenting this idea as to make it palpable to his fellow-men. He told Sterling he did not mind whether he talked "pantheism or pottheism,"—a mild joke which he so frequently repeated as to indicate that he rather overrated its excellence,— so long as it was true; and he meant, I fancy, by being true, not so much corresponding to fact, as expressing adequately the constant effort of his own great imagination to see the finite in some graphic relation to the infinite. Perhaps the central thought of his life was in this passage from *Sartor Resartus*: "What is man himself, but a symbol of God ? Is not all that he does symbolical, —a revelation to sense of the mystic God-given power that is in him, a gospel of freedom, which he, the 'Messias of Nature,' preaches, as he can, by act and word? Not a hut he builds but is the visible embodiment of a thought, but leaves visible record of invisible things, but is, in the transcendental sense, symbolical as well as real." Carlyle was far the greatest interpreter our literature has ever had of the infinite forces working through society, of that vast, dim background of social beliefs, unbeliefs, enthusiasms, sentimentalities, superstitions, hopes, fears, and trusts, which go to make up either the strong cement, or the destructive lava-stream, of national life, and to image forth some of the genuine features of the retributive providence of history.

MR. CARLYLE ON VERSE

STUDENTS of Mr. Carlyle will not have been surprised at the outbreak against verse which was
published the other day in his letter to Dr. Bennett.
Nearly twenty years ago he first publicly broached
the same heresy in his life of John Sterling, whom
he strenuously advised—perhaps in that case wisely
—to give up verse and stick to prose, but on grounds
which were many of them equally applicable to all
men and without reference to the individual faculty
of the man. "Why *sing* your bits of thoughts if you
can contrive to speak them ? By your thought, not
your mode of delivering it, you must live or die,"
urged Mr. Carlyle to his discouraged friend. And
again :— "Beyond all Ages, our Age admonishes
whatsoever thinking or writing man it has,—'Speak
to me some wise, intelligible speech; your wise
meaning in the shortest and clearest way ; behold,
I am dying for want of wise meaning and insight
into the devouring fact : speak, if you have any
wisdom !' As to song so called, and your fiddling
talent,—even if you have one, much more if you
have none, — we will talk of that a couple of
centuries hence, when things are calmer again.
Homer shall be thrice welcome ; but only when
Troy is *taken* ; alas ! while the siege lasts, and the

battle's fury rages everywhere, what can I do with
the Homers? I want Achilles and Odysseus, and
am enraged to see them trying to be Homers."
And again, " Why follow that sad, 'metrical' course,
climbing the loose sandhills, when you have a firm
path across the plain?" And now, it appears, Mr.
Carlyle holds this doctrine still more strongly than
when he did his best to discourage Sterling from
verse-making. He says to Dr. Bennett, — who
actually had the intellectual nerve to send Mr.
Carlyle a sonnet of his own composition :—

It is one of my constant regrets, in this generation,
that men to whom the gods have given a genius (which
means a light of intelligence, of courage, and all manful-
ness, or else means nothing) will insist, in such an earnest
time as ours has grown, in bringing out their divine gift
in the shape of *verse*, which now no man reads entirely
in earnest. That a man has to bring out his gift in
words of any kind, and not in silent divine *actions*, which
alone are fit to express it well, seems to me a great misfortune for him ; but that he should select verse, with its
half-credibilities and other sad accompaniments, when he
might have prose and be wholly credible, if he desired it,
—this I lay at the door of our spiritual teachers (pedants
mostly, and speaking an obsolete dialect), who thereby
incalculably rot the world ; making him who might
have been a soldier and fighter (so terribly wanted just
at present), a mere preacher and idle singer. This is a
fixed perception of mine, growing ever more fixed these
many years ; and I offer it to you, as I have done to
many others in the like case, not much hoping that you
will believe in it all at once. But, certainly, a good,
wise, earnest piece in prose from you would please me
better than the musicallest verses could.

From all which it appears that Mr. Carlyle's objec-

tion to verse consists in this, that there is something
artificial, light-minded, and even falsetto-toned about
it as a mode of conveying meaning between man
and man.

It rather surprises me that a writer who has so
completely made a sort of prismatic prose style for
himself,—a style which to every man who makes
acquaintance with Mr. Carlyle for the first time is
apt to seem (no doubt very untruly and unjustly)
a wonder of artificiality and affectation,—should be
the one to assert that the form and matter of human
thought are quite separable from each other, and
that it is the latter only which has any real importance.   Why, if it were only for Mr. Carlyle's
peculiar comparatives and superlatives of adjectives,
his very profuse employment of abstractions (such
as "credibilities," "Eternities," and so forth), and
a number of other really unique and individual
forms of speech, there would be enough to prove
from the evidence of his own style alone, that
special matter often determines its own form by
some occult law of the inner faculty, and that it is
idle to assume that a man can express his thought
in any way he chooses, or that what would seem
to one man the most true expression of it, is really
the expression of the other's meaning.   And as
for the "earnestness" of our age, Mr. Carlyle's
own mind can hardly be said—except under some
very peculiar use of the term—to want earnestness.
Many would say that he is overstocked with some
forms of that quality.   And how does it show itself ?
Not indeed in climbing "the loose sandhills" of
metre, but, on the other hand, in elaborating a
sort of special language for himself, which is over-
loaded and indistinct with excess of colour, which

combines with a great hunger for the adequate
vision of all physical facts a certain wrathful
melancholy at the littleness of the human world,
and a vain yearning to introduce Titan-worship
into it, in the hope of thereby making it somewhat
less contemptible. This is expressed in Mr. Carlyle's
writings by an illuminated kind of style, in which
the *hinting and suggesting* resources of language are
all developed so as to produce an almost inconceivable sense of high pressure. The crowding of the
colours into a sort of Turneresque shorthand seems
to shadow forth Mr. Carlyle's contempt for mere
speech, and his wish to saturate language with
meaning under the pressure of some half-dozen
atmospheres till it has gained something of the
electric effect of a moral discharge, and become
rather a personal action than a speech. Mr.
Carlyle's sovereign contempt for *minute* moral
phenomena, for "thin" life, for small scrupulosities,
is impressed somehow, chiefly by indirect touches of
style, on every page of his writings. You might
say that his "earnestness" overbalances itself very
often into a lust of the moral-theatrical, which is
on the very borders of falsehood, and that here his
earnestness meets the extreme apparently most
opposed to it. But this again paints itself in his
style, which is far nearer moral theatricality than
good *verse* is capable of being. What, for instance,
does such a sentence as this, among those finding
fault with Sterling for taking orders in the English
Church, express ?—" So dark and abstruse, without
lamp or authentic finger-post, is the course of pious
genius towards the Eternal Kingdom grown. No
fixed highway more ; the old spiritual highways
and-recognised paths to the Eternal, now all torn

up and flung in heaps, submerged in unutterable boiling mud-oceans of Hypocrisy and Unbeliev-ability, of brutal living Atheism and damnable dead putrescent Cant; surely a tragic pilgrimage for all mortals; Darkness and the mere shadow of Death enveloping all things from pole to pole; and in the raging gulf-current offering us Will-o'-the-Wisps for load-stars,—intimating that there are no stars, nor ever were except certain Old-Jew ones, which have now gone out." Translated into common prose, it would mean only that a vast deal of unreal and half-belief is mixed up with all the traditional creeds, that such unreal and half-belief is evil and weak and dangerous, and paralyses what genuine belief there is in its fight with the brutalism of genuine selfishness and self-worship. But this crowd of metaphor, under which Mr. Carlyle sails, adds a great deal of indirect expression to that rather commonplace opinion, and manages to make it ex-press, besides what it does formally say, a vast deal of Mr. Carlyle's personal contempt for antiquated formulæ, for all professions of accurate thinking about infinite subjects, for fanciful solutions of problems of which he recognises no authentic solution, and, generally, for conventional and easy-going religious creeds of all sorts.

Yet one can see dimly why Mr. Carlyle, with all the peculiarity of his speech, hates, as he does, the rhythmical forms of English verse. What verse specially expresses is the imaginative completeness or satisfaction of the poet's mind or feeling, some-times a sense of harmony between his mind and the subject of his thought, more often perhaps (and almost always in lyrical poetry) a sense of complete absorption in the life of his own emotion which, for the moment, is allowed to tinge everything he sees, and create, as it were, a universe for itself. Now neither of these states of mind is what Mr. Carlyle wants to express. In all his writings there is the fundamental wrath and melancholy of a mind in conflict with the world of men as he finds it, and anxiety to express that conflict. A deep revolutionary fire glows in his veins,—not revolutionary in the popular sense, for he is always striving to shadow forth his contempt for the chief revolutionary processes of republican enthusiasm, but in a much deeper sense than the popular, in a sense which goes to the heart of the moral universe as we find it. He wants to see what he calls "silent divine actions" predominant everywhere, to extinguish the idle fret, and gossip, and fussy enthusiasms of the world he sees, and substitute for them organised hosts of obedient souls waiting upon the silent signals of great men, as a servant waits upon the eye of his master. His whole soul protests because he does not find this. He cannot express the contempt with which he looks upon the foolish chaos of actual life as he sees it. And he cannot forget it and sink into himself. However, he has not only no craving for the imaginative rhythm of verse, but he hates it as expressing a fundamental harmony which he cannot hear, and as hiding the anarchy he detests. His grotesqueries of style seem to say the same thing. When he talks of "musicallest verses," it is with a soul that protests against the existence of music in all this moral anarchy, and the odd form of his superlative somehow expresses this. Not that he himself is without a sense of music. On the contrary, his prose expresses often very finely that shriek of the retreating wave before it dashes again on the shore, in which the chronic conflict of earth and ocean is so wonderfully reflected. But in all his music there is the note of discord, which verse drowns. He is at one with the great silent forces of Nature, or tries to be so ; but he no sooner sees man (and he cares very little about anything else) than he lifts up his voice and shrieks or sighs like the wind which precedes a tempest.

I have heard a very able literary man defend Mr. Carlyle's thesis—so far as this goes, at least, that a great deal of the finest poets' thoughts might be just as effectively expressed in prose as in verse— by referring to the fine prose scene in Hamlet (Act ii. Scene 2), where we find Shakespeare putting such thoughts as these, for instance, into Hamlet's mouth and giving them in prose :—"What a piece of work is a man ! how noble in reason ! how infinite in faculty ! in form and moving how express and admirable ! in action how like an angel ! in apprehension how like a god ! the beauty of the world ! the paragon of animals!" Yet nothing could better illustrate Mr. Carlyle's own preference of prose to verse. Hamlet speaks this fine passage in prose, why ? Because he is expressing not so much his intellectual admiration, but the failure of his heart to admire; he is expressing not his feelings, but the *jar* in them. "It goes so heavily with my disposition that this goodly frame, the earth, seems to me a sterile promontory, this most excellent canopy, the air, look you, this brave o'erhanging firmament, this majestical roof fretted with golden fire, why, it appears no other thing to me than a foul and pestilent congregation of vapours." And how does he end his panegyric on the great masterpiece of creation, man ? Why, by saying, "And yet, to me, what is this quintessence of dust? Man delights not me: no, nor woman neither." Indeed, nothing seems to me more remarkable than the use of prose by Hamlet throughout the play, to express that jar in his mind which Mr. Carlyle always feels so keenly. In the earlier part of the play, before the discord is fully developed, he speaks in the usual verse. Throughout, when in soliloquy, and not directly measuring himself against the world, he speaks in verse, which expresses the lyrical pain within him. Even with his mother, since he feels that she can partly respond to his passionate, but tender reproaches, he speaks in verse. But in fencing with Rosencranz and Guildenstern, in his mockery of Polonius, in his harshness with Ophelia, in his bitter comments in the graveyard, in his scornful reception of Osric, he uses a prose nearer in tone and movement to Mr. Carlyle's than almost any other English literature could produce, though, of course, for many reasons different enough.

The truth is, that true poetry could no more be given in prose without a complete failure to express the writer's mind than common, everyday prose could be given in poetry; and Mr. Carlyle himself is one of my best witnesses. Doubtless a great deal of verse is mere prose in conventional fetters; but I doubt whether any of this was worth giving at all, either in prose or verse. Take the one great poet, who most often falls into pure prose, Wordsworth, and wherever you find a prosaic line, you find one which neither in prose nor verse was worth keeping. No doubt Mr. Browning is a great exception to this. Many of his semi-dramatic monologues would have been studied with as much interest if they had been given in prose as in verse, and some of them with a great deal more. The Roman lawyers in "The

Ring and the Book " would have been far more amusing and readable in prose than in verse. But then Mr. Browning, great as he is as an imaginative writer, is hardly a great poet. There is a jar between the acute practical sense in him and the visionary feeling which resounds through a very great part of his verse. But as for such an assertion as that Shelley's, or Tennyson's, or Wordsworth's poetry, or any true poetry whatever, loses " earnestness " by its form of verse, it seems to me simply ludicrous. Just imagine how this wail would gain in " earnestness " by being expressed in prose :—

> When the lamp is shattered,
> The light on the dust lies dead ;
> When the cloud is scattered,
> The rainbow's glory is shed ;
> When the lute is broken,
> Sweet tones are remembered not ;
> When the lips have spoken,
> Love's accents are soon forgot.

Any cry of the spirit of this sort would, I take it, lose indefinitely in earnestness by its translation into prose ; and to take quite another sort of composition, who would venture to distort and torture into prose even the highest specimens of specifically " earnest " poetry, Milton's " Samson Agonistes," or Wordsworth's " Ode to Duty " ?—

> Stern Lawgiver ! yet thou dost wear
> The Godhead's most benignant grace ;
> Nor know we anything so fair
> As is the smile upon thy face :
> Flowers laugh before thee on their beds
> And fragrance in thy footing treads ;

Thou dost preserve the stars from wrong;
And the most ancient heavens, through Thee, are
fresh and strong.

No ; Mr. Carlyle's objection to verse is the objection of a noble mind out of tune, which is always craving to mark the discords of its own depths. Verse is the natural and only possible instrument of expression both for overpowering lyrical feeling and for complete imaginative insight.

MRS. CARLYLE

IF Mrs. Carlyle married for ambition, as Mr. Froude reports, it is probable that she has gained what most ambitious people hope to gain,—whether they ultimately value what they have gained or not,—a name of her own in literature, and not merely the name of a faithful companion to her famous husband. Never were letters, unless they were the letters of Cowper, so full of fascination as Mrs. Carlyle's. Her letters surpass those of her husband in every quality which letters should have except vividness, —in variety, naturalness, lightness of touch; in the rapid, but never abrupt, change from tender to satirical, from satirical to imaginative, and from imaginative, again, to the keen, shrewd, matter-of-fact of mother-wit; while in a few of them there is a wild, gipsy kind of waywardness which is, of course, entirely foreign to Mr. Carlyle's sphere. But I am not going to discuss Mrs. Carlyle's letters, but to attempt to reconstruct, so far as it is possible, from the insight they give, the figure of the author of the letters, who, while linked with a man of marvellous, though narrow, genius, made for herself— quite unconsciously too—a fame which shines distinctly enough even in the immediate neighbourhood of his, and which shines by no reflected light.

We are told in these volumes that Mrs. Carlyle's grandmother was grandniece to a notable gipsy, Matthew Baillie, who came to be hanged, and whose wife was the original of Scott's "Meg Merrilies." Mr. W. E. Forster, to whom Mrs. Carlyle mentioned this gipsy descent, is said to have replied that this information was the first thing to make her mind intelligible to him as a cross between that of a gipsy and that of John Knox (from whom also she was descended). But, so far as I can see, there was but little of John Knox in Mrs. Carlyle. She had no taste for abstract doctrine, or, indeed, for the abstract in any shape. Nor was she didactic. The gipsy clearly predominated in her over the Calvinist divine. Like the gipsies, she loved a certain wilful order, an order improvised out of chaos; and one great source of her suffering in the extreme repression of her life with Carlyle was that he had no love for these snatches of fitful and changeful energy, and wanted nothing so much as constant protection against surprise. A brother of General Cavaignac, who was intimate with the Carlyles, used to say of Mrs. Carlyle that hers was a genius for "detail"; and so it was,—as well for the imagination as for the execution of detail. She could always see how much really skilful detail could effect; and to this, we believe, she owed much of her extraordinary power of managing others,—ranging from the power of pacifying Carlyle to the power of "writing-down a parrot." Considering how wonderfully tender and accessible were her sympathies,—at one time she, justly enough, called her head "a perfect chaos of other people's disasters and despairs,"— her answer to the question, "Why do women marry?" —because, "like the great Wallenstein, they do not

find scope enough for their genius and qualities in
an easy life," would scarcely have been a sufficient
one, for she could have found scope for her genius
and qualities in almost any life. But undoubtedly
the enormous difficulties of engineering Carlyle's
life for him did make an impression on her
ambitious imagination, and launched her into the
pursuit of an ideal which she often found quite too
hard for her. Perhaps the reason why it was often
too hard for her was her gipsy pride. As a
Haddington cooper told her, twenty years after her
departure from Haddington, she had been, even as a
girl, "not just to call proud, very reserved in her
company," and it was this proud and reserved side
of her which rendered her life with Carlyle often
so much more unhappy than it otherwise need have
been. For though she was sweet, pitiful, and
fascinating to those who leaned upon her, she had
a keen sense of her own dignity, and could not
endure to be herself treated as a mere detail of life;
and this was how Carlyle not unfrequently treated
her. What she loved best was to queen it over
men, and Carlyle was not the man to let his wife
queen it over him. And how could she queen it!
Long after she was a middle-aged woman she could
pick up chance acquaintances in a coach and so
fascinate them, that when she left her parasol in
that coach one would compete eagerly and secretly
against the other for the chance of recovering and
restoring it to her. In her old age,—indeed a year
or two before her death,—when she had partially
recovered from a most dangerous illness, middle-
aged men of the world burst into tears at the sight
of her whom they had never hoped to see again,
and quivered all over with the joy of recovering her.

She owed this power of fascination, no doubt, partly to her ready tenderness of sympathy, partly to her volleys of gentle scorn. It is clear that women who cannot make themselves feared seldom gain the same empire as those who *can* make themselves feared as well as loved. It was this double power, obviously, which gave Lady Harriet Baring, afterwards Lady Ashburton, that victory over Mrs. Carlyle which embittered some eight years or so of Mrs. Carlyle's life. Lady Harriet, though she can hardly have had Mrs. Carlyle's literary power,—otherwise *some* of her letters, at least, would surely have been preserved,—combined with her intellectual brightness and wit the great advantage of genuine high breeding, an advantage which Mr. Carlyle, with his vivid perceptions and his own peasant breeding, was the first to perceive and enjoy. That was how Lady Harriet placed Mrs. Carlyle at a disadvantage, for Mrs. Carlyle, thorough lady as she was, had never queened it over the kind of men who were at Lady Harriet's feet, and had, in spite of that pride and reserve which distinguished her as a middle-class woman, nothing like the distinction which marked her rival. And bitterly did Mrs. Carlyle feel the defeat. It is obvious that she who never fretted over the most homely tasks before, chafed passionately against having — for example — to mend Mr. Carlyle's trousers at the very time when Mr. Carlyle wanted to go and worship a woman to whom servile domestic tasks were things of little meaning,—rumours of the servants' hall. For I do not believe that the sore heart which Mrs. Carlyle bore about with her through some seven or eight years of her married life would have been anything like

as sore as it was through jealousy alone. She was
not a jealous woman, and I should doubt if she
had any of that passionate feeling for her husband
which stirs jealousy to its depths. But she was a
very proud woman, and it crushed and humiliated
her to be slaving for the man who was so captivated
by the air of royalty borne by one who had never
thus slaved for him. It is the queen trodden under
the foot of the conquering queen who groans so
bitterly in Mrs. Carlyle's diary of 1855. And she
groans, as she is well aware, not as that conquering
queen, if she in her turn had been trodden down,
would groan, but with less scorn for herself and
more of middle-class self-pity, and more, too, of
those feminine consolations which she derived from
dwelling on her own power of painting her misery.
Mrs. Carlyle never succumbs to her misery. She
fights it vindictively. Throughout it you see that
it is Mr. Carlyle's indifference to her, his scorn, as
she understood it, his cool exactingness, when she
felt that the right to exact was hers rather than
his, that stung her to the quick. Had anything
but her personal pride been wounded, she would
hardly have suffered so much. As it was, she never
fathomed the deepest depth of wretchedness, for
she never quite lost the pleasure of painting vividly
the inward wrath with which she was overflowing
at this preference of the aristocratic queen to the
gipsy queen of Carlyle's earlier life. And evidently,
too, she frequently met Carlyle's imperious *exigeance*
with rapier thrusts that wounded him keenly.

I have said that Mrs. Carlyle had little con-
versance with dogma or creed of any kind, but she
had imagination enough, and critical faculty enough,
to let in gleams of speculative wonder on her

life, and some of these sceptical touches have a
marvellous force of their own. In the dialogue
between her watch and her canary, she makes the
watch reprove the canary for complaining of its
prison. " Alas ! my bird ! here sit prisoners. There,
also, do prisoners sit. This world is all prison,
the only difference for those who inhabit it being
in the size and aspect of the cells ; while some
of these stand revealed in cold, strong nakedness
for what they really are, others are painted to look
like sky overhead and open country all around,
but the bare and the painted walls are alike impassable, and fall away only at the coming of the
Angel of Death." Nothing could better present
her impression of the universe, for while Mrs.
Carlyle had apparently no faith but an imaginative
one, she had imagination enough to paint the bare
walls of her universe for herself, and with a fresco
of no mean beauty. She was keen enough to see
through the hollowness of false creeds, and to
penetrate now and then to some of the more
beautiful aspects of true creeds ; but even while
she could appreciate the dreariness of a Church
of which she could say, "Anything so like the
burial - place of revealed religion you have never
seen, nor a rector more fit to read the Burial
Service," she was quite unprepared to contend
that there should be a burial-place prepared for
revealed religion, and that the time for reading
its burial service had arrived. Her religion consisted in glimpses of noble ideals, and in the
gracious human charities for which, when her pride
was not touched, she was always more than ready.
She had a humour, too, that combined with her
natural tenderness to make life, by fitful gleams,

radiant as well as interesting. But on the whole, it is the gipsy queen whom we see in her,—the wild, lively queen whose mission it was to bring order out of chaos by the help of her fine genius for "details"—who fascinated most men's hearts, but smarted under her inferiority to a choicer type of queenhood, and who chafed bitterly against the sense of imprisonment which the constant society of such a man as Carlyle necessarily imposed on a character so full of vivacity, and so eager to feel the consciousness of its own power. Such is the picture impressed on the mind by the perusal of Mrs. Carlyle's frank, charming, playful, and bitter letters, eloquent now with tenderness, and now, again, with impatient wrath and a mortification hardly rising to the point of scorn.

BIOGRAPHY IN MORTMAIN

MRS. OLIPHANT and Mr. Venables both take up the cudgels against Mr. Froude in current numbers of the May magazines,—Mr. Venables in the *Fortnightly*, and Mrs. Oliphant in the *Contemporary*,—both intimating that Mr. Froude has done his duty very ill, and is responsible for representing the relation between Mr. and Mrs. Carlyle as much less satisfactory than it really was. For my own part, I have done my best to show that the public impression on this head was very hasty, and that for a very large part of her life, at least, Mrs. Carlyle was obviously as devoted as a wife as she was brilliant as a woman. But apart from the question as to the proper inferences to be drawn from the facts; I must say that Mrs. Oliphant, whose very vigorous attack on Mr. Froude is much the more formidable of the two, has not at all sufficiently weighed what was Mr. Carlyle's share of this responsibility and what was Mr. Froude's. She writes as if the publication of the fragment of diary rested on Mr. Froude's sole responsibility, whereas, as I understand Mr. Froude, Mr. Carlyle had himself selected for publication a part, and a most painful part, of the diary, though affording no clue to the bitterness of Mrs. Carlyle's tone.

"A part only of the following extracts," says Mr. Froude in giving extracts from the diary, "was selected by Mr. Carlyle, a part sufficient merely to leave a painful impression, without explaining the origin of his wife's discomfort." Mrs. Oliphant represents it as if no part of the bitter diary of 1855-56 had been selected by Mr. Carlyle at all, but only fragments of letters which seemed to demand explanation, and that Mr. Froude had out of his head hunted up the diary to expose the black spot in the relations between husband and wife. If I have understood the matter rightly this is not so. Mr. Froude is, indeed, I suppose, responsible for obtaining and publishing the indiscreet and highly-coloured letter from Miss Jewsbury, with which the extracts from the diary conclude, and is also responsible, I suppose, for some extension of the extracts taken from the diary, but not— so I understand what seems to me his explicit statement — for authorising the publication of passages which reveal the blackness of desolation in which Mrs. Carlyle was sunk at the time this diary was written. It is quite another question, of course, whether Mr. Carlyle was not exceeding greatly the right of a husband in authorising, without her consent, the publication of passages which could not but draw public attention to the bitterness of soul in which his wife at one time seemed to be lost,—passages which, I am well inclined to believe, with Mrs. Oliphant, that Mrs. Carlyle herself would never have written had she thought it possible that they would one day see the light. But if we are to blame any one, let us at least blame fairly, and not make Mr. Froude the whipping-boy on whom to vent all our indignation.

It seems to me that Mr. Froude has responsibilities
enough to answer for. He has to answer for the
literary reduplications which have extended what
would have made two charming volumes of unique
letters into three volumes of letters abounding in
repetitions and monotonies. He is responsible for
inviting Miss Jewsbury to add an evidently over-
coloured and *ex parte* criticism to the most painful
part of the correspondence. He is responsible, as
I understand him, for revealing the explanation of
Mrs. Carlyle's darkest moods — the indignation
which she felt at the intellectual charm exercised
over her husband by Lady Harriet Baring. But
he is not responsible for revealing the fact that
these moods were at one time very dark. Mr.
Carlyle himself, apparently as a sort of penance,
had given his sanction deliberately to this revelation,
and had heard with satisfaction that Mr. Froude
acquiesced in that decision. So I understand the
case. And, therefore, Mr. Froude's responsibility
appears to me to consist of three distinct elements
—(1) Responsibility for not dissuading Mr. Carlyle
from an act of questionable penance, but rather
confirming him in it; (2) Responsibility for
bringing out the secret of Mrs. Carlyle's desolation
of heart, instead of leaving it a riddle to the public;
(3) Responsibility for darkening the picture by
adding Miss Jewsbury's comments. I confess that
I think the first of these decisions the most serious
of the three, and the second much the soundest
of the three exercises of discretion—not a mistake
at all, granting that the first course had been
irrevocably decided on; while the third seems to
me an unquestionable mistake of secondary importance. I do not think that if any evidence of the

darker moods which beset Mrs. Carlyle during
some years of her life were to have been given at
all, it would have been wise or fair to Mr. Carlyle
to leave them unexplained. The public imagination
is none too charitable in such matters, and while
I think it certain that before very long the spirit
in which this temporary alienation of feeling
between Mrs. Carlyle and her husband is judged
will not be very harsh, I do not know what might
not have been the inferences drawn if Mr. Froude
had left extracts from the diary showing us Mrs.
Carlyle in her misery, and had not afforded us any
explanation. As for Miss Jewsbury's comments,
they seem unquestionably to make matters worse
than they really were, and, therefore, they should
have been rejected. But they are so obviously
inconsistent with some of the facts, that they will
not exercise any lasting influence on the estimate
of either Mr. or Mrs. Carlyle.   It is clear, however,
that Mrs. Oliphant minimises excessively when she
represents these moods of Mrs. Carlyle as so
transient that on turning a few pages you may
always come again on the old affectionate language.
I believe that for some years, at least, the tone of
Mrs. Carlyle's letters remains more or less proud
and frigid, and that you must turn very many
pages at some parts of the book before you can
find any trace of the old playful affectionateness
and fondness.

To my mind, the primary blunder which Mr.
Froude made was in not dissuading Mr. Carlyle
from the ill-judged act of penance which, unless I
mistake Mrs. Carlyle's nature altogether, she would
herself so strenuously have disapproved and condemned, and so certainly have prevented had she

had anything to do with the decision. There is a
great deal of indignation expended in modern times
on the tyranny of "The Dead Hand," and it is not
I who would contend for the right of "The Dead
Hand" to control, unconditionally, the disposition of
property among the living, seeing that the living
brain is much more competent to judge of the
expediency of continuing these dispositions of
property which a once living brain conceived, than
any brain which had no foresight of the present
exigencies of society possibly could have been.
But if, on the one hand, the Dead Hand controlled
the destinies of the living too much, I am ready to
maintain that it does not control the disclosures
that most concern the owner of that Dead Hand
half enough. It may be maintained, indeed, that
no one has any right of monopoly in his own most
secret history, if in any way whatever, accidental or
otherwise, he puts it out of his own power to keep
the secret. Nor would I go so far as to assert that
a man, say of the tenth century, whose private
history should now be recovered, would have much
claim on us of the nineteenth century to respect his
privacy if it could be shown that the publication
of his story would confer a great benefit on the
modern world. The reason, as I understand it, why
the privacy of a person lately dead—or even dead
within a period so short that the revelation of his
private circumstances would seriously affect a good
many living persons—should be respected is this :
that he (or she) had means inaccessible to any one
else of judging how far it was right or wrong to
divulge those private circumstances, and even if the
wrong of divulging them would ever cease to be a
wrong. To refuse to respect the privacy of the

dead—at all events while the dead are still a felt influence among the living—is to refuse to respect the one judgment which alone was competent to decide on the rightness of privacy or publicity. Thus, supposing we could be sure—as I quite agree with Mrs. Oliphant that we can be all but sure— that Mrs. Carlyle would have protested vehemently against the publication of those of her journals or letters which express either personal dissatisfaction with her husband, or a passionate gloom from which the public could at once have inferred the existence of that dissatisfaction, if not of more than the dissatisfaction which actually existed, we may surely say that it distorts the truth of her character and misrepresents her feeling for her husband, when we, the outside public, receive the confession—even though we know the confession to be involuntary —of feelings which she could never have written down without great qualification, if she could have written them down at all, had she imagined that they would be overheard.

Why is it simply dastardly to go and repeat to an assembled party a soliloquy accidentally overheard, which we well know that the utterer would have cut out his tongue rather than publish? First, because it grossly misrepresents the person who inadvertently says aloud what he believed himself to be saying only to himself. Next, because the reticence he intended to display was in all probability not only for his own sake, but for the sake of others also, and because he was a better judge of the right and wisdom of both kinds of reticence than he who accidentally overhears him can be. Lastly, because we all trust each other not to break the implied confidence we repose in each other in this way.

Precisely in the same way the same reason applies, in my opinion, to this unauthorised revelation of Mrs. Carlyle's journal. So far as Mr. Carlyle was the only one to suffer by it, he might, perhaps, be excused for thinking that he had the right to give the permission. But then, in the first place, he was not the only person to suffer by it. In the opinion of many of us, Mrs. Carlyle's character has suffered as much, and in part unjustly, because her whole soul would have revolted from this seeming disloyalty to her husband, from which, nevertheless, our knowledge of its involuntary character cannot wholly absolve her. In the next place, even so far as the revelation affects our judgment of Mr. Carlyle himself, surely her judgment was entitled to much weight. No one knew him so well. No one would have been more eager to assert that these crude journals, never intended for the public eye, would misrepresent the truth as to Carlyle himself, even though we know we are, as it were, eavesdroppers, listening to her private soliloquies, and not taken by her into her willing confidence. Now, should not these things weigh with us? Is it fair to her to overhear her in her moods of anguish talking to herself? Is it fair to her husband? Is it fair, indeed, to the present generation to give it notice that if we can but overhear its secrets,—or, worse still, if we can overhear what it might like us to fancy its secrets, supposing it could be sure that we should try to worm them out and publish them,— we shall have no scruple in betraying those secrets? To my mind, the very same reasons which make it so undesirable that " The Dead Hand " should govern the disposition of modern wealth and energies, of which the brain which governed that hand had no anticipative grasp, make it in the highest degree desirable that it should govern the responsibility of giving or withholding confidences to the world which survives it, of the wisdom and delicacy of which no one living could have the same power or right to judge as belonged to the dead. No doubt that right diminishes with every distinct remove from the generation which those confidences would be the most likely to fascinate and interest, because the reasons for reticence or disclosure gradually expire with those removes. But, as it seems to me, "The Dead Hand" has not half enough power to suppress one-sided and inadequate materials for biography, the communication of which in their present form would have given the most exquisite pain, and caused the most exquisite self-reproach, to the mind and conscience which directed that hand. But in this case, at all events, I blame Mr. Carlyle even more than I blame Mr. Froude.

RALPH WALDO EMERSON

THE great American thinker, who has been so often compared to Carlyle, and who in some respects resembles, whilst in many more he is profoundly different from him, and who has so soon followed him to the grave, will be remembered much longer, I believe, for the singular insight of his literary judgments than for that transcendental philosophy for which he was once famous. It is remarkable enough that Carlyle and Emerson both had in them that imaginative gift which made them aim at poetry, and both that incapacity for rhythm or music which rendered their regular verses too rugged, and too much possessed with the sense of effort, to sink, as verse should sink, into the hearts of men. Carlyle's verse is like the heavy rumble of a van without springs; Emerson's, which now and then reaches something of the sweetness of poetry, much more often reminds one of the attempts of a seeress to induce in herself the ecstasy which will not spontaneously visit her. Yet the prose, both of Carlyle and Emerson, falls at times into that poetic rhythm which indicates the highest glow of a powerful imaginative nature, though of such passages I, at least, could produce many more from Carlyle than from Emerson. I should say

that a little of Emerson's verse is genuine poetry,
though not of the highest order, and that none
of Carlyle's is poetry at all ; but that some of
Carlyle's prose is as touching as any but the noblest
poetry, while Emerson never reaches the same
profound pathos.   Nor is this the only side on
which these two contemporary thinkers resemble
each other.   As thinkers, both were eager trans-
cendentalists, and, at the same time, rationalists too.
Both were intended for divines, and both abandoned
the profession, though Emerson filled a pulpit for
a year or two, while Carlyle never even entered on
the formal study of theology.   Both, again, were
in their way humourists, though Emerson's humour
was a much less profound constituent of his character than Carlyle's.   And, finally, both would have
called themselves the spokesmen of " the dim,
common populations," the enemies of all selfish
privilege, of all purely traditional distinctions
between man and man, of all the artificial selfishness of class, of all the tyranny of caste, and the
cruelty of custom.

Yet Emerson and Carlyle were in their way
remarkable contrasts.   Emerson was benignant
and gentle as Carlyle was arrogant and bitter.   Mr.
Ruskin has asked, " What can you say of Carlyle,
except that he was born in the clouds, and struck
by lightning ? "   Of Emerson it might, perhaps, be
also said that he was born in the clouds, but
assuredly not that he was struck by lightning.
There is nothing scathed or marred about him,
nothing sublime, though something perhaps better
—a little of the calm of true majesty.   He has
the keen kindliness of the highest New-England
culture, with a touch of majesty about him that

no other New-England culture shows.   He has
the art of saying things with a tone of authority
quite unknown to Carlyle, who casts his thunder-
bolt, but never forgets that he is casting it at some
unhappy mortal whom he intends to slay.   That
is not Emerson's manner; he is never aggressive.
He has that regal suavity which settles a trouble-
some matter without dispute.   His sentences are
often like decrees.   For example, take this, on the
dangers of the much-vaunted life of action,—"A
certain partiality, headiness, and want of balance is
the tax which all action must pay.   Act if you
like, but you do it at your peril"; or this, on
the dangers of speculation,—"Why should I vapour
and play the philosopher, instead of ballasting the
best I can this dancing balloon"; or this, on the
dangers of hero-worship,—"Every hero becomes a
bore at last.   We balance one man with his
opponent, and the health of the State depends upon
the see-saw"; or this, on the Time-spirit,—"We
see now events forced on which seem to retard or
retrograde the civility of ages.   But the World-
spirit is a good swimmer, and storms and waves
cannot drown him."   There is no thinker of our
day who, for sentences that have the ring of oracles,
can quite compare with Emerson.   Mr. Arnold, in
a sonnet written nearly forty years ago, on Emerson's
essays, said,—

> A voice oracular has pealed to-day ;
> To-day a hero's banner is unfurled.

And the first line at least was true, whatever may
be said of the second.   No man has compressed
more authoritative insight into his sentences than
Emerson.   He discerns character more truly than

Carlyle, though he does not describe with half the
fervent vigour. Carlyle worships Goethe blindly,
but Emerson discerns the very core of the poet.
"Goethe can never be dear to men. His is not
even the devotion to pure truth, but to truth for
the sake of culture." And again,—Goethe, he says,
"has one test for all men : *What can you teach me ?*"
Hear him of Goethe as artist,—" His affections help
him, like women employed by Cicero, to worm out
the secrets of conspirators." Or take this, as
summing up Goethe as a poet :—" These are not
wild, miraculous songs, but elaborate poems, to
which the poet has confided the results of eighty
years of observation . . . Still, he is a poet of a
prouder laurel than any contemporary, and under
this plague of microscopes (for he seems to see out
of every pore of his skin) strikes the harp with a
hero's strength and grace." There is something far
more royal and certain in Mr. Emerson's insight
than in all the humorous brilliance of Carlyle.

Still, if I were to compare the two as transcendental thinkers, I should not hesitate to declare
Carlyle much the greater of the two. Emerson
never seems to me so little secure of his ground as
he is in uttering his transcendentalisms, — Carlyle
never so secure. Emerson on "Nature," Emerson
on the "Over-soul," Emerson on the law of
"Polarity," Emerson on "Intuition," does not seem
to me even instructive. He aims too wide, and
hits only the vague. When he tells us, in his
Representative Men, that "animated chlorine knows
of chlorine, and incarnate zinc of zinc," he
only attempts to state his peculiar pantheism in
words which not only do not make it more intelligible, but rather illustrate the untruth of the

general assertion that only like can perceive like.
"Shall we say," he adds, "that quartz mountains
will pulverise into innumerable Werners, von
Buchs, and Beaumonts, and that the laboratory of
the atmosphere holds in solution I know not
what Berzeliuses and Davys?"—a question to
which I, at least, would reply with a most emphatic
"No," if, at least, the object be, as it no doubt is,
to explain discoverers by their latent affinity with
the thing discovered.   Suppose it is put thus,—
"Animated bacteria know of bacteria, incarnate
lymph of vaccine:"—who would not see the
absurdity?   Is there really more of the bacteria in
Professor Pasteur or Professor Koch than there is
in the cattle inoculated by the former, or the con-
sumptive patients who die from the presence of
tubercular bacteria, according to the teaching of the
latter; that Professors Pasteur and Koch discover
their presence, while the patients themselves discover nothing of the nature of their own complaints?
Of course, Emerson would have said that he did
not mean his statements to be thus carnally
understood.   Very likely not; but have they any
real meaning at all, unless carnally construed?   Mr.
Emerson's transcendental essays are full of this
kind of dark and vague symbolism, which carries
weight only in proportion to the extent of our
ignorance, not to the extent of our knowledge.
Now, Carlyle, so far as he was a transcendentalist,
stuck to the very truth and reality of nature.   He
showed us how small a proportion of our life we
can realise in thought; how small a proportion of
our thoughts we can figure forth in words; how
immense is the difference between the pretensions
of human speech and the real life for which it

stands; how vast the forces amidst which the
human spirit struggles for its little modicum of
purpose; how infinite the universe, both in regard
to space and time, on which we make our little
appearances only to subside again before we can
hope materially to change the great stream of
tendencies which contains us; and he made us feel,
as hardly any other has made us feel, how, in spite
of all this array of immensities, in which we are
hardly a distinguishable speck, the Spirit whose
command brings us into being requires of us the
kind of life which defies necessity, and breathes
into the order of our brief existence the spirit of
impassioned right and indomitable freedom. This
was but a narrow aim, compared with that of Mr.
Emerson's philosophy, but it succeeded, while
Emerson's did not. The various philosophic essays,
in which Emerson tried to assert the absolute unity
of the material and spiritual laws of the Universe,
have always seemed to me, though decidedly
interesting, yet unquestionable failures. You can
drive a coach and six through almost any of the
generalisations which pass for philosophy in these
vague and imaginative, but unreal speculations.

Inferior in genius, as a man Emerson will compare favourably with Carlyle. He certainly possessed
his soul in patience, which Carlyle never did. He
had a magnanimity in which Carlyle was altogether
wanting. He sympathised ardently with all the
greatest practical movements of his own day, while
Carlyle held contemptuously aloof. Emerson was
one of the first to strike a heavy blow at the
institution of slavery. He came forward to encourage his country in the good cause when slavery
raised the flag of rebellion. He had a genuine

desire to see all men really free, while Carlyle only
felt the desire to see all men strongly governed,—
which they might be without being free at all.
Emerson's spirit, moreover, was much the saner and
more reverent of the two, though less rich in power
and humour. His mind was heartily religious,
though his transcendentalism always gave a certain
air of patronage to his manner in speaking of any
of the greater religions. One of his youthful sermons
was thus described by a lady who heard it:—"Waldo
Emerson came last Sunday, and preached a sermon,
with his chin in the air, in scorn of the whole human
race." That is caricature, but whenever Emerson
spoke on any religion which claims a special revelation, even in later life, his chin seemed to be "in the
air" still. He had the democratic transcendentalist's
jealousy of any one who claimed to be nearer God
than the race at large. He was contemptuous of
the pretensions of special access to God, and this, to
my ear at least, always spoils his tone when he
speaks of Christ and Christianity. But towards
man he is always reverent,—which Carlyle seldom
is,—and he is always reverent, too, in relation to the
Divine Mind itself. "I conceive a man as always
spoken to from behind," he once wrote, "and unable
to turn his head and see the speaker. In all the
millions who have heard the voice, none ever saw
the face. As children in their play run behind each
other, and seize one by the ears, and make him walk
before them, so is the Spirit of our unseen pilot."
Those are the words of a truly reverent mind,
though of a mind as jealously devoted to a sort of
false spiritual democracy as it is reverent in its
attitude and poetic in its inmost thought.

LONGFELLOW

"THE fact is, I hate everything that is violent,"
said the poet whom the world has just lost to some
friend who had been with him during a thunder-
storm, and to whom he was excusing himself for the
care with which he had endeavoured to exclude
from his house the tokens of the storm; and one
sees this in his poetry, which is at its highest point
when it is most restful, and is never so happy in its
soft radiance as when it embodies the spirit of a
playful or childlike humility. I should not claim
for Longfellow the position of a very great or
original poet; it was his merit rather to embody
in a simple and graceful form the gentleness
and loveliness which are partially visible to most
men's eyes, than to open to our sight that which is
hidden from the world in general. To my mind,
"Hiawatha" is far the most original of his poems,
because the happy nature-myths which best expressed the religious genius of the American Indians
appealed to what was deepest in himself, and found
an exquisitely simple and harmonious utterance in
the liquid accents of his childlike and yet not un-
stately verse. His material in "Hiawatha" was so
fresh and poetical in itself, as well as so admirably

suited to his genius, that in his mind it assumed
its most natural form, and flowed into a series of
chants of childlike dignity and inimitable grace.
The story of Nature has never been told with so
much liquid gaiety and melancholy,—so much of
the frolic of the childlike races, and so much of their
sudden awe and dejection,—as in "Hiawatha," which
I, at least, have never taken up without new delight
in the singular simplicity and grace, the artless art
and ingenuous vivacity, of that rendering of the
traditions of a vanishing race. How simple and
childlike Longfellow makes even the exaggerations
so often found in these traditions, so that you
enjoy, where you might so easily have sneered!
How spontaneously he avoids anything like disserta-
tion on the significance of the natural facts portrayed,
leaving us the full story and poetry of impersonation,
without any attempt to moralise or dilate upon its
drift! How exquisitely the account of the first
sowing and reaping of the Indian corn, of Hiawatha's
revelation of agriculture to his people, is told in
his three days' wrestling with Mondamin, in his
conquest over him, and the sowing of the bare grain,
that the green and yellow plumes of Mondamin may
wave again over his grave! And how eerie is the
tale of the first warning of spiritual truths, the
return of spectres from beyond the grave to warn
Hiawatha that for him, too, there are secrets which
it will need a higher revelation than his to reveal :—

> One dark evening, after sun-down,
> In her wigwam Laughing Water
> Sat with old Nokomis, waiting
> For the steps of Hiawatha
> Homeward from the hunt returning.

On their faces gleamed the firelight,
Painting them with streaks of crimson,
In the eyes of old Nokomis
Glimmered like the watery moonlight,
In the eyes of Laughing Water
Glistened like the sun in water;
And behind them crouched their shadows
In the corners of the wigwam,
And the smoke in wreaths above them
Climbed and crowded through the smoke-flue.

Then the curtain of the doorway
From without was slowly lifted;
Brighter glowed the fire a moment,
And a moment swerved the smoke-wreath,
As two women entered softly,
Passed the doorway uninvited,
Without word of salutation,
Without sign of recognition,
Sat down in the farthest corner,
Crouching low among the shadows

From their aspect and their garments
Strangers seemed they in the village;
Very pale and haggard were they,
As they sat there sad and silent,
Trembling, cowering with the shadows.

Was it the wind above the smoke-flue,
Muttering down into the wigwam?
Was it the owl, the Koko-koho,
Hooting from the dismal forest?
Sure a voice said in the silence:
"These are corpses clad in garments,
These are ghosts that come to haunt you,
From the kingdom of Ponemah,
From the land of the Hereafter!"

Homeward now came Hiawatha
From his hunting in the forest,
With the snow upon his tresses,

And the red deer on his shoulders.
At the feet of Laughing Water
Down he threw his lifeless burden ;
Nobler, handsomer she thought him,
Than when first he came to woo her ;
First threw down the deer before her,
As a token of his wishes,
As a promise of the future.

Then he turned and saw the strangers,
Cowering, crouching with the shadows ;
Said within himself, "Who are they ?
What strange guests has Minnehaha ?"
But he questioned not the strangers,
Only spake to bid them welcome
To his lodge, his food, his fireside.

When the evening meal was ready,
And the deer had been divided,
Both the pallid guests, the strangers,
Springing from among the shadows,
Seized upon the choicest portions,
Seized the white fat of the roebuck,
Set apart for Laughing Water,
For the wife of Hiawatha ;
Without asking, without thanking,
Eagerly devoured the morsels,
Flitted back among the shadows
In the corner of the wigwam.

Not a word spake Hiawatha,
Not a motion made Nokomis,
Not a gesture Laughing Water ;
Not a change came o'er their features ;
Only Minnehaha softly
Whispered, saying, "They are famished ;
Let them do what best delights them ;
Let them eat, for they are famished."

. . . . . .

Once at midnight Hiawatha,

Ever wakeful, ever watchful,
In the wigwam dimly lighted
By the brands that still were burning,
By the glimmering, flickering firelight,
Heard a sighing oft repeated,
Heard a sobbing as of sorrow.

From his couch rose Hiawatha,
From his shaggy hides of bison,
Pushed aside the deer-skin curtain,
Saw the pallid guests, the shadows,
Sitting upright on their couches,
Weeping in the silent midnight.

And he said : " O guests ! why is it
That your hearts are so afflicted,
That you sob so in the midnight ?
Has perchance the old Nokomis,
Has my wife, my Minnehaha,
Wronged or grieved you by unkindness,
Failed in hospitable duties ? "

" Then the shadows ceased from weeping,
Ceased from sobbing and lamenting,
And they said, with gentle voices :
" We are ghosts of the departed,
Souls of those who once were with you.
From the realms of Chibiabos
Hither have we come to try you,
Hither have we come to warn you.

" Cries of grief and lamentation
Reach us in the Blessed Islands ;
Cries of anguish from the living,
Calling back their friends departed,
Sadden us with useless sorrow.
Therefore have we come to try you ;
No one knows us, no one heeds us,
We are but a burden to you,
And we see that the departed
Have no place among the living.

"Think of this, O Hiawatha!
Speak of it to all the people,
That henceforward and for ever
They no more with lamentations
Sadden the souls of the departed
In the Islands of the Blessed."

There you see Longfellow at his best, rendering
with a singular mixture of simplicity and dignity
legends of which the very essence is a mixture of
simplicity and dignity, yet a mixture so rare, that
the least false note would have destroyed the whole
poetry of the tradition.

But Longfellow, singularly happy as he was in
catching the spirit of the American-Indian nature-
myths, could yet render with hardly less success—
though here he shared his success with scores of
other poets not less skilful—the grace and culture
of a thoughtful criticism of the past. Many have
equalled, I think, though few have surpassed, the
beauty of such a sonnet as this on Giotto's famous
tower, for the thought it expresses was one so deeply
ingrained in Longfellow's own mind, that he seemed
to be breathing out the very heart of his own
Christian humility in thus singing the glory of the
incomplete :—

How many lives, made beautiful and sweet
    By self-devotion and by self-restraint,
    Whose pleasure is to run without complaint
    On unknown errands of the Paraclete,
Wanting the reverence of unshodden feet,
    Fail of the nimbus which the artists paint
    Around the shining forehead of the saint,
    And are in their completeness incomplete !

In the old Tuscan town stands Giotto's tower,
The lily of Florence blossoming in stone,—
A vision, a delight, and a desire,
The builder's perfect and centennial flower,
That in the night of ages bloomed alone,
But wanting still the glory of the spire.

Longfellow certainly, though often ineffective and commonplace in his treatment of a subject, had a true genius for touching the subject of humility in any form, and is never more successful than when relating the legend how Robert, King of Sicily, was taught the truth of those words in the "Magnificat" —"He hath put down the mighty from their seat, and hath exalted the humble and meek"; or when finding in the midnight chimes of the belfry of Bruges,—he heard fitfully in sleep,—the best type of the sort of half-accidental power which the poet exerts over the careless and preoccupied spirit of man :—

But amid my broken slumbers
Still I heard those magic numbers,
As they loud proclaimed the flight
And stolen marches of the night ;
Till their chimes in sweet collision
Mingled with each wandering vision,
Mingled with the fortune-telling
Gipsy-bands of dreams and fancies,
Which amid the waste expanses
Of the silent land of trances
Have their solitary dwelling.
All else seemed asleep in Bruges,
In the quaint old Flemish city.

And I thought, how like these chimes
Are the poet's airy rhymes,

All his rhymes and roundelays,
His conceits, and songs, and ditties,
From the belfry of his brain,
Scattered downward, though in vain,
On the roofs and stones of cities !
For by night the drowsy ear
Under its curtains cannot hear,
And by day men go their ways,
Hearing the music as they pass,
But deeming it no more, alas !
Than the hollow sound of brass.

Yet perchance a sleepless wight,
Lodging at some humble inn
In the narrow lanes of life,
When the dusk and hush of night
Shut out the incessant din
Of daylight and its toil and strife,
May listen with a calm delight
To the poet's melodies,
Till he hears, or dreams he hears,
Intermingled with the song,
Thoughts that he has cherished long ;
Hears amid the chime and singing
The bells of his own village ringing,
And wakes and finds his slumbrous eyes
Wet with most delicious tears.

It will be gathered that I do not particularly admire
the pieces which one oftenest hears quoted from
Longfellow — "Excelsior," "A Psalm of Life,"
"The Light of Stars," and so forth, all of which
seem to me to express commonplace feelings with a
certain picturesque and conventional eloquence, but
without anything of individual or unique power.
Longfellow is too apt to take up the conventional
subjects of poetry and deck them out with a pretty

patch of colour that does not redeem them from
commonplaceness, but does make their commonplaceness agreeable to the popular mind ; and when
he does this, though I perfectly understand why he
is so popular, I also perfectly understand why so
many of the poets think of him as falling short of
the true poetic standard.   But though I cannot feel
any enthusiasm for the remark that,

> Our hearts though stout and brave,
> Still like muffled drums are beating
> Funeral marches to the grave,

I do hold that Longfellow was not only a poet, but
a poet whom the critics will appreciate better the
more they turn their attention away from the
pieces which, by a sort of trick of sentimental
metaphor, have caught hold of the ear of the public,
to those which are less showy and more restful.

It has been said, and truly said, that there was
very little of the local genius of the New World in
Longfellow's poetry ; that he was as Conservative
at heart as a member of the oldest European
aristocracy, that even the form of his poetic thought
was not bold, or striking, or unique.   And this is
undoubtedly true ; but after the first period of *ad
captandum* writing, which almost every young man
of talent passes through, he gained that singular
grace of perfect simplicity—simplicity both instinctive and cultivated — which rejects everything
adventitious with a sure and steady antipathy ; and
this it was which enabled him, when he had secured
a fine subject, to produce such a poem as " Hiawatha,"
or, again, so graceful and tragic a picture as that
embodied in the following verses :—

KILLED AT THE FORD.

He is dead, the beautiful youth,
The heart of honour, the tongue of truth,
He, the life and light of us all,
Whose voice was blithe as a bugle-call,
Whom all eyes followed with one consent,
The cheer of whose laugh, and whose pleasant word,
Hushed all murmurs of discontent.

Only last night, as we rode along
Down the dark of the mountain gap,
To visit the picket-guard at the ford,
Little dreaming of any mishap,
He was humming the words of some old song :
" Two red roses he had on his cap,
And another he bore at the point of his sword."

Sudden and swift a whistling ball
Came out of a wood, and the voice was still ;
Something I heard in the darkness fall,
And for a moment my blood grew chill ;
I spake in a whisper, as he who speaks
In a room where some one is lying dead ;
But he made no answer to what I said.

We lifted him up to his saddle again,
And through the mire and the mist and the rain
Carried him back to the silent camp,
And laid him as if asleep on his bed ;
And I saw by the light of the surgeon's lamp
Two white roses upon his cheeks,
And one, just over his heart, blood-red !

And I saw in a vision how far and fleet
That fatal bullet went speeding forth
Till it reached a town in the distant North,
Till it reached a house in a sunny street,

Till it reached a heart that ceased to beat
Without a murmur, without a cry ;
And a bell was tolled in that far-off town,
For one who had passed from cross to crown,
And the neighbours wondered that she should die.

It would be hard, I think, to convey better the
strange contrast between the gay and picturesque
courage of youth, and the sudden sentence which
absolutely ended the story of life and love, than it
is conveyed in these few stanzas ; their simplicity
has no nakedness in it ; it is the simplicity which
avoids detail, because detail only obscures the effect,
not the simplicity which says a thing crudely or
poorly. Longfellow, like all poets who had not
any great originality of initiative, was singularly
dependent on his subjects for his success ; but
when his subject suits him, he presents it with
the simplicity of a really great classic, with all its
points in relief, and with nothing of the self-conscious
or artificial tone of one who wants to draw attention
to the admirable insight with which he has grasped
the situation. He can be very conventional when
the subject is conventional. When it is not, but is
intrinsically poetical, no one gives us its poetry more
free from the impertinences of subjective ecstasy
than he. He was not a great poet, but he was a
singularly restful, singularly simple-minded, and—
whenever his subject suited him, as in one very
considerable and remarkable instance it certainly
did—a singularly classical poet, who knew how to
prune away every excrescence of irrelevant emotion.

ROBERT BROWNING

THERE is hardly any English poet who has had a
greater power of delivering an electric shock than
Mr. Browning. His is the verse which flashes,—as
a galvanic battery,—flashes that make the nerves
tingle and the eyes involuntarily close. Whatever
else he fails in, he never fails to be an awakening
poet when he is understood at all. Of course, in
his impatience to wake us up, he sometimes fails
to make us understand his highly compressed and
often merely hinted drift ; and then, in spite of the
vigorous jolts which he administers to the imagination, we may doze off, as a man wearied by a very
rough cart will doze off, through sheer intellectual
fatigue. But this never happens in Mr. Browning's
greatest works. His own mind was never obscure.
It was his shorthand style that obscured it, not any
obscureness in his own perceptions or his own conceptions. He was as vigorous and keen-sighted as
a weather-beaten sailor, and as rough in his tenderness, when he was tender, as in his boldness, when
he was bold. Mr. Buchanan, in his earlier days,
hit him off most skilfully when he said :—

With eye like a skipper's cocked up at the weather,
Sat the vice-chairman Browning, thinking in Greek.

Nothing is more remarkable than his love for Italy, its mellow atmosphere, and its soft, rich landscape, when we think of the weather-beaten *brusquerie* of his thought and speech. He was shrewd with the shrewdness of a man of business, plain with the plainness of an old sailor, and yet, above all, he was idealist, deeply convinced that the realities of the spiritual world are the most real of all realities,—and also the most significant of human destiny. He loved spiritual power better than spiritual grace, the sublime better than the beautiful, the picturesque and the grotesque better than the harmonious. But in his idealism he was never shadowy or unreal. He could not bear to evade a difficulty, to ignore a dread, or to shut his eyes to a peril. His great imaginative impulse was to grasp the nettle that threatened to sting him, and he often grasped it so forcibly as to destroy not merely its stinging power, but its very tissue, and wake up to wonder whether he had ever been in danger of a sting at all.

His genius has been miscalled dramatic. That is, I think, a mistake. His insight into character was very keen, but he never lost himself in the characters he depicted. He translated them all into Browningese forms. Bishop Blongram is Browning posing as a worldly Bishop. The Bishop who orders his tomb at St. Praxed's Church is Browning posing as a sensual, superstitious Italian Bishop. Ogniben, the Papal Legate in " A Soul's Tragedy," is Browning posing as ecclesiastical diplomatist. You never lose the Browningite manner of deliverance. You never forget that the artist is telling you what *he* sees in the picture he is painting, and that he himself is the interpreter, though a very acute interpreter, of what he sees. Even the

malignant monk who soliloquises in the Spanish
cloister, soliloquises with the abrupt manner, and
with the darting, forked-lightning tongue of a
Spanish Browning.   You see his piercing, critical
eye in every delineation, however objective it may
seem to be, of woman's passion or man's meditation.
The Arab physician, Karshish, gives his diagnosis of
the case of Lazarus in the keen, abrupt, zigzag of
Browning's thought.   Even the free-living artist,
Fra Lippo Lippi, talks in Browning's sudden, impatient, up-and-down style :—

> A fine way to paint Soul by painting body
> So ill, the eye can't stop there, must go further
> And can't fare worse !   Thus yellow does for white
> When what you pick for yellow's simply black,
> And any sort of meaning looks intense
> When all beside itself means and looks naught.
> Why can't a painter lift each foot in turn,
> Left foot and right foot, go a double step,
> Make his flesh liker and his soul more like
> Both in their order ?   Take the prettiest face,
> The Prior's niece . . . Patron saint—is it so pretty
> You can't discover if it means hope, fear,
> Sorrow, or joy !   Won't beauty go with these ?
> Suppose I've made her eyes all right and blue,
> Can't I take breath and try to add life's flash,
> And then add soul and heighten them threefold ?
> Or say there's beauty with no soul at all
> (I never saw it—put the case the same),
> If you get simple beauty and nought else,
> You get about the best thing God invents,—
> That's somewhat.

Surely a more remarkable reproduction of Browning's dialectic method by a mediæval Italian painter
can hardly be imagined.

Yet Browning may be said almost to have found himself in the delight he had in reading other persons' souls. In this way his greatest work was certainly the " Ring and the Book," in which he gave full swing to his delight in all sorts of people, from a gentle Italian girl to a cruel and spiteful profligate, from keen and crabbed Roman lawyers to a Pope brimming over with the most magnanimous charity and the most latitudinarian theology. They all talk, as Browning talked, about their own hearts and their own lives. But Browning really found himself in thus interpreting the great variety of characters he had delighted to study, for he had the most eager pleasure in this intellectual species of sympathy, this reconstruction for his own enjoyment of the tragedies and comedies of other men's and women's lives. The late Professor Clifford used to maintain that everything, however material, from a stone or a footstool to the human body, had a certain amount of " mind-stuff " at its core, — the stone and footstool very little, the human body a great deal. How he proved this to his own satisfaction Professor Clifford never explained. But his phrase was a happy one to describe the art of Mr. Browning. What he loved to portray was the "mind-stuff" behind all sorts of characters, from the most malignant and viperish to the noblest and most forgetful—most self-forgetful ; but often, I suspect, he put a great deal more "mind-stuff" into his interpretations than could have been found in the originals. For example, his "Grammarian's Funeral," one of the most characteristic of his poems, certainly attributes a great deal more " mind-stuff " to the slaving Grammarian than men of his type can usually boast :—

Was it not great ? did not he throw on God,
    (He loves the burthen)—
God's task to make the heavenly period
    Perfect the earthen ?
Did not he magnify the mind, show clear
    Just what it all meant ?
He would not discount life, as fools do here,
    Paid by instalment.
He ventured neck or nothing—Heaven's success
    Found, or earth's failure :
" Wilt thou trust Death or not ? " he answered, "Yes :
    Hence with Life's pale lure ! "
That low man sees a little thing to do,
    Sees it and does it :
This high man, with a great thing to pursue,
    Dies ere he knows it.
That low man goes on adding one to one,
    His hundred's soon hit :
This high man, aiming at a million,
    Misses an unit.
That, has the world here—should he need the next,
    Let the world mind him !
This, throws himself on God, and unperplext
    Seeking shall find him.
So, with the throttling hands of death at strife,
    Ground he at grammar ;
Still, thro' the rattle, parts of speech were rife :
    While he could stammer
He settled *Hoti's* business—let it be !—
    Properly based *Oun*—
Gave us the doctrine of the enclitic *De*,
    Dead from the waist down.

All that is rather Mr. Browning's " mind-stuff " than
that of the poor old Grammarian, but it was "mind-
stuff" which came to light in him from studying
some poor old Grammarian. He was really a part

of all whom he had met, but he himself contributed generally at least as much to the subjects he studied as they contributed to him.

One of the most curious features of Mr. Browning's poetry is his love for music, and his unusually unmusical and even jolting verse. Yet he could write verse of exquisitely musical rhythm,—witness "A Tocatta of Galuppi's," which, read by a musical voice in sympathy with the writer, is like a burst of exquisite music,—but for the most part he really preferred the jolting of such lines as I have just quoted. That the poet who wrote such stanzas as the following should so seldom have filled his song with musical cadences is passing strange. Perhaps he loved music all the more that he was usually too brusque and too impatient to subdue it to his own soul :—

As for Venice and her people, merely born to bloom and
   drop
Here on earth, they bore their fruitage, mirth and folly
   were the crop ;
What of soul was left, I wonder, when the kissing had to
   stop ?
"Dust and ashes !" So you creak it, and I want the
   heart to scold.
Dear dead women, with such hair too,—what's become of
   all the gold
Used to hang and brush their bosoms ? I feel chilly and
   grown old.

The poet who poured forth the lines which end with these sad stanzas had a genuine melody in his soul, though he drew forth melody from others by the use of a truly Socratic irony, and often a very elaborate apparatus of dissonance.

BROWNING AND TENNYSON

In some respects the two greatest imaginative poets of our day are striking contrasts. Browning is careless and impatient in execution; Tennyson careful and elaborate. Browning is rough and ungainly; Tennyson smooth and stately. Browning trots or gallops; Tennyson walks or canters. Browning almost gasps out his meaning, omitting half the articles and particles which weave speech into a flexible texture; Tennyson touches and retouches the form till it is no less perfect, or even more perfect, than the thought or emotion to be expressed, so that the artistic workmanship sometimes attracts even more attention than the imaginative substance on which it is expended. Again, Tennyson studies poems; Browning, it might almost be said, studies the neglect of these qualities, or, if that be exaggeration, at least ignores them altogether, and hews away right and left, like a pioneer in a jungle, instead of shaping anxiously and lovingly as a sculptor shapes his marble. Tennyson treats words and all their associations with the utmost sympathy and reverence; Browning tumbles them about and rolls them over almost as a tempest does the rocks of an Alpine valley, sometimes producing very weird

effects with them, but effects which have a great
deal of the appearance of rough play about them,
like the casts in some giant's game at bowls.
Tennyson not infrequently wears the graceful negligence of manner appropriate to one who is on
easy terms with the Muses; Browning is apt to
play them tricks, and indulge in familiarities with
them which suggest that he does not revere them
as Muses at all.

Yet, in spite of all these marked contrasts, there
are points of resemblance which are due partly to
the common interests of the social world in which
both these poets have lived, partly to the intellectual tendencies of the time. Both are at heart
idealists, with a strong desire not to ignore the
realities with which idealists must deal. Both are
possessed by Christian convictions: Both are eager
students of the philosophy of Faith. Both have
made elaborate studies of ecclesiastical eccentricities
—Tennyson of St. Simeon Stylites, Browning of
the Bishop who orders his tomb at St. Praxed's
Church. Both have given the most anxious attention to provincial and vernacular peculiarities,—
Tennyson in his two "Northern Farmers," his
"Grandmother," and just now in his "Owd Roä"—
Browning in his Yorkshire Halbert and Hob, and
his study of Bunyan's coarse converts, Ned Bratts
and his wife. And both, with a very strong desire
to master the religious attitude of a world far
removed from our own,—Tennyson the mysticism
of the age of chivalry, Browning the peculiarities
of mediæval or modern superstition,—have been
intensely modern; modern in their faith and in
their sympathies, in their confidence that they are
"heirs of all the ages," and that they stand on a

summit of knowledge and experience higher than
that of even the greatest of their predecessors.

But though we may recognise the similarity of
some of the ideal aims pursued by Tennyson and
Browning, and of such even of their methods as the
realism of their times has suggested to them,
nothing can minimise the contrast between the
method of a poet to whom charm of manner is
generally essential—one might almost say as to
much of his early poetry, almost too essential, so
essential as to become a mannerism — and the
method of the poet who despises charm of manner
altogether, and appears to be abrupt, purposely and
by preference ; between the manner of a poet who
sings—

> I asked thee, " Give me immortality,"
> Then didst thou grant mine asking with a smile,
> Like wealthy men who care not how they give.
> But thy strong Hours indignant work'd their wills,
> And beat me down and marr'd and wasted me ;
> And tho' they could not end me, left me maim'd
> To dwell in presence of immortal youth,
> Immortal age besides immortal youth,
> And all I was in ashes,

and the manner of a poet who sings in his fine
study of the old Grammarian, that—

> He settled *Hoti's* business—let it be !
>   Properly based *Oun*—
> Gave us the doctrine of the enclitic *De*,
> Dead from the waist down.

Here are contemporary poets of the self-same
country, both idealists in aim, both feeling the
imperious necessity of not being too much of idealists

to recognise fully the vulgarities, the dust, and, so to say, the lumber of life, one of whom yet strives to give dignity where he can to all his visions, and either grace or ease where dignity is impossible; while the other almost strives to *avoid* giving any trace of an artistic manner or finish to anything that he has to say, nay, who makes it more familiar than is quite natural, by using such phrases as "Settled *Hoti's* business," or blurting out in his eager, shorthand style, "Put case," without the definite article, which would naturally, even in familiar dialogue, precede the word "case" and soften the hurry of his speech. The Poet-Laureate, in his boyish days at least, was so great a lover of graceful manner, that his attitude of speech often suggested posture-making. The vivid and graphic thinker whom we have just lost was so great a lover of the familiar, that he invented angularities of style which no ordinary man could have discovered, and evidently preferred "settling *Hoti's* business" to explaining the principles which govern its use in the Greek syntax. And no doubt the former phrase is a great deal more awakening than the latter. Its very familiarity gives a shock to conventional habits of thought, and that is really at the bottom of Browning's love of familiarity and abruptness of style. He wants to turn versification into a spur rather than a pleasure. He oftener uses rhyme and rhythm to prick the drowsy mind, than directly to exalt the commonplace mind. And no doubt the view that all verse should have a sweetness of its own had been overdone in modern times before Browning arose to contradict it. The Virgilian use of verse is not the only use. The great Greek dramatists can hardly be said to have made "charm" the chief feature of their versification. Many of their choruses are very rugged, and much of their dialogue is plain even to homeliness. Dante often abounds in crabbed speech, even I suppose (for I speak on the authority of others) where there is no doubt about the text. And even Goethe, lucid and harmonious as he loved to be, did not shrink from being jerky and obscure where his subject required it, as he evidently thought it did in his Walpurgisnacht on the Brocken. It is a mistake to suppose that verse has no function except that of lending harmony, beauty, and grandeur to the thought. Sometimes, as in the case of Tennyson's "Northern Farmer," rhythm only answers the purpose of a frame to isolate and give the impression of care, condensation, and study to a sketch of a very rough and coarse figure. Sometimes, as in the case of "Hudibras," as well as with a great many of Browning's poems, the jerk and the jingle are as essential to the grotesque effect intended, as want of proportion may be to an effective caricature. Indeed, with poets who, like Tennyson, are great masters of both metre and rhyme, the rhythm of the finer blank metre is more satisfying, exactly because there is less exuberance of sweetness in it than in the most beautiful of the rhymed verses. The former has something of the dignity and simplicity of sculpture about it; the latter has too soft and luxurious an air for the most exalted themes. And for the same reason in the Greek poetry, in which there was no such thing as rhyme, and, except in the Homeric hexameter, very little even of the silver rhythm of Virgil, we find a greater wealth of majesty than even poets of the highest order could have produced

under the conditions of modern rhyme. It may
well be questioned whether rhyme has not added
too much sweetness to modern poetry, and made it,
so to say, too "sugary." Are not Tennyson's greatest
achievements effected without it, or in that modified
rhyme of "In Memoriam," where the distance
between the two enclosing rhymes in the first and
fourth lines keeps the ear waiting long enough to
prevent the full sweetness of rhyme from cloying
the sense? Browning, however, uses rhyme with a
very different object from poets in general, not to
add to the beauty or harmony of the effect, but to
multiply surprises and shocks, to take your breath
away, sometimes to flog you into alertness, sometimes to laugh you into confusion, sometimes, again,
to make you laugh heartily at his humour. To use
his own happy and latest phrase, he "hitches the
thing into verse," rather than expresses in verse,
because he loves the rhythmical movement and the
cry which it is capable of yielding. He often uses
verse as a conjuror uses sleight-of-hand, to astonish
you with his ingenuity, with his resource, with his
agility, with his presence of mind,—or as a tight-
rope dancer uses the nimbleness and flexibility of
his limbs. In a word, Browning does not aim at
setting life to music, though music was so dear to
him. To him music was one thing and poetry
another; the greatest part of life, and that which
he cared most to study, was quaint and odd rather
than beautiful and sublime; and especially quaint
and odd when you compared it with the spiritual
ends for which Browning believed that man had
been created. It was his great aim to show *how*
quaint and odd life really is, how different from the
standards of the eternal world, and yet how much

influenced by those standards. He loved to make men see the strange irregularity, the astounding unevenness, the almost incredible failures, which we are compelled to recognise in a world in which the hunger and thirst for nobler things are yet always breaking through; and he thought he could do this better by using verse freely to familiarise to us the incongruities of the world as it is, than by using it to make the world—either as it is or as it should be—fascinating. To Browning life is a medley of grotesques, with a glowing horizon beyond it. And he used his poetic ingenuity quite as much to help us enter into the grotesqueness, as to help us see the sunlit distance.

THE POETIC PLACE OF MATTHEW ARNOLD

MR. ARNOLD'S most fascinating little volume of selections from his own poems, with an exquisitely embellished title-page, marks a certain maturity of stage in a poet's life and development, and reminds one that Mr. Arnold has really been so long familiar to us, that it is no longer difficult to form some estimate of what he has done, or even of what relative place he occupies, in one's mind, among the other English poets.

What strikes one first about Mr. Arnold is that he, more perhaps than any poet who has ever used the English language, is a poet of precision. His language is chosen with the purity of taste and purity of feeling to which Dr. Newman alone of other English writers has fully accustomed us. Nothing could be more different in many ways than the best poetry in the *Lyra Apostolica* and the best poetry in Matthew Arnold's volumes. Their tendency is, for the most part, opposite. Their subjects are usually very different. But in the finely-chiselled outline of the thought, in the delicate discrimination between the various associations carried by words, in the curious lucidity, often rising into lustre, of the expression, I know nothing

like Matthew Arnold outside the prose and poetry
of Dr. Newman.   Take Dr. Newman's marvellous
description of David :—

> Twofold praise thou shalt attain,
> In royal court and battle-plain ;
> Then comes heart-ache, care, distress,
> Blighted hope and loneliness ;
> Wounds from friend and gifts from foe,
> Dizzied faith and guilt and woe ;
> Loftiest aims by earth defiled,
> Gleams of wisdom sin-beguiled,
> Sated Power's tyrannic mood,
> Counsels shared with men of blood,
> Sad success, parental tears,
> And a dreary gift of years.

There is no other poet, living or dead, for whose
work, so far as I know, that verse might possibly,
and without ignominious blundering, be mistaken by
one who did not know its author, except Matthew
Arnold.   The nearest thing I know to this in
English poetry is Mr. Arnold's delineation of a very
different figure, Goethe :—

> When Goethe's death was told, we said :
> Sunk, then, is Europe's sagest head.
> Physician of the iron age,
> Goethe has done his pilgrimage.
> He took the suffering human race,
> He read each wound, each weakness clear ;
> And struck his finger on the place,
> And said : *Thou ailest here, and here!*
> He looked on Europe's dying hour
> Of fitful dream and feverish power ;
> His eye plunged down the weltering strife,
> The turmoil of expiring life—

> He said : *The end is everywhere,*
> *Art still has truth, take refuge there!*
> And he was happy, if to know
> Causes of things, and far below
> His feet to see the lurid flow
> Of terror, and insane distress,
> And headlong fate, be happiness.

Or perhaps one might compare Dr. Newman's lines still more aptly to the picture of a physician of sick souls groping in vain for some remedy for spiritual decay and despair, in Mr. Arnold's beautiful poem, the "Scholar Gipsy." In speaking of those who wait in vain "the spark from Heaven" which shall show them what to do, he wrote :—

> Yes, we await it !—but it still delays,
>   And then we suffer ! and amongst us one,
>   Who most has suffer'd, takes dejectedly
>   His seat upon the intellectual throne ;
>   And all his store of sad experience he
>   Lays bare of wretched days ;
>   Tells us his misery's birth and growth and signs,
>   And how the dying spark of hope was fed,
>   And how the breast was soothed, and how the head,
>   And all his hourly varied anodynes.

In the predominance of language of precision, and yet language exquisitely pure and poetical, full of the light and air of poetry, Mr. Arnold has all the skill and delicacy and discriminating felicity of Dr. Newman.

But Mr. Arnold is not only a poetic sculptor in the exquisite clearness of his outlines ; he is also a poetic water-colour painter of the purest school,— the school which regards what is technically called "body-colour" as a sin, and aims at making trans-

parency of effect almost as important as truth of
effect itself. Here Mr. Arnold reminds us of the
poet Gray, who paints with the same lucid touch,
though certainly with much less richness of impression. There is a good deal in Mr. Arnold's
poetry which reminds me, in its style of colouring,
more of the celebrated "Elegy in a Country
Churchyard" than of any other English poem.
But the difference is, that Mr. Arnold is more
original in his touches. Gray is full of beauty, but
his pictures, both of humanity and of nature, are
slightly conventional in their cast; they are exquisitely painted, but painted without marking that
the poet's mind has ranged beyond the common
horizon, though it has got a far more than common
command over the instruments for calling up in
others what he sees vividly himself. It is otherwise
with Mr. Arnold. He hardly ever paints a lovely
scene without some phrase which adds to your
knowledge of its charm. This verse, for instance,
is like Gray in style, but a good deal above Gray
in originality of painting :—

> But on the stairs what voice is this I hear,
> Buoyant as morning and as morning clear?
> Say, has some wet, bird-haunted English lawn
> Lent it the music of its trees at dawn?
> Or was it from some sun-flecked mountain brook
> That the sweet voice its upland clearness took?

That is quite in Gray's style of painting, but the
"wet, bird-haunted English lawn" is a touch too
original and exquisite for Gray. As a painter in
transparent water-colours, however, Mr. Arnold has
perhaps never surpassed, though he has very often
approached the beauty of that contrast in "Thyrsis"

between a stormy and a brilliant summer, which the
June and July of the present year must have often
recalled to Mr. Arnold's many admirers :—

So, some tempestuous morn in early June,
    When the year's primal burst of bloom is o'er,
      Before the roses and the longest day—
    When garden-walks and all the grassy floor
      With blossoms red and white of fallen May
        And chestnut flowers are strewn—
So have I heard the cuckoo's parting cry,
    From the wet field, through the vext garden-trees,
    Come with the volleying rain and tossing breeze :
    The bloom is gone, and with the bloom go I!

Too quick despairer, wherefore wilt thou go ?
    Soon will the high midsummer pomps come on,
      Soon will the musk carnations break and swell,
    Soon shall we have gold-dusted snapdragon,
      Sweet-William with his homely cottage-smell,
        And stocks in fragrant blow ;
Roses that down the alleys shine afar,
    And open, jasmine-muffled lattices,
    And groups under the dreaming garden-trees.
And the full moon, and the white evening star.

For purity and lustre of colour that picture has
never been surpassed in English verse.   It takes up
the style of Gray, gives it a freshness and originality
not belonging to Gray, while keeping all his purity,
freshness, and transparency.   In finish, fastidiousness, and grace, Mr. Arnold is Gray's equal; in
buoyancy, freshness, and lustre, greatly his superior.
  But while in clearness and sharp definition of
outline, and purity and delicacy of colour, Mr.
Arnold has rarely been equalled by any of our
English poets, it is, of course, to be understood that

his subjects are limited to those which can be
treated with so fine a pencil and so transparent a
style as his. Thought is always uppermost in his
mind. His observation itself is always tranquil and
full of the definiteness of intellectual discrimination. He never breaks out into singing or wailing
like Shelley. He never masses his colours with the
force and passion of Byron. He never mixes his
effects with the lavish hand of Tennyson, so as
almost to bewilder you with the multiplicity and
variety of impressions. He keeps in one stratum,
the intellectual and reflective stratum, even in his
narrative poems. He is animated by one predominating emotion, the emotion of a sort of grandiose
spiritual compassion. So far as he has a clear
affinity with any of the greater poets of England, it
is obvious that his affinity is with Wordsworth;
and that, though he has not Wordsworth's rapture
or Wordsworth's sublimity, he has learnt more
from Wordsworth than from any other, while he has
brought to the treatment of Wordsworth's themes
a more delicate and tender workmanship, a greater
richness and subtlety of intellect, a considerable
narrative power, of which Wordsworth can hardly
be said to have possessed even the germs, and a
much larger historical and philosophical horizon.
Still, Wordsworth was and doubtless will continue
to be recognised as a poet of much greater weight
of natural genius, of far more hardy power, of far
deeper impulses. Mr. Arnold can hardly be called
a true disciple of Wordsworth, deeply as he has
drunk at the spring of Wordsworth's genius. It
may be said of him that he has been fascinated and
charmed by Wordsworth's thoughts, without being
truly conquered by them; that he has been

diverted from his intellectual troubles by Wordsworth, but has failed to be consoled. He says of
Wordsworth in the beautiful memorial verses
transferred to this little volume :—

> And Wordsworth !—Ah, pale ghosts, rejoice !
> For never has such soothing voice
> Been to your shadowy world conveyed,
> Since erst, at morn, some wandering shade
> Heard the clear song of Orpheus come
> Through Hades, and the mournful gloom.
> Wordsworth has gone from us—and ye,
> Ah, may ye feel his voice as we !
> He too upon a wintry clime
> Had fallen—on this iron time
> Of doubts, disputes, distractions, fears.
> He found us when the age had bound
> Our souls in its benumbing round ;
> He spoke, and loosed our hearts in tears.
> He laid us as we lay at birth
> On the cool flowery lap of earth,
> Smiles broke from us and we had ease ;
> The hills were round us, and the breeze
> Went o'er the sunlit fields again ;
> Our foreheads felt the wind and rain.
> Our youth returned ; for there was shed
> On spirits that had long been dead,
> Spirits dried up and closely furl'd,
> The freshness of the early world.

But that, eloquent as it is, is not the kind of way
in which Wordsworth himself would have wished
to be commemorated. He would have regarded the
faint classical hope expressed on behalf of the
"pale ghosts" as utterly removed from the school
of his hardy and humble though buoyant faith.
He would not have desired his poetry to be looked

upon as an alleviation of human lots,—as a sweet interlude in the iron courts of human destiny,— but rather as the announcement of one who had discerned with prophetic glance the ultimate divinity of this unintelligible world. He went about with deep exultation in his heart, not, like Mr. Arnold, with an exalted compassion and a serene fortitude. Where Wordsworth said "rejoice," Mr. Arnold says "endure." While Wordsworth's rapture was the rapture of illumination from the source of all light, Mr. Arnold's is but an ambiguous and hesitating joy in the buoyancy of his own soul. The affinities of Mr. Arnold with Wordsworth, and the still graver contrasts between them, will not be adequately seen by the readers of this little volume of "Selections" only. It is in such poems as "Resignation," "The Youth of Nature," and the two fine poems on the author of "Obermann" that Mr. Arnold's true philosophy,—his rejection of Wordsworth,—his relegation of Wordsworth to the position of a poet who charms us chiefly by ignoring "the half of human fate," is to be found. Still, Mr. Arnold can never be understood by one who has not grasped his relation to Wordsworth, his deep delight in Wordsworth, his long study of him, and his fundamental rejection of him.

On the whole, I should say that Mr. Arnold will live in English literature as one who recalls Gray by his cool, pure, and delicate workmanship; Newman by the severe and lucid sharpness of his outlines; and who represents a survival from the school of Wordsworth, having carried off from it a good deal of its habit of thought and buoyancy of feeling, while rejecting its main current of meditative faith. In the delineation of human passion, Mr. Arnold has limited himself almost to a single phase of it, but in the delineation of that phase he is supreme.   No English poet ever painted so powerfully the straining of emotion against the reins of severe intellectual repression. In Mr. Arnold there is a deep love of excitement, and a deep fear of it, always struggling.   He may be said to have gained his reputation as a poet by the vigour with which he paints the conflict.

> I staunch with ice my burning breast,
> With silence balm my whirling brain,

might almost be transferred from one of his poems to the title-page, as the motto of his whole poetry, both narrative and reflective.

POETIC CHARM

MR. E. R. RUSSELL, the editor of the *Liverpool Daily Post*, whose critical essays often evince a delicate subtlety as well as a keen insight, has just printed a paper on Matthew Arnold, read before the Literary and Philosophical Society of Liverpool, of which I will venture to say that it is nearer to the kind of paper which one might have expected Matthew Arnold to write upon his own prose works, if he had had (as perhaps he had) the detachment of mind to put himself at a distance from his own thought, than anything else on the critic whom we have lost, that has come under my notice. Mr. Russell quotes from some former criticism of his own on Matthew Arnold, which I have never had the good fortune to meet with, some strictures on "the lack of energy and climax" in Matthew Arnold, on "the curious absence of strong flow in the ripples of his pellucidity," on "his resigned sequesterment from the broad channels of life and action," and on "the too negative quality of his lucidity,"— all sound criticisms, but all, I think, directed rather to Matthew Arnold's prose than to his poetry ; and I confess that, for my own part, I would not buy all the prose Matthew Arnold ever wrote, including even the finest of his *Essays in*

Criticism, at the sacrifice of one of his elegiac
pieces,—the "Memorial Verses," for example, on
Byron, Goethe, and Wordsworth. There is again
but little reference, I think, to the poetry, when
Mr. Russell speaks of "the unconventional *naïveté*
which gave its charm of egoistical attraction to
Matthew Arnold," or in the very happy remark on
the "cunning over-accentuation" which Mr. Russell
regards as one of "the tricks of his pretty, but
never frivolous art," though I object to the word
"pretty" as hardly ever applicable to Matthew
Arnold's prose, while it would be quite unduly
depreciating to the singular grace and classical
simplicity of his poetry, which seldom, indeed,
descends to prettiness, being characterised by
qualities almost inconsistent with "prettiness,"—a
word which to my ears implies something small and
accidental in the nature of its attractiveness, something evidently wanting in unity of effect. But
much as I admire Mr. E. R. Russell's general vein
of criticism on Matthew Arnold, if one regards it
as applying only to his prose, I observe with some
surprise that he says so little of his poetry, and that
little it seems to me quite inadequate, and that he
even selects for special attention those of the poems
in which, to my thinking, Matthew Arnold was
attempting what did not suit his genius. The
"Requiescat," which some friend of Mr. Russell's
selected for special praise, and which Mr. Russell
himself speaks of as a delightful poem, seems to me
to end in genuine bathos when it congratulates the
tired heart on having at last inherited the "vasty
halls of death." The lines on "Dover Beach" are,
I should say, inferior in their kind to almost all
Matthew Arnold's poems in the same key ; and the

description of Rachel, the great actress, is ineffective
as a criticism and uninteresting as a poem; while
the extract from the remarkable verses on "Heine's
Grave" enunciates quite the least happy of Arnold's
criticisms, and perhaps the only one in that particular
and very noble poem which I should have thought
absolutely false. Matthew Arnold is trying to
explain the failure of Heine's wonderful genius to
do what it might have done, and he declares, no
doubt rightly, that it was the deficiency of love in
Heine which jarred his life and wrecked him as
a poet. But then Matthew Arnold goes on to
announce as a great truth, what is very far indeed
from a great truth, and is especially refuted by his
own work as a poet,—the doctrine that "love is the
fountain of charm," and, by implication, that it is
love which draws us to every poet:—

> Charm is the glory which makes
> Song of the poet divine,
> Love is the fountain of charm.
> How without charm wilt thou draw,
> Poet! the world to thy way?
> Not by the lightnings of wit—
> Not by the thunder of scorn!
> These to the world, too, are given;
> Wit it possesses, and scorn—
> Charm is the poet's alone.

And because Heine had not "love, the fountain of
charm," he was conscious of failure:—

> Therefore a secret unrest
> Tortured thee, brilliant and bold!
> Therefore triumph itself
> Tasted amiss to thy soul.

> Therefore, with blood of thy foes,
> Trickled in silence thine own.
> Therefore the victor's heart
> Broke on the field of his fame.

No juster criticism could have been passed on Heine. It was the caustic in him which burned into his own soul, and had he really had more of love in him he at least would have had more of the fountain of charm. But is it in the least true that love is the universal fountain of poetic charm,—say, in Milton, for instance, or Sir Walter Scott, or Matthew Arnold himself? Mr. Russell does not endorse Matthew Arnold's great doctrine, but he does not traverse it, and yet no poet ever produced poetry that had more charm in it than Matthew Arnold, and the greatest of its charms is often as remote from "love" as it is from hatred. But the doctrine, as a universal principle, has no root at all in reality. What is the great charm of Milton? As Matthew Arnold has himself told us, it is his grand style, the style which overawes us all, for instance, when we read :—

> But let my due feet never fail
> To walk the studious cloister's pale,
> And love the high embowered roof
> With antic pillars massy proof
> And storied windows richly dight
> Casting a dim religious light.
> There let the pealing organ blow
> To the full-voiced quire below,
> In service high and anthems clear,
> As may with sweetness, through mine ear,
> Dissolve me into ecstasies,
> And bring all Heaven before mine eyes

Now, it is certainly not the love of "the high
embowered roof," nor yet the love of Heaven to
which the high anthems, whereon Milton dwelt
in so grand a strain, were to introduce him, that
gives their "charm" to these grand lines. It is
not in any natural sense love at all, but the richness and stateliness of the man's inner nature, the
feeling there was in him of a complex inner music
answering to the complex outward music which
he so powerfully delineated. Just so, when he
describes the dim solitude where—

> Glowing embers through the room
> Teach light to counterfeit a gloom,

we at once catch ourselves thinking that in that
noble but highly artificial image, Milton must have
expressed the sense of mysterious half-light in
which his own religious meditations may often
have expired. Most assuredly, if I understand
aright the charm of Milton's grand and sometimes
grandiose images, — such characteristic images,
for instance, as "smoothing the raven down of
darkness till it smiled,"—the secret of the charm
of Milton is not at all to be found in love, but
rather in a certain pomp and majesty, both of
feeling and of movement, which moulded all he
wrote, and is as different as it can be from love.

So, again, with Sir Walter Scott: is there any
charm in his poetry like that which his verse
displays when it expresses the joy of battle, the
glory of strife ?—

> Go sound the trumpet, fill the fife,
>   To all the sensual world proclaim,
> One crowded hour of glorious life
>   Is worth a world without a name ;

or in the grand description of the wild bull ?—

> Through the huge oaks of Evendale,
>   Whose limbs a thousand years have worn,
> What sullen roar comes down the gale
>   And drowns the hunter's pealing horn ?
>
> Mightiest of all the beasts of chase
>   That roam in woody Caledon,
> Crashing the forest in his race,
>   The mountain bull comes thundering on.

Whatever is the charm there, and the charm is great, surely it is not the charm of love; and, to my mind, the charm of almost every distinct poet is a different charm, and though there may be many poets whose charm is capable of resolution into that which Matthew Arnold singles out as the secret of all charm, there are certainly a great many more whose charm cannot by any possibility be so resolved.

And surely the secret of the charm of Matthew Arnold himself is not capable of any such resolution. The charm of the writer who could describe Byron as bearing "from Europe to the Ætolian shore, the pageant of his bleeding heart"; who painted the isolation of all human hearts in the splendid lines :—

> And bade, betwixt their shores to be,
> The unplumbed, salt, estranging sea ;

who could picture Obermann's desolation in the powerful words :—

> A fever in these pages burns
>   Beneath the calm they feign ;
> A wounded human spirit turns
>   Here, on its bed of pain ;

who could describe the Roman noble's miserable
unrest so vividly :—

> In his cool hall, with haggard eyes,
> The Roman noble lay;
> He drove abroad, in furious guise,
> Along the Appian way.

> He made a feast, drank fierce and fast,
> And crowned his hair with flowers—
> No easier nor no quicker passed
> The impracticable hours;

—the poet who touched his highest, in passages of
this kind, certainly could not boast that the
fountain of his charm was love. It would be
less untrue, though not true, to say that the
fountain of Matthew Arnold's charm was lovableness, for certainly his poetry has in it a tenderness
and lovableness which is a very different quality
from love. Love is one thing, and lovableness
another, and sometimes those who have most love
seem on the surface to be least lovable, and *vice
versâ*. Matthew Arnold is often lovable, lovable
for his grace, his tenderness, his sedate purity, his
tranquil and collected patience, his wistful regrets.
But hardly anywhere does the secret of his charm
seem to me to be the power of his love. He is
serene, gentle, reasonable, gracious, with a keen
eye for the cooler beauties of life, and a fine ear
for all the flute-like voices of Nature; but he is
not the poet of love, though he may be the poet
of insight, and especially of insight into the faith
that is seen in retrospect. For my own part, I
should say that poetic charm has no single fountain,

but is almost as manifold in its secret sources as it is in its modes of expression,—being one thing in Homer, another in Dante, a third in Milton, a fourth in Shelley, and a multitude of separate things in Shakespeare.

MATTHEW ARNOLD'S LETTERS

MR. RUSSELL, in his graceful and skilful preface to his perhaps too copious collection of Matthew Arnold's letters, says with great truth that the charm of the poet's letters lies in their perfect naturalness. But he adds, with what seems to me less truth, that they are *himself,*—which does not seem quite adequate,—nay, they are, I think, a good deal less than himself, if Mr. Russell means by being "himself" that they give you the glow and the essence of the man. On the contrary, I should say that their charm is not at all up to the charm of his poetry; not at all up to the charm of his conversation. They are to those who knew him delightful letters, as recalling the man; but they do not fill you with the sense of buoyancy,—though often it was buoyant sadness, not buoyant joyousness,—with which his poems fill you, or even with the sense of buoyancy with which his conversation filled you. They are, as most letters are, a good deal *less* than the man, not as a very few letters are, as Cowper's and Grey's letters have been, more than the man. More even in Cowper's case than his poems; or as some other letters—Mrs. Carlyle's for instance —have been, the letters of one in a specially exuberant frame of mind, filled with the exhilaration of

282

firing off a kind of volley of well-aimed shots which the reserve of ordinary social intercourse might have checked.   There is no sense in reading Matthew Arnold's correspondence that the act of letter-writing stimulated and exalted him, and that is what we find with Cowper's letters and Grey's letters, and, so far as the stimulating goes, with Byron's letters (though in Byron's case the act of correspondence made him a different man, something of an actor as well as a correspondent).   Matthew Arnold was not at his full height in letter-writing, as he was in writing his poems.   His letters are pleasant, affectionate, wholly unaffected, but they are a faint reflection of the poet, and not even a bright or vivid reflection of his conversation.   They are himself, a little subdued, not as the letters of a born letter-writer should be, himself a little exalted. Compare, for instance, what he says of the composition of that lovely little poem on his favourite dog's death, "Geist's Grave," in his letters, with what I heard him say of it in his conversation, and one misses at once the spring and emphasis and *élan* of his high-strung personality :—

My darling Boy :—I hoped to have sent you to-day my lines about your dear, dear little boy (Geist), but I have not yet been able to get a correct copy from the printer.   You shall have it by next week's mail.   At least, I hope so—and you will then get it a fortnight sooner than if we waited for the magazine containing it to be published.   The daily miss of him will wear off, but we shall never forget him, and I am very glad to have stamped him in our memories by these lines, written when he was fresh in our minds.   I like to think of all the newspapers having his dear little name in them when the Christmas number of *The Fortnightly*

Review is advertised, and I hope people will like the
lines, and that will lead to his being more mentioned,
and talked about, which seems to me a sort of continua-
tion of him in life, dear little fellow, though it is but a
hollow and shadowy one, alas !

That is simple and natural and fascinating. But
those who heard him talk of the composition of
that poem miss all the singular rapture of the
manner in which he said, "I assure you I wrote it
with the tears streaming down my face," and with
a simple sort of delight in the full consciousness of
the emotion with which the mere attempt to recall
the poor little dog's affectionateness and grace of
manner had excited within him.   Now any one
who reads the poem will feel, just as those who heard
Arnold speak of it would feel, that he did write it
in a passion of tenderness and sorrow, in a sort of
summer storm of the heart :—

> Only four years those winning ways,
>   Which make me for thy presence yearn,
> Called us to pet thee or to praise,
>   Dear little friend ! at every turn ?
>
> That loving heart, that patient soul,
>   Had they indeed no longer span,
> To run their course, and reach their goal,
>   And read their homily to man ?
>
> That liquid, melancholy eye,
>   From whose pathetic, soul-fed springs
> Seem'd surging the Virgilian cry,
>   The sense of tears in mortal things—
>
> That steadfast, mournful strain, consoled
>   By spirits gloriously gay,
> And temper of heroic mould—
>   What, was four years their whole short day ?

There you see, as you saw in the curious mixture of grief and triumph with which he told his friends of the storm of tears with which he had written the poem, the curious buoyancy as well as the curious scud of passion with which "Geist's" death was commemorated. But you would never gather it from the letter, touching and pleasant as the letter is. Indeed, the verse recalling "that steadfast, mournful strain consoled by spirits gloriously gay," exactly expresses not only poor little "Geist," but still more the poet himself, whose exquisite elegiac poems are at least as remarkable for their elasticity as for their melancholy, for the elation with which he wept, as for the sense of desolation with which he exulted in his own tenderness.

Matthew Arnold's letters of travel, again, hardly suggest the vividness with which his imagination brooded over the loveliness of the scenes he visited. They are pleasant letters of travel, but they do not in any sense supplement or lend new colour to the poems. Take the letters from Switzerland. They are lively, unaffected letters, but they do not glow at all as the poems glow. We never see him pouring out his heart in his letters as we do in his poems. This is the kind of letter which I most enjoy ; he is descending the Maloja Pass into Italy :—

We stopped at Vicosoprano, the chief town of the Swiss part of the valley, to lunch, and here a melancholy thing happened. I had been looking at a small cat, the colour of William's cat, running backwards and forwards across the street. It was in beautiful condition and high spirits, with a small bell round its neck like the bells worn here by the cows—evidently a favourite. I went a little way towards the bridge over the river to see if I

could find any plants, and met a voiturier with four
horses driving fast into the place.   Presently I returned,
saw a crowd, went up to it, and there was my poor little
cat lying quite dead in a pool of blood.   The voiturier
had run over it—not by his fault, I believe—but it had
darted into the street at the moment he was passing; the
wheels had gone over its neck, and it had died instantly,
but it was not mutilated.   It made quite a sensation, and
presently a young man took the little thing up and
laid it under the wall of the side street from which it
had just before been darting out full of prettiness and
play.   I know the girls will be interested in this sad
story; the sudden end of the poor little cat quite afflicted
me.   We went on in the diligence presently, and, passing
through a gorge, came into a new world; chestnuts,
walnuts, and mulberries began as if by magic, and vine-
yards on the hillsides, and all the Italian landscape which
is so beautiful.   In the grass under the chestnuts I saw
more flowers than I have yet seen this time in Switzerland,
but no cyclamens, though we found them, if you remember,
in a like country from Premia downwards.

Here it is more the pity which the poor little cat's
fate excites in him than the scenery which chiefly
charms us.   I find no transcript in the letters of
travel of such poems as the two to the author of
" Obermann," or those on the "Grande Chartreuse."
There is nothing even of that kind of genius for
geography which Arnold had inherited from his
father, and which comes out so vividly in his poems
on the English lakes and on the Swiss passes.   I
seldom even recall such descriptions as that of the
Gemmi Pass :—

> In front the awful Alpine track
>   Climbs up its rocky stair ;
> The autumn storm-winds drive the rack,
>   Close o'er it in the air.

Behind are the abandoned baths,
Mute in the meadows lone,
The leaves are on the valley paths,
The mists are on the Rhone.

The truth is that it took something more than
letter-writing fully to kindle Matthew Arnold.
The sympathy elicited by living personal intercourse did it, and the mingled toil and passion of
imaginative composition did it, but correspondence
did not usually do it. His letters are genial,
tender, sometimes playful, but they are not often
passionate in the sense in which his poems are
passionate,—that is, written in the mood in which
the inner depths of his nature showed themselves.
In a very interesting letter to his sister, Mrs.
Forster, written from Martigny in 1858, he expresses his sympathy with Goethe's feeling that he
could not write his best while distracted by practical
duties and cares. Goethe, he says, thought that he
could have written several good tragedies, but that
in order to write them he must have been "sehr
zerrissen,"— in other words, moved to the very
bottom of his heart,—and that he dared not be so
moved while there was so much that he needed a
calm judgment and a busy mind in order to do well.
And Arnold felt the same. His mind was too full
of his practical duties to spare for poetry the full
room needed to kindle intense imaginative life.
His letters are pleasant, interesting, simple, unaffected, often even lively. But they have not the
buoyancy and *élan* either of his poetry or even of
his conversation. He was not excited by letter-
writing. He only half realised that living contact
of mind with mind, which sometimes kindles corre-

spondence even more than it kindles talk.   He was
not a reserved man in talk.   He seems almost a
reserved man in his letters.   They are written in
a tone much more subdued than that of his talk
or of his compositions whether in verse or often
even in prose.

OUR GREAT ELEGIAC POET

I SHOULD hardly have thought Lord Coleridge's comparison between Matthew Arnold and Horace, in the interesting speech which he delivered when the new bust of Matthew Arnold was unveiled in the Baptistery of Westminster Abbey, a very apposite one. One would hardly call Horace, whose finest poems were many of them what we should now call exquisite *vers de société*, a great elegiac poet, which Matthew Arnold certainly was, —the greatest, I am disposed to think, in the English language, certainly very much greater than Gray. He is always at his best in elegy. "Thyrsis" and "The Scholar-Gipsy" will stand by the side of, if not above, Milton's "Lycidas," I believe, in the estimate of the best critics of the future. His magnificent elegies on De Senancour, the author of "Obermann," are as much more touching than Gray's Elegy in a country churchyard as they are richer in true vision. The lines on "Rugby Chapel" and on "Heine's Grave" are amongst the most vivid pictures in the language of two great figures in the first half of the present century. The "Southern Night," in which he commemorates his brother William Delafield Arnold, is perhaps the most musical expression of pro-

found yet gentle and subdued regret that English
literature contains; the "Memorial Verses" on
Byron, Goethe, and Wordsworth are living studies
penetrated by that "sad lucidity of soul" which
Matthew Arnold has himself illustrated with so
much power in the singularly fine lines called
"Resignation." The little poem "By a Death-Bed,"
also called "Youth and Calm," is of the very
essence of elegy. And the main beauty even of
the longer poems, of "Sohrab and Rustem," of
"Tristram and Iseult," of "The Sick King of
Bokhara," lies in the elegiac terminations and the
modulated beauty of those trains of thought which
lead up to those terminations. Again, "The
Forsaken Merman" and "The Church of Brou"
would hardly be true poems at all without their
elegiac tone; while some even of the most beautiful
of all his elegies are devoted to his little dog
"Geist," in the poem on "Geist's Grave," and to
his little daughter's canary, in "Poor Matthias."
Lord Coleridge knows Horace a thousand times
better than I do, but I should never have thought
that Horace would be regarded as most at home
in his elegiac mood. No doubt the two beautiful
passages which Lord Coleridge quotes from Horace
are both elegiac, but surely that is not Horace's
most common nor even his most frequently
successful attitude of mind. I should have thought
Horace a considerably greater artist in the lighter
lyrical vein than Arnold, but not nearly so great
an elegiac poet. Elegy demands that special
"sad lucidity of soul" which Gray poured forth
with such exquisite tenderness in the celebrated
Elegy, and in the Ode on the distant prospect of
Eton. It is a mood of regret, but of calm regret

which heightens instead of disturbing and confusing the power of vision—nay, which seems to
lend to the apprehension of the external object
treated a singular discernment of its finest atmo-
spheric conditions, a halo of its own, transforming
mere sight into vision.   To illustrate what I mean
by contrast: Browning is hardly ever elegiac, I
should not suppose him ever to have known the
mood at all, but for the lines, "O lyric love, half-
angel and half-bird," in "The Ring and the Book,"
and the elegiac ring in the "Tocatta of Galuppi."
But though elegy must be suffused with feeling,
it must not rise to what Arnold has himself called
the lyrical cry.   Principal Shairp was quite wrong,
in the fine lines quoted by Lord Coleridge, when
he spoke of Arnold as pouring forth in his songs
"the calm which is not calm but agony."   Shelley
does that, in such lines, for instance, as those
beginning, "When the lamp is shattered, the light
in the dust lies dead," or in the lines "Written in
Dejection at Naples"; but there is not a poem
in all Arnold's volumes that seems to me to suggest
anything approaching to agony, anything beyond
a lofty and calm regret.   Take the lines on his
brother's death :—

> But now that trouble is forgot ;
>   Thy memory, thy pain, to-night,
> My brother ! and thine early lot,
>   Possess me quite.

> The murmur of this Midland deep
>   Is heard to-night around thy grave,
> There, where Gibraltar's cannon'd steep
>   O'erfrowns the wave.

For there, with bodily anguish keen,
  With Indian heats at last fordone,
With public toil and private teen—
    Thou sank'st, alone.

Slow to a stop, at morning grey,
  I see the smoke-crown'd vessel come ;
Slow round her paddles dies away
    The seething foam.

A boat is lower'd from her side ;
  Ah, gently place him on the bench !
That spirit—if all have not yet died—
    A breath might quench.

Is this the eye, the footstep fast,
  The mien of youth we used to see,
Poor, gallant boy !—for such thou wast,
    Still art, to me.

The limbs their wonted tasks refuse ;
  The eyes are glazed, thou canst not speak ;
And whiter than thy white burnous
    That wasted cheek !

Or compare Arnold's calm steadfastness in declaring
the faith in our Lord's Resurrection an illusion,
with the passion of Clough's despair when he
embodies in verse the same conviction. This is
Arnold's language :—

Ay, ages long endured his span
Of life—'tis true received—
That gracious Child, that thorn-crown'd Man !
—He lived while we believed.

While we believed, on earth he went,
And open stood his grave.
Men called from chamber, church, and tent ;
And Christ was by to save.

> Now he is dead ! Far hence he lies
> In the lorn Syrian town ;
> And on his grave, with shining eyes,
> The Syrian stars look down.

There is no agony there, only calm elegy over a
lost faith, a dispelled illusion; only another
replica of the splendid elegy over a lost faith contained in the "Stanzas at the Grande Chartreuse."
It is a more poetical and regretful form of the
denial which he expressed more dogmatically and
positively in his prose writings, when he said that
the objection to miracles was that "they do not
happen." Clough's tone is indeed different; that
is indeed agony and not elegy at all :—

> Through the great sinful streets of Naples as I past,
>   With fiercer heat than flamed above my head
> My heart was hot within me ; till at last
>   My brain was lightened when my tongue had said,
>   Christ is not risen !
>   Christ is not risen, no—
>   He lies and moulders low
>   Christ is not risen !

> What though the stone were rolled away, and though
>   The grave found empty there ?—
>   If not there, then elsewhere ;
> If not where Joseph laid Him first, why then
>   Where other men
> Translaid Him after, in some humbler clay.
>   Long ere to-day
> Corruption that sad perfect work hath done,
> Which here she scarcely, lightly had begun :
>   The foul-engendered worm
> Feeds on the flesh of the life-giving form
> Of our most Holy and Anointed One.

> He is not risen, no,—
> He lies and moulders low ;
>   Christ is not risen !

What if the women, ere the dawn was grey,
Saw one or more great angels, as they say
(Angels, or Him himself) ?   Yet neither there, nor then,
Nor afterwards, nor elsewhere, nor at all,
Hath He appeared to Peter or the ten ;
Nor, save in thunderous terror, to blind Saul ;
Save in an after Gospel and late Creed,
      He is not risen indeed,—
         Christ is not risen !

That is no elegy ; that is the burning passion of
an agonised denial, due mainly to Clough's deep
sense of the sinfulness of the world which should
have been, yet was not, redeemed, and partly to his
sceptical intellect weighing the evidence which
then, at all events, he found wanting.   But more
passionate throes in renouncing a great faith
have never been depicted in the English tongue.
Matthew Arnold never rose into that mood.
Throughout his poems the grief and regret are
always gentle and always mellow.   His poetic
pain is never anguish ; it never confuses, but only
stimulates his vision.   His grief seldom rises even
above that sweet and tender grief depicted in the
perfect poem on "Geist's Grave."   When he
commemorated—

> That liquid, melancholy eye,
>   From whose pathetic soul-fed springs
> Seem'd surging the Virgilian cry,
>   The sense of tears in mortal things,

he himself said that his own eyes were streaming
with tears ; but they were gentle tears, the tears

of sweet elegiac regret, which brings with it a
keener and brighter vision, not that stormy anguish
which troubles and bedims the whole earthly scene.
To my mind Matthew Arnold was the greatest
elegiac poet in our literature, though not a very
great lyric poet.   Indeed, the only perfect lyrics
in his volumes are also elegiacs—the songs of
Callicles in "Empedocles on Etna," which com-
memorate the visionary beauty of the old Greek
mythology.

MATTHEW ARNOLD'S POPULARITY

MATTHEW ARNOLD can hardly be called a popular poet, but yet he is a poet who is probably more especially popular with the literary class than any other poet of our day. Messrs. Macmillan have just issued the thirteenth reprint of the selected poems as he himself chose them in 1878, so that there has been a reprint of this little volume of Selections very nearly once in every year since it was first issued. Yet I should have thought that a small volume of selected poems would hardly have sold so well, in the case of an author the bulk of whose whole poetical work was so moderate, as the poems themselves. And it is likely enough that this may be actually the case. For it is very probable that the greater number of those who buy the selected poems for their small size, may really possess some complete edition of the poems as well, using the Selections only for the purpose of carrying about from place to place. Fascinating as the selected poems are, I can hardly say that they are at all more fascinating, in proportion to their bulk, than the poems from which they are selected. It cannot even be asserted that they contain specimens of all Matthew Arnold's most characteristic work; for they do not contain either

"Geist's Grave" or "Poor Matthias," though the poems on his dog and his daughter's canary are some of the most unique and characteristic of all his productions. Nor have they "The Sick King of Bokhara"; nor the fine poems on the author of "Obermann" — perhaps the finest he ever wrote; nor, again, the stanzas from "The Grande Chartreuse"; nor the lines at Heine's grave, which contain the great passage on England, as the weary Titan, "with labour-dimm'd eyes, staggering on to her goal, bearing, on shoulders immense, Atlantean, the load, well-nigh not to be borne, of the too vast orb of her fate." Now, almost all these I have just named are poems which are specially character-istic of Matthew Arnold, and of which those who know him well think at once whenever they wish to discriminate what is most individual in his genius; so that it certainly cannot even be main-tained that there are specimens of all his most typical poems in the little volume of Selections, though there are hardly a dozen of the number that one would be willing to exchange for others of equal length. Wordsworth is positively improved by judicious selection; so, indeed, is Shelley, and Browning, and Buchanan, and so, most of all, is Swinburne. But Matthew Arnold was so select in what he wrote, that any selection necessarily ex-cludes what it seems almost barbarous to exclude, and what cannot be excluded without sacrificing a special feature of his poetry, as well as mere *replicas* of a class. There are few poets, indeed, the poetical effect of whose works you would not positively improve by weeding out some fifty or even a hundred of their poems. But you could hardly leave out more than a score of Matthew Arnold's

poems without gravely injuring the total effect.
Nothing can better show how little he wrote that
was not of fine and separate quality.

The first characteristic I should select from
amongst those which make his poems popular with
the literary class, is that rare carving of words,
which makes so many of his single lines and phrases
intellectually memorable.   For instance, this of
Shakespeare :—

> We ask and ask.   Thou smilest and art still,
> Out-topping knowledge.

Of Death :—

> Though nothing can *dismarble* now
> The smoothness of that limpid brow.

Of the flatteries of love :—

> Ah, not the nectarous poppies lovers use,
>   Nor daily labour's dull Lethæan spring,
> Oblivion in lost Angels can infuse
>   Of the soil'd glory and the trailing wing.

Of the solitude of the heart :—

> And bade betwixt our shores to be
> The unplumb'd, salt, estranging sea.

Of a momentary relaxation in the poignancy of
remorse :—

> I staunch with ice my burning breast,
>   With silence balm my whirling brain,
> Oh Brandan to that hour of rest !
>   The Joppa beggar's ease was pain.

Of the helplessness of memory :—

> And we forget because we must,
> And not because we will.

Of the frugality of the will :—

> And tasks in hours of insight will'd
> May be in hours of gloom fulfill'd.

Of the insatiable soul of the Roman noble :—

> He made a feast, drank fierce and fast
>   And crown'd his hair with flowers ;
> No easier nor no quicker pass'd
>   The impracticable hours.

Of the hurry of the English practical man :—

> We see all sights from pole to pole,
>   And glance and nod and bustle by,
> And never once possess our soul
>   Before we die.

And instances like these of perfect carving in a few short words I could multiply largely with the greatest ease.

Then how great and refreshing was Arnold as a descriptive poet. Shall we ever have again such soul-resting pictures of the Thames, of the scenery near Oxford, of " those wide fields of breezy grass, where black-wing'd swallows haunt the glittering Thames," amid the "red loose-strife and blonde meadow-sweet " of the summer term ? And when again shall we have such cool, enchanting pictures of the green Alps of Switzerland, and see

——darkness steal o'er the wet grass,
  With the pale crocus starr'd,
And reach that glimmering sheet of glass
  Beneath the piny sward
Lake Leman's waters far below,

as we have so often had in his singularly cool and
refreshing poems? I know no poet—not even
Gray—whose descriptive poetry refreshes and rests
the soul like Matthew Arnold's.

But I have left Arnold's great characteristic still
untouched. It is as a poet of elegy, as a singer of
regret, that Matthew Arnold was greatest, at once
so pathetic and so buoyant. Even in his passion
of regret for his favourite dog, written, as I
remember hearing himself attesting, with tears
literally raining down his cheeks, his pathos is at
once pathetic and elastic. You feel his grief profoundly, and yet there is an elasticity in the poem
which makes even the grief comparatively soothing.
No poet gives us the buoyancy which, though it
offers no consolation, nay, often expressly refuses
it, yet bears you along the current of a passionate
regret with such a sense of life, rather than loss,
in the singer, as Matthew Arnold does in his elegies.
He reminds his sister in the fine lines headed
"Resignation" (which do not really describe resignation at all, but a very different thing, that bounding
of the heart underneath the sense of irreparable loss
which promises new life beyond the loss), how, as
children, they had crossed one of the passes in the
Westmoreland hills and got down to the sea,
probably somewhere near Whitehaven :—

But, Fausta, I remember well,
That as the balmy darkness fell

> We bath'd our hands with speechless glee,
> That night, in the wide glimmering sea.

And somehow even in the saddest of his elegies
you seem to find him bathing his hands, not exactly
with speechless glee, but with a certain bounding
of the heart that defies regret to paralyse him, "in
the wide glimmering sea." Take the two poems
to the author of "Obermann"; both of them are
in the essence of their doctrine almost hopeless
poems, or at least the hope to which they cling is
so fanciful, so much of a mere straw, that if that
were all, you would say their teaching was pure
despair; and yet the buoyancy and elasticity in
them is quite irresistible. He says farewell to
Obermann in the first of these thus:—

> Farewell! Under the sky we part,
>   In this stern Alpine glen.
> O unstrung will! O broken heart!
>   A last, a last farewell!

But the whole poem conveys that, whether M. de
Senancour's will was unstrung and his heart broken
or not, Matthew Arnold's certainly was not. He
was clearly off to fresh woods and pastures new.
It is the same with the second poem addressed to
the author of "Obermann." He closes that fine
poem with the following buoyant verses:—

> Still in my soul the voice I heard
>   Of Obermann!——away
> I turned; by some vague impulse stirr'd,
>   Along the rocks of Naye.
>
> Past Sonchaud's piny flanks I gaze
>   And the blanch'd summit there
> Of Malatrait, to where in haze
>   The Valais opens fair,

> And the domed Velan, with his snows,
>   Behind the upcrowding hills,
> Doth all the heavenly opening close
>   Which the Rhone's murmur fills ; —
>
> And glorious there, without a sound,
>   Across the glimmering lake,
> High in the Valais-depth profound
>   I saw the morning break.

Evidently that dawn brought Mr. Arnold more brightness than " Obermann " had brought him gloom. And the stanzas from " The Grand Chartreuse," though they take leave of his passionately regretted faith, end with the same note of almost triumphant life. " The Buried Life," again, is one of the most characteristic of these poems of buoyant sadness—poems with no consolation in them, but with a spring of life so fresh that it seems to defy the need of consolation. He describes first the airs and floating echoes " that convey a melancholy into all our day," and then he goes on :—

> Only—but this is rare—
> When a belovèd hand is laid in ours,
> When, jaded with the rush and glare
> Of the interminable hours,
> Our eyes can in another's eyes read clear,
> When our world-deafen'd ear
> Is by the tones of a loved voice caress'd—
> A bolt is shot back somewhere in our breast,
> And a lost pulse of feeling stirs again.
> The eye sinks inward, and the heart lies plain,
> And what we mean, we say, and what we would,
>   we know.
> A man becomes aware of his life's flow
> And hears its winding murmur ; and he sees
> The meadows where it glides, the sun, the breeze.

That is Matthew Arnold's mood all through his
exquisite elegies.   They are all sad, but buoyant in
their sadness.   They discourage faith and chill
hope, but they have such a high pulse beating in
them that they never leave the reader cheerless in
spite of their melancholy.

THE UNPOPULARITY OF CLOUGH

THE appearance of Mr. Waddington's admiring and sympathetic "monograph" on Clough—why call, by the way, a publication of this kind a monograph, which properly means a study of something artificially separated from its natural context?—affords me a good opportunity of asking why Clough is not better known than he is in modern English literature; why his fame is not greater, and his often magnificent verse more familiar to modern ears. In Mr. Haweis's hasty and scrappy book on the *American Humourists*, Mr. Haweis scoffs parenthetically at the present American Minister's "curious notion that Clough was, after all, the great poet of the age" (*American Humourists*, p. 83); and even one of Clough's most intimate friends, Mr. F. T. Palgrave, has lent some authority to Mr. Haweis's scoff, by the remark—to me as amazing as it appears to some good critics candid— that "one feels a doubt whether in verse, he (Clough) chose the right vehicle, the truly natural mode of utterance." I can only say in reply, that Clough seems to me never to touch verse without finding strength, never to attempt to speak prose without losing it and becoming half-articulate. But there clearly must be some reason or quasi-reason in a view which a whole generation of lovers of poetry have not disproved, but to some extent verified by the relative neglect in which, during a time when verse has secured an immense amount of attention, Clough's touching and often stirring and elevating poetry has been left. Mr. Waddington, I am sorry to see, does not address himself to this question, and throws but little light on it. And with all his genuine appreciation of Clough, his study is wanting in the strong outlines and massiveness of effect which might have done something to secure for Clough the public esteem which he certainly will one day secure. Mr. Waddington is too discursive, and does not bring the great features of his subject into sufficiently strong relief. His essay might increase the vogue of a public favourite, but will hardly win popularity for one who has never yet emerged from the comparative obscurity of a singer delightful to the few, though his name even is hardly recognised by the many.

For my own part, though I should not assert that Clough is the great poet of our age, I should agree heartily with Mr. Lowell that he will in future generations rank among the highest of our time, and that especially he will be ranked with Matthew Arnold, as having found a voice for this self-questioning age—a voice of greater range and richness even, and of a deeper pathos, though of less exquisite sweetness and "lucidity" of utterance, than Matthew Arnold's own—a voice that oftener breaks, perhaps in the effort to express what is beyond it, but one also that attempts, and often achieves, still deeper and more heart-stirring strains. Clough had not Mr. Arnold's happy art of interweaving delicate fancies with thoughts and emotions.

Poems like "The Scholar-Gipsy" and "Thyrsis,"
like "Tristram and Iseult," "The Sick King of
Bokhara," and the stanzas on "The Author of
'Obermann,'" were out of his reach. And, no
doubt, it is precisely poems of this kind into
which, across the bright web of rich and stimulating
fancy, Mr. Arnold has woven lines of exquisitely-
drawn and thoroughly modern thought and feeling,
that have gained for Mr. Arnold his increasing,
though not as yet overwhelming, popularity.
Clough had nothing of this fanciful art. He was
realist to the bottom of his soul, and yet, though
realist, he looked at all the questions of the day
from the thinker's point of view, and not from the
people's point of view. He did not frame his
pictures, as his friend does, in golden margins of
felicitous fancy. He left them almost without a
frame, or, at any rate, with no other frame than
that furnished by the plain outline of his story.
This might have but increased his popularity, had
Clough's subjects been like Burns's subjects, the
common joys and sorrows of the human heart.
But it was not so. His subjects, for the most part,
have a semi-scholastic ring, but do not embody
those elaborate artistic effects which soften a
scholastic ring to the ear of the people. He was a
self-questioner who did not cast over his questionings that spirit of imaginative illusion which in Mr.
Arnold's poetry sometimes makes even self-questionings sound like the music of a distant and brighter
sphere. Clough's poetry is full of direct, home-
thrusting questioning—concerning character in the
making, faith in the making, love in the making;
and powerful as it is, this analytic poetry no doubt
needs more than any kind of poetry, for its im-

mediate popularity, the glamour which Mr. Arnold's artistic framing throws round it.

Nor is this the only difference. The charm of Clough's humour, the strength of his delineation is so great that, if the only difference between him and Matthew Arnold were the difference between a plain and an attractive setting, that advantage of Mr. Arnold's might, I think, have been counterbalanced by the deeper pathos of Clough's pictures and the stronger lines in which he draws. But there is another difference. Matthew Arnold, negative as the outcome of his thought too frequently is, never leaves you in any kind of doubt as to what he means. His lines are always sharply chiselled. He is dogmatic even in his denials of dogma. Lucid and confident to the last degree, he never leaves the mind without a very sharply-marked impression of a clear thought. And even where that thought is not popular—even where it is the reverse of popular—such sharp, distinct lines, gracefully graven, are likely to gain more readers and admirers than lines of freer sweep, but more uncertain drift. Compare, for instance, some of Mr. Arnold's finest lines on the dearth of true revealing poets, with some of Mr. Clough's finest on the same subject. Mr. Arnold, after bewailing the loss of Goethe and Wordsworth, turns to the hermit of the Alps, M. de Senancour (his "Obermann"), and addresses him thus :—

> And then we turn, thou sadder sage,
> To thee ! We feel thy spell !
> —The hopeless tangle of our age,
> Thou too has scann'd it well !
>
> Immovable thou sittest, still
> As death, composed to bear !

Thy head is clear, thy feeling chill,
And icy thy despair.

Yes, as the son of Thetis said,
I hear thee saying now :
Greater by far than thou art dead ;
Strive not ! die also thou !

Ah ! two desires toss about
The poet's feverish blood.
One drives him to the world without,
And one to solitude.

The *glow,* he cries, *the thrill of life,*
Where, where do these abound ?—
Not in the world, not in the strife
Of men, shall they be found.

He who hath watch'd, not shared, the strife,
Knows how the day hath gone.
He only lives with the world's life,
Who hath renounced his own.

Now hear Clough, on the same subject :—

Come, Poet, come !
A thousand labourers ply their task,
And what it tends to scarcely ask,
And trembling thinkers on the brink
Shiver, and know not how to think.
To tell the purport of their pain,
And what our silly joys contain ;
In lasting lineaments pourtray
The substance of the shadowy day ;
Our real and inner deeds rehearse,
And make our meaning clear in verse :

Come, Poet, come ! for but in vain
We do the work or feel the pain,
And gather up the seeming gain,
Unless before the end thou come
To take, ere they are lost, their sum.

Come, Poet, come !
To give an utterance to the dumb,
And make vain babblers silent, come ;
A thousand dupes point here and there,
Bewildered by the show and glare ;
And wise men half have learned to doubt
Whether we are not best without.
Come, Poet ; both but wait to see
Their error proved to them in thee.

Come, Poet, come !
In vain I seem to call.   And yet
Think not the living times forget.
Ages of heroes fought and fell
That Homer in the end might tell ;
O'er grovelling generations past
Upstood the Doric fane at last ;
And countless hearts on countless years
Had wasted thoughts, and hopes, and fears,
Rude laughter and unmeaning tears,
Ere England Shakespeare saw, or Rome
The pure perfection of her dome.
Others, I doubt not, if not we,
The issue of our toils shall see ;
Young children gather as their own
The harvest that the dead had sown,
The dead forgotten and unknown.

One feels the difference at once between the picture
of the lucid insight of solitary renunciation, and the
ardent invocation addressed to a new teacher of a
dimly-anticipated lesson.   The one poet is distinct,
the other vague, and though the more distinct teaching is the less hopeful, it sinks more easily into the
reader's mind.   Yet, for my part, I find a richer
music in the vague hope of Clough, than even in the
sweet, sad despondency of Arnold.

Further, Clough not only sings finely of the

immature stage of moral character, but of the
immature stage of faith and the immature stage
of love.   He studies both in the making—admitting
it to be a riddle how that making will end.   Here,
for instance, is a fine poem on faith in the making,
which will be popular one day, as describing a
stage which many will then have passed through,
but which has not found popularity yet :—

> What we, when face to face we see
> The Father of our souls, shall be,
> John tells us, doth not yet appear ;
> Ah ! did he tell what we are here !
>
> A mind for thoughts to pass into,
> A heart for love to travel through,
> Five senses to detect things near,
> Is this the whole that we are here ?
>
> Rules baffle instincts—instincts rules,
> Wise men are bad—and good are fools,
> Facts evil—wishes vain appear,
> We cannot go, why are we here ?
>
> O may we for assurance' sake,
> Some arbitrary judgment take,
> And wilfully pronounce it clear,
> For this or that 'tis we are here ?
>
> Or is it right, and will it do,
> To pace the sad confusion through,
> And say :—It doth not yet appear,
> What we shall be, what we are here ?
>
> Ah yet, when all is thought and said,
> The heart still overrules the head ;
> Still what we hope we must believe,
> And what is given us receive ;

Must still believe, for still we hope
That in a world of larger scope,
What here is faithfully begun
Will be completed, not undone.

My child, we still must think, when we
That ampler life together see,
Some true result will yet appear,
Of what we are, together, here.

And here once more is a curiously subtle passage
on love "in the making," which must wait, I suppose, for its popularity till the human heart under-
stands itself better, and is franker with itself, but
which will have its popularity then. It is from
"The Bothie of Tober-na-Vuolich," the most buoyant
and humorous poem of the higher kind produced
in England during the present century. The
enthusiast of the poem is descanting on the
beauty which physical labour adds to the charm of
women :—

Well, then, said Hewson, resuming ;
Laugh if you please at my novel economy ; listen to this,
    though ;
As for myself, and apart from economy wholly, believe
    me,
Never I properly felt the relation between men and
    women,
Though to the dancing-master I went perforce, for a
    quarter,
Where, in dismal quadrille, were good-looking girls in
    abundance,
Though, too, schoolgirl cousins were mine—a bevy of
    beauties—
Never (of course you will laugh, but of course all the
    same I shall say it),
Never, believe me, I knew of the feelings between men
    and women,

Till in some village fields in holidays now getting stupid,
One day sauntering "long and listless," as Tennyson has
    it,
Long and listless strolling, ungainly in hobbadiboyhood,
Chanced it my eye fell aside on a capless, bonnetless
    maiden,
Bending with three-pronged fork in a garden uprooting
    potatoes.
Was it the air? who can say? or herself, or the charm
    of her labour?
But a new thing was in me; and longing delicious
    possessed me,
Longing to take her and lift her, and put her away from
    her slaving.
Was it embracing or aiding was most in my mind? hard
    question!
But a new thing was in me; I, too, was a youth among
    maidens:
Was it the air? who can say? but in part 'twas the
    charm of the labour.
Still, though a new thing was in me, the poets revealed
    themselves to me,
And in my dreams by Miranda, her Ferdinand, often I
    wandered,
Though all the fuss about girls, the giggling and toying
    and coying,
Were not so strange as before, so incomprehensible purely;
Still, as before (and as now), balls, dances, and evening
    parties,
Shooting with bows, going shopping together, and hear-
    ing them singing,
Dangling beside them, and turning the leaves on the
    dreary piano,
Offering unneeded arms, performing dull farces of escort,
Seemed like a sort of unnatural up-in-the-air balloon-
    work
(Or what to me is as hateful, a riding about in a carriage),

Utter removal from work, mother earth, and the objects
   of living.
Hungry and fainting for food, you ask me to join you in
   snapping—
What but a pink-paper comfit, with motto romantic
   inside it?
Wishing to stock me a garden, I'm sent to a table of
   nosegays;
Better a crust of black bread than a mountain of paper
   confections,
Better a daisy in earth than a dahlia cut and gathered,
Better a cowslip with root than a prize carnation without
   it.
That I allow, said Adam.

              But he, with the bit in his teeth, scarce
Breathed a brief moment, and hurried exultingly on
   with his rider,
Far over hillock, and runnel, and bramble, away in the
   champaign,
Snorting defiance and force, the white foam flecking his
   flanks, the
Rein hanging loose to his neck, and head projecting
   before him.
Oh, if they knew and considered, unhappy ones! Oh,
   could they see, could
But for a moment discern, how the blood of true gallantry
   kindles,
How the old knightly religion, the chivalry semi-quixotic,
Stirs in the veins of a man at seeing some delicate
   woman
Serving him, toiling—for him, and the world; some
   tenderest girl, now
Over-weighted, expectant, of him, is it? who shall, if
   only
Duly her burden be lightened, not wholly removed from
   her, mind you,

Lightened if but by the love, the devotion man only can
    offer,
Grand on her pedestal rise as urn-bearing statue of
    Hellas ;—
Oh, could they feel at such moments how man's heart, as
    into Eden
Carried anew, seems to see, like the gardener of earth
    uncorrupted,
Eve from the hand of her Maker advancing, an help meet
    for him,
Eve from his own flesh taken, a spirit restored to his
    spirit,
Spirit but not spirit only, himself whatever himself is,
Unto the mystery's end sole helpmate meet to be with
    him ;—
Oh, if they saw it and knew it ; we soon should see them
    abandon
Boudoir, toilette, carriage, drawing-room, and ball-room,
Satin for worsted exchange, gros-de-naples for plain
    linsey-woolsey,
Sandals of silk for clogs, for health lackadaisical fancies !
So, feel women, not dolls ; so feel the sap of existence
Circulate up through their roots from the far-away centre
    of all things,
Circulate up from the depths to the bud on the twig that
    is topmost !
Yes, we should see them delighted, delighted ourselves in
    the seeing,
Bending with blue cotton gown skirted up over striped
    linsey-woolsey,
Milking the kine in the field, like Rachel, watering cattle,
Rachel, when at the well the predestined beheld and
    kissed her,
Or, with pail upon head, like Dora beloved of Alexis,
Comely, with well-poised pail over neck arching soft to
    the shoulders,
Comely in gracefullest act, one arm uplifted to stay it,

Home from the river or pump moving stately and calm
  to the laundry ; ⁄
Ay, doing household work, as many sweet girls I have
  looked at,
Needful household work, which some one, after all, must
  do,
Needful, graceful therefore, as washing, cooking, and
  scouring,
Or, if you please, with the fork in the garden uprooting
  potatoes.

That is not a picture of love, but a picture of the
initial stages of love, and of that which often prevents love from ripening.   Nor can such a picture
be popular while the mind shrinks from looking in
the face the poor beginnings of its own highest
powers.   One day, however, Clough will vindicate
the justice of Mr. Lowell's judgment on him, though
that day may not be yet.   Arnold will, perhaps,
grow to even greater popularity before the growth
of Clough's popularity begins.   But begin it will,
and wax, too, to a point as high, perhaps, as Arnold's
ever will be, for Clough's rapture and exultation,
when they reach their highest points, are beyond
the rapture and exultation of Arnold, though his
music is less carefully modulated, and his pictures
less exquisitely framed.

AMIEL AND CLOUGH

Mrs. Humphrey Ward, in the interesting introduction which she prefixes to her beautiful translation of *Amiel's Journal*, indicates, though not as I should have been disposed to do, the close analogy between Amiel's dread of practical life and Clough's dread of practical life. And there certainly was a close analogy, as well as a wide difference between their views. Amiel, it is clear, never did anything at all equal to his powers, through a jealous regard for his own intellectual independence. He could not bear to commit himself to any practical course which would mortgage, as it were, his intellectual freedom. "The life of thought alone," he wrote, "seems to me to have enough elasticity and immensity to be free enough from the irreparable; practical life makes me afraid." And yet he knew that a certain amount of practical life was essential even to a true intellectual life, only he was anxious to reduce that practical life to a minimum, in order that the intellectual life might remain as free as possible.

Clough, too, had ₂the greatest distrust of the practical ties into which he felt that the tenderness of his nature would bring him. The whole drift of his *Amours de Voyage* was to show that fidelity to the intellectual vision is inconsistent with the class

316

of connections into which the sentiments of a tender
heart bring men; not only inconsistent with them,
but so superior to them, that sooner or later the
intellect would assert its independence and break
through the dreams to which, under the influence
of feeling, men submit themselves. The difference
between the two men's views was in substance this
—Amiel rather condemned himself for his fastidious
assertion of intellectual freedom, and held that had
his character been stronger, he would have embarked
more boldly on practical life, and would have made
a better use of his talents in consequence; Clough,
on the contrary, rather condemned himself for the
weakness that allowed him to drift into the closer
human ties. He speaks of them as more or less
unreal, as more or less illusions, out of which he
must some day recover, and return to the assertion
of his intellectual freedom. Amiel reproached
himself for not trusting his instincts more, and for
living the self-conscious life so much; Clough
reproached himself for letting his instincts dispose
of him so much, and for not resisting the illusions
into which his instincts betrayed him. It is very
curious to compare the different modes in which the
Genevan student of Hegelian philosophy and the
English student of Greek thought, writing at very
nearly the same time, express the same profound
terror of embarrassing themselves by all sorts of ties
with the narrowness and imperfections of the human
lot. To Amiel's case, however, in spite of the moral
self-reproach with which he viewed his intellectual
fastidiousness, it was undoubtedly in great measure
the contagion of Hegelian Pantheism which made
him fancy that he could identify himself with the
universal soul of things; and, on the other hand,

it was the timidity of an excessive moral sensitiveness which made it intolerable to him to enter into
the very heart of practical life, with the fear before
his eyes that he might create for himself a lifelong
regret by taking an irreparable false step. This,
he seems to say, was the reason why he never
married, just as it was in part the reason why
Clough, in his *Amours de Voyage*, makes his hero
reproach himself for his desire to marry. Amiel
felt that to enter into a relation of which he had the
highest ideal, and then to find it far below his ideal,
would entail on him a shame and remorse which he
would simply be unable to endure. And at the
very close of his life, he writes, with much less of
his usual feeling of self-reproach, a sort of defence
of his own detachment from the world. He
declares that to have done anything voluntarily,
which should bring upon him an inner shame,
would have been unendurable to him. " I think,"
he says, "I fear shame worse than death. Tacitus
said, 'Omnia serviliter pro dominatione.' My tendency is just the contrary. Even when it is voluntary,
dependence is a burden to me. I should blush to
find myself determined by interest, submitting to
constraint, or becoming the slave of any will whatever. To me, vanity is slavery, self-love degrading,
and utilitarianism meanness. I detest the ambition
that makes you the liege man of something or some
one—I desire simply to be my own master. If I
had health, I should be the freest man I know.
Although perhaps a little hardness of heart would
be desirable to make me still more independent . . .
I only desire what I am able for; and in this way I
run my head against no wall, I cease even to be
conscious of the boundaries which enslave me. I

take care to wish for rather less than is in my power,
that I may not even be reminded of the obstacles
in my way. Renunciation is the safeguard of
dignity. Let us strip ourselves if we would not be
stripped." There you have the moral secret of
Amiel's pride without the self-blame with which he
usually accompanied it. His pride was due partly
to a moral dread of incurring responsibilities he
could not bear,—"responsibility," he said, "is my
moral nightmare,"—and partly to the dread of
appearing ridiculous and contemptible to himself if
he could find himself unequal to them. That reminds me very much of the spirit which Cardinal
Newman, as a young man,—before he entered his
great Tractarian mission,—rebuked in himself :—

> Time was I shrank from what was right
> From fear of what was wrong ;
> I would not brave the sacred fight
> Because the foe was strong.

> But now I cast that finer sense
> And sorer shame aside ;
> Such dread of sin was indolence,
> Such aim at Heaven was pride.

Amiel's feeling is absolutely described in these lines,
though the keen censure cast upon it by Dr.
Newman was probably not reflected—at least in
the latter part of his career—in Amiel's own
conscience. But, as I have already hinted, there
was doubtless another and a more intellectual
strand of feeling—the deep impression that by
binding himself in a number of complex relations to
only half-known or utterly unknown human beings,
—to persons who might disappoint him bitterly,

and to children unborn who might turn out anything but beings to whom he could sustain the close
tie of fatherhood—he should fritter away the
power of reverie in which he took such delight.
Under the spell of some of the more ambitious
German philosophies, he fancied he could identify
himself with the soul of things; and this dreaming
power he valued, as it seems to me, much beyond
its real worth, if indeed that worth were real at
all :—

My privilege is to be the spectator of my own life-
drama, to be fully conscious of the tragi-comedy of my
own destiny, and, more than that, to be in the secret of
the tragi-comedy itself—that is to say, to be unable to
take my illusions seriously, to see myself, so to speak, from
the theatre on the stage, or to be like a man looking
from beyond the tomb into existence.   I feel myself forced
to feign a particular interest in my individual part, while
all the time I am living in the confidence of the poet
who is playing with all these agents which seem so
important, and knows all that they are ignorant of.   It
is a strange position, and one which becomes painful as
soon as grief obliges me to betake myself once more to
my own little rôle, binding me closely to it, and warning
me that I am going too far in imagining myself, because
of my conversations with the poet, dispensed from taking
up again my modest part of valet in the piece.   Shakespeare must have experienced this feeling often, and
"Hamlet," I think, must express it somewhere.   It is a
Doppelgäugerie, quite German in character, and which
explains the disgust with reality, and the repugnance
to public life, so common among the thinkers of
Germany.   There is as it were a degradation, a Gnostic
fall in thus folding one's wings and going back again
into the vulgar shell of one's own individuality.   Without
grief, which is the string of this venturesome kite, man

would soar too quickly and too high, and the chosen souls would be lost to the race, like balloons which, save for gravitation, would never return from the empyrean.

This passage gives the intellectual facet of the moral feeling at the root of Amiel's "finer sense" and "sorer shame"—the moral feeling that made him shrink from all sorts of practical responsibility, lest he should undertake what was beyond him, or lose his complete detachment from the narrowness of life. The two feelings together—the love of reverie in the larger sense, and the dread of responsibility, —sealed up his life almost hermetically in his own bosom, and made him a stranger to the world. He longed to free himself from the narrow shell of his own individuality, and consequently dreaded accepting duties and obligations which would have made that individuality more definite and more oppressive. And yet Amiel felt himself tied down to this narrower life by one string which he could not ignore. When he felt the touch of grief, which, as Mrs. Browning says, is something more than love, since "grief, indeed, is love, and grief besides," then he was aware that he was hemmed within the conditions of a distinct individual lot, that he was seeking something which he could not obtain, while yet he could not suppress, or even wish to suppress, his desire to obtain it. Grief brought home to him the strict limits of his individuality as nothing else brought them home. He could deny himself the more intimate ties of life, but he could not deny himself grief for the severance of such ties as he had. He could not soar above his own individual nature when his heart was bleeding. Then he felt that it was not for him to look at his own life with an impartial imagination, as he would look at any other person's, or as Shakespeare might have looked at one of the characters he had created; for then he felt that throb of anguish which he could not evade by any soaring or imaginative wings, however lofty and free the flight. His intellect was held captive by his griefs,—otherwise, as he said, he might almost have lost his individuality in the ecstacy of reverie.

Clough's attitude of mind towards these practical ties, of which he, too, dreaded the constraining power, was very different. He evidently regarded the intellectual life as the true life, and the life of ordinary man as more or less a condescension to conditions within which his nature could never suffer itself to be long confined. He looked at the actual experience of his sensitive and tender nature with a little amusement and a good deal of contempt. This is how he makes his hero lecture himself, for instance, when he finds himself gradually falling in love :—

Yes, I am going, I feel it,—I feel and cannot recall it,—
Fusing with this thing and that, entering into all sorts
    of relations,
Tying I know not what ties, which whatever they are,
    I know one thing,
Will and must, woe is me, be one day painfully broken—
Broken with painful remorses, with shrinkings of soul
    and relentings,
Foolish delays, more foolish evasions, most foolish
    renewals,
But I have made the step, have quitted the ship of
    Ulysses.
Quitted the sea and the shore, passed into the magical
    island ;
Yet on my lips is the *moly*, medicinal, offered of Hermes.

I have come into the precinct, the labyrinth closes
   around me,
Path into path rounding slyly; I pace slowly on, and
   the fancy,
Struggling awhile to sustain the long sequences, weary,
   bewildered,
Fain must collapse in despair ; I yield, I am lost, and
   know nothing ;
Yet in my bosom unbroken remaineth the clue ; I shall
   use it.
Lo, with the rope on my loins I descend through the
   fissure, I sink, yet
Inly secure in the strength of invisible arms up above
   me ;
Still, wheresoever I swing, wherever to shore, or to
   shelf, or
Floor of cavern untrodden, shell sprinkled, enchanting,
   I know I
Yet shall one time feel the strong cord tighten about
   me,—
Feel it, relentless, upbear me from spots I would rest in ;
   and though the
Rope swing wildly, I faint, crags wound me, from crag
   unto crag re-
Bounding, or, wide in the void, I die ten deaths, ere the
   end I
Yet shall plant firm foot on the broad lofty spaces I
   quit, shall
Feel underneath me again the great massy strengths of
   abstraction,
Look yet abroad from the height o'er the sea whose
   salt wave I have tasted.

Evidently to Clough's mind "the great massy
strengths of abstraction" were the levels on which
he could tread firmly, while all the experiences he
was destined to undergo in the region of feeling

were a sort of illusion, a sort of dream. To Amiel, grief was the cord that kept him from soaring into aimless reverie. To Clough, thought was the rope that kept him from sinking into the enchantments of a world of illusions. He trusted his thoughts, not his feelings. Clough's feelings charmed him away from the life of thought, and thought brought him home again to the real and solid. Amiel's thoughts charmed him away from the life of feeling, and his feelings brought him home again to the real and solid.

Was either of them right? I should say not. Thought undoubtedly does correct, with most salutary inseparability, the illusions of feeling. And, again, feeling does correct, and correct with equally salutary inseparability, the day-dreams of thought. The man who habitually distrusts his feelings is just as certain to live in a world of illusions as the man who habitually distrusts his thoughts. But undoubtedly Amiel, who allowed the illusions of imaginative reverie and intellectual freedom to govern his career much more absolutely than Clough allowed his faith in "the massy strengths of abstraction" to govern his career, made the greater mistake of the two. Had Amiel not been so sedulous to ward off the pressure of re- sponsibilities to which he did not feel fully equal, he might doubtless have made mistakes, and entered into relations which he would have found painful to him and a shock to his ideal. But the truth is those relations, which are not all we desire them to be in human life, which are not ideal relations, are of the very essence of the discipline of the will and of the affections, and no man ever yet escaped them without escaping one of the most useful experiences of human life. Amiel, like Clough, was far too much afraid of hampering the free play of his intellect. No man ever yet did great work in the world without hampering the free play of his intellect. And yet it is no paradox to say that no man ever yet had the highest command of his intellect who had not, times without number, hampered its free play, in order that he might enter more deeply into the deeper relations of the human heart.

BENJAMIN JOWETT

THOSE who wish to know what the late Master of Balliol really was, should not content themselves with reading Mr. Lionel Tollemache's very interesting sketch of him, which has just been republished with additions by Edward Arnold, but should study also the *College Sermons*, which the Dean of Ripon has just edited and Mr. Murray published. Mr. Tollemache, who himself evidently agrees more with the sceptical side of Jowett than with his spiritual side, more with his head than with his heart, tells us very justly that the secret of his friend's unique fascination lay in this, that while his head was the head of a sceptic, his heart was the heart of a saint; but he does not add what I think is the truth, and was almost equally of his essence, that while those who felt fascinated by the saint were sure to hear from him reproofs that came from the sceptic, those who were fascinated by the sceptic were sure to hear from him reproofs that came from the saint. In the present state of English religion nothing is more remarkable than the almost equal balance in many minds between Tennyson's "Two Voices." Mr. Tollemache has happily prefixed to his sketch three verses from

that beautiful poem, the most characteristic of
which tells us of men—

> Who, rowing hard against the stream,
> Saw distant gates of Eden gleam,
> And did not dream it was a dream.

Jowett can hardly be described as "rowing hard
against the stream," for he alternately drifted with
it and rowed against it; but to those who drifted
with it he seemed to be rowing against it, and to
those who rowed against it he seemed to be drifting
with it. Mr. Tollemache tells us that Jowett once
said of one of the apologists for Christianity, "He
is trying to pitch the standard of belief too high
for the present age." That exactly describes what
Jowett endeavoured, with his whole strength, to
avoid. He tried, on the contrary, to pitch the
standard of belief just as high as he thought the
present age would bear, but no higher. He endeavoured to hit the present age between wind and
water, between the incredulity of scientific doubt
with its higher criticism, and the faith of the
believing heart. He was a Platonist who could not
endure the naked and negative school of incredulous
criticism, but who was equally unable to endure
the devout paradoxes of the saintly believer. He
encouraged his pupils to seek success in the worldly
sense, success in their professions, success in their
ambitions, success in their intellectual endeavours.
But he had no sooner persuaded them to aim at
such success than he added, in the true spirit of
the saint, "But what is success? not in the mere
vulgar sense of the term, as when we speak of men
succeeding in life who obtain riches, honours, great
offices, or preferments; but what is success in the

higher sense, the success of the mind, if I may use such a term, in which man is raised not only above other men, but above himself; in which he becomes more and more his own master, and is not over-powered by circumstances, but is lord over them." (*College Sermons*, p. 250.) The two voices are heard even in this attempt to raise the standard of young men's ambitions, for Jowett goes on to say that his hearers should not fix their minds too exclusively on the higher kind of success :—

Not excluding, then, this humble care of making a livelihood, I will ask once more, What is success; and what idea of it shall we propose to ourselves? To have carried out some one purpose or design during twenty or thirty years, to have contributed sensibly to the happiness of others, or to have kept a family together; to have obtained a fair share of this world's goods; to have added something real, if not very great, to the stock of human knowledge; to have been a good teacher; to have succeeded in a profession and yet to have risen above it; —whoever seeks or obtains any of these aims cannot be said to have lived in vain; as the world goes, he may fairly claim to be called a successful man. There may be success of a still higher kind, of which I will hereafter say a few words. But speaking generally, the above may be regarded as a tolerably accurate description of what men call success in life such as we should desire for ourselves or our friends.

There the Master of Balliol was very careful not "to pitch his standard too high for the present age." But he recurs to the higher strain before he concludes :—

The considerations which have been placed before you in this sermon relate chiefly to our earthly life, and yet they may receive correction and enlargement from the thought of another. For there is an eternal element even in worldly success, when, amid all the rivalries of this world, a man has sought to live according to the will of God, and not according to the opinion of men. Whatever there was of justice, of purity, or disinterestedness in him, or Christ-like virtue, or resignation, or love of the truth, shall never pass away. When a man feels that earthly rewards are but for a moment, and that his true self and true life have yet to appear; when he recognises that the education of the individual beginning here is continued hereafter, and, like the education of the human race, is ever going on; when he is conscious that he is part of a whole, and himself and all other creatures are in the hands of God;—then his mind may be at rest: he has nothing more to fear; he has attained to peace, and is equally fit to live or die.

Yet no one would, I think, gather from Mr. Tollemache's little book that he often pressed the more saintly view of life upon his pupils with as much earnestness as passages of this last kind embody. The difference between Tennyson's "Two Voices" and Jowett's "Two Voices" was this, that while Tennyson intended to make the higher voice silence the lower, Jowett intended to reconcile them so far as "The heavy and the weary weight of all this unintelligible world" would admit of their reconciliation.

Now, as a matter of fact, these two voices hardly do admit of complete reconciliation. And Jowett's fascination for the more eager spirits of our modern life consisted in his readiness to talk, and to talk earnestly, in both strains. Even intellectually he spoke with both voices. No question could be more critical for the ethical ideal of our life than the question of Determinism and Free-will, and even there he followed the cue of his great master and sided with Plato, who, while an idealist in all his yearnings, was a determinist in his theory. There is no passage in Mr. Tollemache's little sketch more characteristic than his account of Jowett's attitude on the question of Determinism and Free-will. Mr. Tollemache tells us that Jowett sometimes, as in his essay on Casuistry, seemed to recommend acquiescence in conventional morality, but sometimes "faced about and became a moralist of the first water" (p. 118). And then he goes on to give us this characteristic story :—

Another question bearing on that of the heinousness of sin is the question of Philosophical Necessity. One of the " stodgy questions " which, as an undergraduate, I put to Jowett was whether he believed in Necessity or in Free-will. *J.*—" I believe in Necessity in the sense of believing that our actions are determined by motives." *T.*—" That admission seems to me to cover the entire ground. But would it do to act on the belief ?" *J.*—(laughing)—" If we begin to act on the belief, we shall have to turn you out of the College. (More seriously) No, whatever one may think about the abstract question, one does not mean that it is the same thing to be walking along the street of one's Free-will and to be dragged along it against one's will. Necessity, when rightly understood, remains a sort of theory in the background, and one acts in much the same way whether one believes in it or not."

Yet, if it be true, as Jowett once said in his introduction to Plato's *Phædo*, that " we are more certain of our ideas of truth and right than we are of the existence of God," it must be evident that the conviction that we are all determined by our motives, and never determine them for ourselves, would *over-*

ride our religious feelings and the authority of our consciences, instead of submitting itself to the authority of conscience. Jowett was always attempting to reconcile the language of the higher of Tennyson's "Two Voices" to the lower, but always failed in the attempt. Mr. Tollemache recognises this somewhat too clearly for a "disciple," unless he really thinks that it is right to acquire a certain "obliquity of vision," for he says in one place that Jowett "tried to be a philosopher, moralist, and preceptor all at once. As a philosopher, he looked at the world from the outside, and, so looking, he dimly perceived—or (what is much the same thing) he was conscious of trying not to perceive—that all is vanity. As a moralist he looked at the world from the inside, and almost convinced himself that all is an intense reality. I hope it is not an overstrained metaphor to add that, if he looked at the world with one eye, as it were, from the outside, and with the other eye from the inside, the result could hardly fail to be an occasional obliquity of mental vision." And in another place he says that Jowett let his two jarring personalities "go careering about in opposite directions," and concludes that "to any logical disciple of Jowett's, as well as to any disciple of Pattison's, the sense of sin has a ghostly impressiveness, and indeed has much in common with the representation of a ghost on the stage,— he distinctly sees it, but *also he sees through it*" (p. 125).

Yet Jowett's heart sometimes completely mastered his head. In the singularly touching and much more than pathetic, almost overwhelming, message which he sent to the College from his sick-bed in October 1891, the higher of Tennyson's "Two Voices" is heard in lonely supremacy, and there is no attempt at all to reconcile it with the lower voice. He begins with a message, but the message soon passes into a prayer, which is all the more overpowering for the perfectly simple and unpretentious accent with which it opens :—

Most of us have been wanting in the clear desire and wish to serve God and our fellow-men. At the critical times of life we have not done justice to ourselves. We have not tried enough to see ourselves as we are, or to know the world as it truly is. We have drifted with society, instead of forming independent principles of our own. We have thought too much of ourselves, and of what is being said about us. We have cared more for the opinion of others than for the truth. We have not loved others in all classes of society as Thou, O Lord, hast loved us. We have not thanked Thee sufficiently for the treasures of knowledge, and for the opportunities of doing good which Thou hast given us in this latter day. We have worried ourselves too much about the religious gossip of the age, and have not considered enough the fixed forms of truth. We have been indolent, and have made many excuses for falling short in Thy work. And now, O Lord, in these difficult times, when there is a seeming opposition of knowledge and faith, and an accumulation of facts beyond the power of the human mind to conceive ; and good men of all religions, more and more, meet in Thee ; and the strife between classes in society, and between good and evil in our own souls, is not less than of old ; and the love of pleasure and the desire of the flesh are always coming in between us and Thee ; and we cannot rise above these things to see the light of Heaven, but are tossed upon a sea of troubles ;— we pray Thee be our guide, and strength, and light, that, looking up to Thee always, we may behold the rock on which we stand, and be confident in the word which Thou hast spoken.

I hardly know any other passage in the literature of our religious life which is more subduing in the simplicity of its adoration than that.   It seems to embody the whole drift of the Apostle John's language—"The world passeth away and the lust thereof, but he that doeth the will of God abideth for ever."   Surely that is not only a victory of faith, but a retractation, like one of St Augustine's retractations, of much that Jowett had said when he earnestly endeavoured not to pitch "the standard of faith too high for the present age."   Here judgment is passed on "the highest criticism of the age," and the decision of what he had sometimes treated as "the Ultimate Court of Appeal" is solemnly reversed.

A GREAT POET OF DENIAL AND REVOLT

NOT many years ago Sir Joseph Arnould, one of our Bombay judges, decided a suit in favour of the heir of the Chief of "the Assassins,"—the man known and feared among the Crusaders as "the Old Man of the Mountain." I have now before me a translation of one of the great poems of the world, written apparently by the intimate college friend, as we might say, of "the old Man of the Mountain" in question, Omar Khayyám, a great Persian astronomer, who rectified the Calendar, and was educated by the same Mohammedan sage as that Hassan of sinister celebrity to whom I have referred. The story, preserved by a grand vizier of the Sultan of Khorassan, is that he himself, Hassan, and this Omar Khayyám, subsequently the poet-astronomer of whom I am writing, made a boyish league together that whichever of them prospered in life should share his wealth equally with his two friends. Nizam-ul-Mulk was the fortunate one in question, rising, as I have said, to be grand vizier of the Sultan, and his friends claimed his performance of the promise : Hassan asking wealth and office, and betraying his friend when it was granted, even to the point, it is said, of afterwards ordering, as Chief of the Assassins,

334

the assassination of his patron ; and Omar Khayyám asking only protection, leisure, and a moderate competence, to enable him to study and think in peace. It was he who composed the wonderful poem of which Mr. Edward Fitzgerald's marvellously fine translation now lies before me,—together with Mr. Schütz-Wilson's interesting essay in the *Contemporary Review*, which has called the attention of English literary men to it not too soon, for indeed it is somewhat a disgrace to us that such a translation of such a poem should have been amongst us for fifteen years without becoming generally known.

I cannot, however, agree with Mr. Schütz-Wilson's estimate of the poem in other respects. It should, I think, take rank rather as the poem of Revolt and Denial, the song of speculative Nihilism and cynical sensualism, than as a poem of the stamp which the *Contemporary* Reviewer claims for it,— namely, one which "denies divinely the divine," and is full of "the unconscious faith which complains to the Deity of its inability to comprehend the divine." Of this character I confess that I cannot find a trace in Mr. Edward Fitzgerald's magnificent translation,—a translation which confessedly selects all the finest verses of the Oriental poem, and leaves only the most sensual still under the veil of the Persian original. With something of the cynical force of Byron, and something, too, of the humorous and familiar ease of Goethe, the writer of this poem (though a contemporary, as Mr. Schütz-Wilson reminds us, of Henry II. and fair Rosamond) expends his whole power in showing what a mockery of man is implied in irreversible laws of creation ; and he accomplishes his task with all the grasp of a thinker of first-rate calibre and all the bitterness of a defiant heart. As for nobleness in any moral sense, it seems to me utterly absent from this fine poem, which of course should be judged by a Mohammedan, and not by a Christian standard. What we have to ask of a poet of this grasp and depth of reflectiveness is this,—has he seized and kept faithful to the nobler elements in the religion in which he was brought up, while revolting against its unrealities and insincerities? Is the defiance due only to refusing to believe a lie, or is it due also to impatience of the yoke of a spiritual restraint? Now, when even a Mohammedan poet has nothing to preach but the intolerableness of the iron law of necessity, the wisdom of plunging into sensual delights, and the futility of spiritual hopes, it seems to me pretty certain that his defiance is compounded equally of affinity for what is evil in Mohammedanism and resistance of what is good in it,—a scorn for its incredible conception of a despotic Omnipotence, and of impatience of its actual demands for sobriety and justice. Add to this that Omar Khayyám was, as I have already said, a great astronomer, who rectified the Calendar by a correction better than that which determined the Julian year, and little inferior to that which determined the Gregorian, and that in spite of his love of science and knowledge of it, through the whole of this poem there runs no less cynical a scorn of the speculative intellect than of the moral law, and we shall have some reason to suppose that while Mohammedanism was unquestionably far too small for his intellect, it was not the mere narrowness of that creed which induced him to rebel against it, but also some of its imperious demands on his better nature.   Also, had he been a true disciple of the sciences into which he had plunged so deeply, he would at least have maintained the grandeur of speculative truth against the rude fatalism of the Mohammedan system, which, however, he certainly does not do, for, as a poet at least, Omar had no respect for human knowledge. He writes :—

LV

You know, my Friends, with what a brave carouse
I made a second marriage in my house ;
   Divorced old barren Reason from my bed,
And took the daughter of the Vine to spouse.

.   .   .   .   .   .

LVII

Ah, but my computations, people say,
Reduce the year to better reckoning ?   Nay,
   'Twas only striking from the Calendar
Unborn to-morrow and dead yesterday.

LVIII

And lately, by the tavern-door agape,
Came shining through the dusk an Angel-shape
   Bearing a vessel on his shoulder ; and
He bid me taste of it ; and 'twas—the Grape !

LIX

The Grape that can with logic absolute
The two-and-seventy jarring Sects confute ;
   The sovereign Alchemist that in a trice
Life's leaden metal into gold transmute :

LX

The mighty Mahmúd, Allah-breathing Lord
That all the misbelieving and black horde
  Of fears and visions that infest the soul,
Scatters before him with his whirlwind sword.

LXI

Why, be this juice the growth of God, who dared
Blaspheme the twisted tendril as a snare ?
  A blessing, we should use it, should we not ?
And if a curse—why, then, who set it there ?

LXII

I must abjure the balm of Life, I must,
Scared by some After-reckoning ta'en on trust,
  Or lured with hope of some diviner drink,
To fill the cup—when crumbled into dust !

LXIII

Oh, threats of Hell and hopes of Paradise !
One thing at least is certain—*this* life flies ;
  One thing is certain, and the rest is lies ;
The flower that once has blown for ever dies.

That is not the song of the sage whose reason has
merely broken through the trammels of a narrow
system, but of one who has lost his faith in
reason as much as he has lost it in moral law,—
and partly, perhaps, on the same ground,—that
the yoke of both was irksome to him.

The finest thread in the poem, in a moral sense,
is the vibrating chord of tenderness for the frailty
of human existence which rings through it. In

this respect there is no cynicism.   The advice to
eat and drink, for to-morrow we die, which is the
burden of the song from beginning to end, at least
does not choke the poet's pity for those who have
eaten and drunk and died, and who, he thinks,
have vanished like bubbles from the surface of
the stream.   There is a real passion, for instance,
in the tone of these fine verses on the frailty of
human hopes and joys :—

XVI

The worldly hope men set their hearts upon
Turns ashes—or it prospers ; and anon,
    Like snow upon the desert's dusty face
Lighting a little hour or two, was gone.

XVII

Think, in this batter'd caravanserai
Whose portals are alternate night and day,
    How sultan after sultan with his pomp
Abode his destined hour, and went his way.

XVIII

They say the lion and the lizard keep
The courts where Jamshýd gloried and drank deep ;
    And Bahrám, that great hunter—the wild ass
Stamps o'er his head but cannot break his sleep.

XIX

I sometimes think that never blows so red
The Rose as where some buried Cæsar bled ;
    That every hyacinth the garden wears
Dropt in her lap from some once lovely head.

XX

And this reviving herb whose tender green
Hedges the river-lip on which we lean—
     Ah, lean upon it lightly! for who knows
From what once lovely lip it springs unseen !

The tenderness of that last verse, with its Oriental
turn of expression, is as exquisite as any touch I
know in poetry of the same stamp.   But the
tenderness of Omar for extinguished happiness,
though it shows a kindly heart, is not, as far as I
can see, at all akin to the love which is too intense
to believe the world a mockery,—too humble to
believe that there is no better love at the source
of things than exists in an ephemeral human heart.
On the contrary, the lyrical pain with which Omar
contemplates the evanescence of all human joy
is not so deep but what it is assuaged by the
tribute of a poetical tear, after which it loses
itself in its usual burden of *carpe diem*, which it
repeats this time with even more than usual ardour.
This is the verse which follows the tender regrets
I have just quoted :—

XXI

Ah ! my belovéd, fill the cup that clears
To-DAY of past regret and future fears ;
     To-MORROW ?—why, to-morrow I may be
Myself with yesterday's seven thousand years.

Great as is Omar's command of all the imagery
of human despondency, it takes a great deal of
imagination to find in this poem, as Mr. Schutz-
Wilson finds in it, "the unconscious faith which
complains to the Deity of its inability to com-

prehend the divine." If there be any passage
which approaches such faith at all, it is perhaps
this :—

XLIX

Would you that spangle of existence spend
About THE SECRET ? quick about it, friend !
   A hair, perhaps, divides the false and true,
And upon what, prithee, does life depend ?

L

A hair, perhaps, divides the false and true ;
Yes, and a single Aleph were the clue—
   Could you but find it—to the treasure-house ;
And peradventure to *the Master* too—

LI

Whose secret presence, through creation's veins
Running quicksilver-like, eludes your pains ;
   Taking all shapes from Máh to Máhi ; and
They change and perish all—but He remains.

LII

A moment guessed—then back behind the fold,
Immerst of darkness round the drama rolled,
   Which for the pastime of eternity,
He does Himself contrive, enact, behold.

But even here the theism, or rather pantheism,
which is certainly asserted or approached, takes
a cynical turn, and the whole stage of life is said
to be a drama enacted for the pastime of eternity.
That is infinitely lower in tone than the noble
pantheism of Shelley, which in mode of thought
it so closely approaches :—

The One remains, the many change and pass,
　Heaven's light for ever shines, Earth's shadows fly ;
Life like a dome of many-coloured glass
　Stains the white radiance of Eternity.

But if Omar does not approach even Shelley in the reverence with which he views the power which runs through all the arteries and minute veins of life, certainly Shelley never expressed with anything like Omar's magnificence of grasp, and hardly did Professor Tyndall, or any other prophet of the "potentialities" of matter, even imagine, as he has done, the true emptiness of the world regarded in the light in which modern materialism regards it, as the vain pageantry engendered by a store of Proteus-like physical force :—

LXIV

Strange, is it not ? that of the myriads who
Before us passed the door of darkness through,
　Not one returns to tell us of the road,
Which to discover we must travel too.

LXV

The revelations of devout and learn'd
Who rose before us, and as prophets burn'd,
　Are all but stories which, awoke from sleep,
They told their fellows and to sleep return'd.

LXVI

I set my soul through the invisible,
Some letter of that after-life to spell,
　And by-and-by my soul returned to me
And answered, " I myself am heaven and hell."

LXVII

Heaven but the vision of fulfill'd desire,
And hell the shadow of a soul on fire,
    Cast on the darkness into which ourselves,
So late emerged from, shall so soon expire.

LXVIII

We are no other than a moving row
Of magic shadow-shapes that come and go
    Round with this sun-illumin'd lantern held
In midnight by the master of the show.

LXIX

Important pieces of the game he plays
Upon this chequer-board of nights and days;
    Hither and thither moves, and checks, and slays,
And one by one back in the closet lays.

LXX

The ball no question makes of Ayes or Noes,
But right or left as strikes the player goes,
    And he that tossed you down into the field—
He knows about it all, he knows, he knows.

LXXI

The moving finger writes, and having writ,
Moves on; nor all your piety and wit
    Shall lure it back to cancel half a line
Nor all your tears wash out a word of it.

LXXII

And that inverted bowl they call the sky,
Whereunder crawling coop'd we live and die;
    Lift not your hands to *it* for help—for it
As impotently rolls as you or I.

LXXIII

With earth's first clay they did the last man knead,
And there of the last harvest sow'd the seed ;
  And the first morning of creation wrote
What the last dawn of reckoning shall read.

LXXIV

YESTERDAY THIS DAY'S madness did prepare
To-morrow's silence, triumph, or despair.
  Drink ! for you know not whence you came nor why,
Drink ! for you know not why you go, nor where.

There is certainly something in the Oriental imagination which surpasses all that Western imagination can effect in attempts to give a glimpse of the infinite or absolute. No poetry existing, of course, approaches the poetry of Isaiah and some of the Psalms in the sweep of its images. But this may be attributed to the divine truth which inspired the thought. Turn, then, to this far from pious poetry, the very poetry of revolt and despair, and observe with what majesty the mere infinitude of the panorama is depicted, even on the author's assumption that the whole panorama is a delusion and a snare. It is not mainly the breath of divine inspiration, I suspect, which gives to the Hebrew prophets their strange ease in conceiving the smallness of human things from a higher and wider point of view,—it is rather the Eastern imagination, which seems much better fitted than the Western for escaping from the limitations of practical life and sweeping the horizon of an infinite world. The sceptic is as much more powerful in sweeping it, from the point of view of a sceptic, as is the believer in sweeping the same universe from the point of view of a divine seer.   And yet, Oriental as he is, Omar is always modern.   Take the following wonderful conversation among the clay images of a potter's shop, which is intended to take off the speculative imbecility of man in dealing with these large problems.   First speak two clay images, who may be said to represent, suppose, the author of a Bridgewater treatise and a Universalist or Unitarian :—

LXXXIV

Said one among them, " Surely not in vain
My substance of the common earth was ta'en
   And to this figure moulded, to be broke
Or trampled back to shapeless earth again."

LXXXV

Then said a second, " Ne'er a peevish boy
Would break the bowl from which he drank in joy,
   And he that with his hand the vessel made
Will surely not in after-wrath destroy."

Whereupon some porcelain representative of the " dangerous classes " takes up the parable thus :—

LXXXVI

After a momentary silence spake
Some vessel of a more ungainly make ;
   " They sneer at me for leaning all awry,—
What ? did the hand, then, of the Potter shake ? "

After which a good-humoured Mephistopheles of Goethe's easy-going kind speaks out,—

" Why," said another, " some there are who tell
Of one who threatens he will toss to Hell
   The luckless Pots he marred in making ;—pish,
He's a good fellow and 'twill be all well ; "

surely no doubtful anticipation of the Mephisto-
phelian speech with which Goethe's "dialogue in
heaven," in the prologue to Faust, ends :—-

> Von Zeit zu Zeit seh' ich den Alten gern,
>   Und hüte mich mit ihm zu brechen,
> Es ist gar hübsch von einen grossen Herrn
>   So menschlich mit dem Teufel selbst zu sprechen.

Indeed, the easy cynicism of this conversation among
the clay pots expresses the profound scorn of the
poet for all human solutions of the great enigma in
a way which makes it really unintelligible how any
one should find a deep faith beneath the tumult of
the poet's soul. Indeed, I rather doubt the tumult.
Pity and scorn are its extreme limits,—no passion of
love or of suffering can be deciphered in it. The
great contemplative intellect of the man of science
sets itself to work to show the futility of attempting a solution of the problem of life. But, while he
drops a tear over the illusions of humanity, he remains calmly satisfied with himself for having found
none, because he is sure that there is none to be
found.

WHY MR. RUSKIN FAILED AS A POET

MISS THACKERAY gave one of her very charming books the very unpromising title of *Miss Williams' Divagations.* No better general reason why Mr. Ruskin failed as a poet can be assigned than by saying that the two heavy volumes of his poetry, which Mr. G. Allen has just published, might properly be entitled "Mr. Ruskin's Divagations." There is really no wholeness in any one of these pieces of verse, no sign, that I have seen, in any one of them of having proceeded out of a vivid imaginative conception which filled his mind and heart, and which he was eagerly struggling to embody in words. And yet Mr. Ruskin, as we all know, is a great artist in speech. Any number of passages could be extracted from his prose writings in which speech is used with the most consummate art, generally to call up some beautiful scene before the eye, sometimes to impress a true criticism on the mind, not unfrequently to satirise playfully or scornfully some weakness or worldliness of modern society. Open, for instance, his *Seven Lamps of Architecture,* and we find this passage in the chapter on "The Lamp of Memory"—analysing the effect of the memory of the past on the impressions produced by a scene in the Jura—a passage in which the

splendour of the description almost rivals the
magnificent vision which it seeks to realise for
us :—"I came out presently on the edge of the
ravine : the solemn murmur of its waters rose
suddenly from beneath, mixed with the singing of
the thrushes among the pine boughs ; and, on the
opposite side of the valley, walled all along as it
was by grey cliffs of limestone, there was a hawk
sailing slowly off their brow, touching them nearly
with his wings, and with the shadows of the pines
flickering upon his plumage from above ; but with
the fall of a hundred fathoms under his breast, and
the curling pools of the green river gliding and
glittering dizzily beneath him, their foam globes
moving with him as he flew.   It would be difficult
to conceive a scene less dependent upon any other
interest than that of its own secluded and serious
beauty ; but the writer well remembers the sudden
blankness and chill which were cast upon it when
he endeavoured, in order more strictly to arrive at
the sources of its impressiveness, to imagine it, for
a moment, a scene in some aboriginal forest of the
New Continent.   The flowers in an instant lost
their light, the river its music ; the hills became
oppressively desolate ; a heaviness in the boughs of
the darkened forest showed how much of their
former power had been dependent upon a life which
was not theirs, how much of the glory of the
imperishable, or continually renewed, creation is
reflected from things more precious in their memories
than it, in its renewing.   Those ever-springing
flowers and ever-flowing streams had been dyed by
the deep colours of human endurance, valour, and
virtue ; and the crests of the sable hills that rose
against the evening sky received a deeper worship,

because their far shadows fell eastward over the iron wall of Joux and the four-square keep of Granson." Or, again, taking up his *Modern Painters*, and, opening it almost at random, we read this fine criticism on the Venetian school of painting :—"Separate and strong like Samson, chosen from its youth, and with the Spirit of God visibly resting upon it ; like him it warred in careless strength, and wantoned in untimely pleasure. No Venetian painter ever worked with any aim beyond that of delighting the eye, or expressing fancies agreeable to himself or flattering to his nation. They could not be either unless they were religious. But he did not desire the religion. He desired the delight. The 'Assumption' is a noble picture because Titian believed in the Madonna. But he did not paint it to make any-one else believe in her. He painted it because he enjoyed rich masses of red and blue, and faces flushed with sunlight. Tintoret's 'Paradise' is a noble picture because he believed in Paradise. But he did not paint it to make any one think of Heaven, but to form a beautiful termination for the hall of the Greater Council. Other men used their effete faiths and mean faculties with a high moral purpose. The Venetians gave their most earnest faith and the lordliest faculty to gild the shadows of an ante-chamber or heighten the splendour of a holiday." Or, again, take this scornful description of the English worship of cruel energy and degraded toil contained in the criticism on Turner's picture of "The Garden of the Hesperides " :—"The greatest man on our England in the first half of the nine-teenth century, in the strength and hope of his faith, perceives this to be the thing he has to tell us of utmost moment, connected with the spiritual world. In each city and country of past time, the master-minds had to declare the chief worship which lay at the nation's heart; to define it; adorn it; show the range and authority of it. Thus in Athens we have 'The Temple of Pallas'; and in Venice 'The Assumption of the Virgin'; here in England is our great spiritual fact for ever interpreted to us,—'The Assumption of the Dragon.' No St. George any more to be heard of; no more dragon-slaying possible; this child, born on St. George's day, can only make manifest the dragon, not slay him, sea-serpent as he is, whom the English Andromeda, not fearing, takes for her lord."

Now, in passages like these there is evidently the richest affluence of artistic speech, but it is not a kind of affluence that is at all disposed to keep within the strict laws of rhyme and rhythm, or to promote that distinct unity of effect which a poem requires. When one turns to Mr. Ruskin's poems they are almost all divagations. They meander, and they meander with much less significance and continuity of purpose than his prose disquisitions, which, with all their wide offings, and their varied points of departure, and their splendid digressions, do generally converge to a definite point at last, and serve to impress some lessons or to proclaim some gospel. In his poetry it is not so; there you see a good deal of Mr. Ruskin's gentle playfulness and of his mild caprice; much more than of his evangelical zeal. His fairies and gnomes are the most arbitrary of beings; his fancies have no real life in them; his stories have no real passion; his musings no heart; and even his descriptions no fire. For example, take this bit of vituperation against the sensuality and slothfulness of a mountain population

in which Mr. Ruskin appears to be quite in earnest,
and yet expresses himself in language much more
marked by caprice than by force :—

> Have you in heaven no hope—on earth no care—
>   No foe in hell—ye things of stye and stall,
> That congregate like flies, and make the air
>   Rank with your fevered sloth—that hourly call
> The sun, which should your servant be, to bear
>   Dread witness on you, with uncounted wane
> And unregarded rays, from peak to peak
>   Of piny-gnomoned mountain moved in vain ?
> Behold, the very shadows that ye seek
>   For slumber, write along the wasted wall
> Your condemnation.   They forgot not, they,
>   Their ordered function, and determined fall,
> Nor useless perish.   But *you* count your day
>   By sins, and write your difference from clay
> In bonds you break, and laws you disobey.
>   God ! who hast given the rocks their fortitude,
>   The sap unto the forests, and their food
> And vigour to the busy tenantry
> Of happy, soulless things that wait on Thee,
> Hast Thou no blessing where Thou gav'st Thy blood ?
>   Wilt Thou not make Thy fair creation whole ?
> Behold and visit this Thy vine for good—
>   Breathe in this human dust its living soul.

" Piny-gnomoned " is an affected phrase which, I
suppose, tries to convey the idea that the shadows
of the pine-trees on the mountain-side tell the
height of the sun, much in the same way in which
the shadows of the gnomon on a sun-dial tell the
hour of the day.   But that just shows how the
fetters of verse appear to constrain Mr. Ruskin
into attempting to express what he utterly fails to
express.   In the comparative freedom of his poetic

prose he would probably have given us a telling
picture of the impressive effect of these natural
sun-dials.   He is more readable when he attempts
less, and simply chats in rhyme, as in the following
" rhyming letter " : —

I hope you will not (moved by the delay
Of mine epistle to this distant day)
Accuse me of neglect ; for if you do,
I can retort an equal blame on you :
For I, who in my study's height sublime,
See every wave of calmly passing time
Flow softly onward in one beaten track—
My only journeys into town and back—
Horace and Homer all I choose between,—
Dulwich or Norwood my sole change of scene,—
Find every hour exactly like its brother,
And scarce can tell the days from one another ;
And cannot find a single circumstance,
As I review, with a reverted glance,
The fast flown autumn months from end to end,
To fill a page, or interest ev'n a friend ;
While you, whose distant wandering steps have trod
The blue lake's glittering shingle and the sod—
The short, crisp sod, which on the mountains high
Braves the unkindness of their cloudy sky,—
Whose velvet tuftings most I love to feel
Result elastic underneath my heel—
You, sir, I say, whose eye hath wandered o'er
Bala's blue wave and Harlech's golden shore,
And seen the sun declining towards the west
Light the lone crags of Idris' triple crest,
And watched the restless waters dash and swell
By Pont y Monach—should have much to tell.

But even there, there is not only little poetry, but
at least one bathos, the extraordinary flatness of

saying that the writer likes to feel the velvet tuftings of the sod "*result* elastic" underneath his heel.   No true poet could have used the word "result" in such a context.

The truth seems to be that, instead of feeling the rhythm of metre and rhyme a stimulus to his imagination, Mr. Ruskin found it a heavy fetter upon his imagination.   His poetical prose delights in its rhetorical freedom.   He loves to pile up touches, each of which adds to the total effect; and, as a rule, the methods of rhetoric are not only not the methods of poetry, but are essentially different in kind from the methods of poetry.   Rhetoric climbs, where poetry soars.   Rhetoric takes long sweeps, where poetry concentrates its meaning in a single word.   Rhetoric loves to use a little exaggeration, where poetry has a passion for the simplicity of absolute truth.   Verse cramps the rhetorician and fires the poet.   Mr. Ruskin's prose is, I admit, the very poetry of rhetoric, but his verse is very far from being the rhetoric of poetry.   The fixed laws and restrained passion of verse do not suit his genius.   He loves a freer hand, and less urgent need to strive for unity of effect.   When he writes in verse he becomes either trivial or unnatural, because he cannot well take those wide sweeps and cumulate so freely those minute effects which are the very materials of his art.   He can chat in verse with a certain grace and playfulness.   One of the best bits I have found in his verse is the description of the shattering and morally confounding effect of a sneeze.   But when he addresses himself to any task of higher passion, he needs plenty of elbow-room, for he cannot make up by intensity and concentration for the want of space wherein to wheel and charge, as it were, against the idols which he wishes to reprobate and denounce.   Judged by his verse, Mr. Ruskin would seem to be a man without passion, and full of whimsical caprice.   Judged by his prose, there is in him a higher and richer rhetoric than any English writer, since Jeremy Taylor, has held at his command.

MR. WALTER BAGEHOT [1]

ENGLAND has lost this week a man of singular power as a political, economical, and literary thinker. And in saying a man of singular power, I do not use the word "singular" as a mere superlative to express a high degree, but in its more exact sense as expressing a very rare and, indeed, an almost unique kind of power, of which I do not know that I could anywhere find another equally well-marked example. Mr. Walter Bagehot, whose essays on finance, on banking, on economy, and on politics have so long been familiar to all the leading statesmen and politicians of England, and to many of those of France and Germany, died this day week at Langport, after two or three days' illness, at the early age of fifty-one. What we have lost in losing the further development of his political and economical principles it is, of course, impossible to conjecture; but of what *kind* that loss is, it is not difficult to say, since, of course, what we should have gained had his life been prolonged, must in all probability have been analogous to the many wise and original lessons which are contained in his various published writings. And

[1] This article on Walter Bagehot appeared in the *Economist*, dated 31st March 1877.

it happens to be easy enough to give a general conception, even in Mr. Bagehot's own words, of the special nature of those lessons.

In an essay published about a year ago in the *Fortnightly Review*—an essay which was to have been one of a series, of which I can only trust that it may still be possible to give others to the world —Mr. Bagehot spoke of the science of political economy as follows :—

It is an abstract science which labours under a special hardship. Those who are conversant with its abstractions are usually without a true contact with its facts; those who are in contact with its facts have usually little sympathy with and little cognisance of its abstractions. Literary men who write about it are constantly using what a great teacher calls " unreal words "—that is, they are using expressions with which they have no complete vivid picture to correspond. They are like physiologists who have never dissected ; like astronomers who have never seen the stars ; and, in consequence, just when they seem to be reasoning at their best, their knowledge of the facts falls short. Their primitive picture fails them, and their deduction altogether misses the mark—sometimes, indeed, goes astray so far that those who live and move among the facts boldly say that they cannot comprehend " how any one can talk such nonsense " ; while, on the other hand, those people who live and move among the facts, often, or mostly, cannot of themselves put together any precise reasonings about them. Men of business have a solid judgment, a wonderful guessing power of what is going to happen, each in his own trade ; but they have never practised themselves in reasoning out their judgments and in supporting their guesses by arguments ; probably, if they did so, some of the finer and correcter parts of their anticipations would vanish. They are like the sensible lady to whom Coleridge said,

"Madam, I accept your conclusion, but you must let me find the logic for it."

Now, what Mr. Bagehot here so vividly describes as the great defect of economical writers who have no living knowledge of business on the one hand, and of men of business who have no true mastery of economical principles on the other hand, is just the defect which his great natural faculties, his careful, theoretical studies, and his large special experience, enabled him to avoid. And this applies not merely to the subjects of which he is specially speaking in this essay, but to all those which he was accustomed to handle. Even to pure literature he brought the keen practical observations, the caustic humour, the illustrative imagination for detail, of a man of the world. Those who do not know the remarkable volume called *Estimates of some Englishmen and Scotchmen*, published now nearly twenty years ago, will find in every essay of that book, almost in every page of it, the evidence of that knowledge of the world which he brought to the illustration of literature, and evidence, too, of the powerful imagination which he brought to bear upon the world. Take, for instance, the essay on Sir Robert Peel, of which the leading idea is contained in the sentence, "A Constitutional statesman is in general a man of common opinions and uncommon abilities,"—an idea which is worked out with the same thorough knowledge of the meaning of our parliamentary system and the same dry humour, which were afterwards displayed in a still higher degree in the book on the *English Constitution*. Mr. Bagehot realised what Constitutional Government really means. He felt vividly,

as every original man has felt, what he himself
called "the tyranny of your next-door neighbour."
"What law is so cruel as the law of doing what he
does ?   What yoke is so galling as the yoke of being
like him ?"   But, unlike most original men, he could
see all the advantages of a political government
which depends on the predominance of average
opinions as conceived by men of more than average
abilities, and he followed out those advantages, and
the inevitable disadvantages associated with them,
into the whole working of the British Constitution.
"You cannot," he said, "though many people wish
you could, go into Parliament to represent yourself.
You must conform to the opinion of the electors,
and they, depend on it, will not be original."   But
it is in the book on the *English Constitution*
that Mr. Bagehot first combined his theoretical
insight with his great knowledge of life, in a manner
so methodical as to make a definite and valuable
addition to political science.   Any one who reads
that book will find the key to many criticisms
which have been found in this journal on the
great political crises of England, France, Germany,
and the United States for many years back.   Read,
for instance, the chapter in that book on the House
of Commons, and note how vividly Mr. Bagehot
makes us feel the marvel of a Constitution where
the centre of power is in a miscellaneous assembly
of 658 more or less ordinary persons, whose opinions
are necessarily conformed to those of millions of
persons even more ordinary and more ignorant than
themselves.   "Of all odd forms of government the
oddest really is government by a *public meeting*."
We see a changing body of miscellaneous persons,
sometimes few, sometimes many, never the same

for an hour ; sometimes excited, but mostly dull
and half-weary, impatient of eloquence, catching at
any joke as an alleviation. These are the persons
who rule the British Empire, who rule England, who
rule Scotland, who rule Ireland, who rule a great
deal of Asia, who rule a great deal of Polynesia,
who rule a great deal of America, and scattered
fragments everywhere." And having made his
readers see the difficulty,—as it is by no means
easy for an Englishman, who is so well used to the
phenomenon, to see it,—he shows us the conditions
—the very rare conditions if we look at the history
of the world—under which alone such a paradox is
not only possible, but beneficial : not, indeed, beneficial on every, or anything like every, subject; for,
Mr. Bagehot shows, "a free government is the most
dull government on matters its ruling classes will
not hear," but still beneficial on the whole, if only
for the political education which it diffuses.

And the happy combination of abstract principles
with a vivid knowledge of the complex facts of
political life, which Mr. Bagehot displayed in his
book on *The English Constitution*, was to a considerable, though of course not to the same, extent,
displayed also in the original little essay on
Physics and Politics, in which he showed the
analogy between the principles determining the
selection of the stronger and more enduring political
states, and the principles determining the selection
of the stronger and more enduring physical organisa-
tions. That book should be read in close connection
with the essay on the *English Constitution*, for
while in the latter he illustrated carefully the
various and very complex conditions which are
needful to make a parliamentary government

possible, in the former he showed how long it was before such conditions existed at all, how dangerous at one time to the cohesion of society and to the authority of government free discussion was, and how much more important it was to the growth of social life that there should be a strong government of some kind—even at the cost of the principle of free discussion—than that truth should be elicited by the fine sifting of evidence and argument. *Physics and Politics* showed Mr. Bagehot's close study of the physical speculations of modern times, and especially of Mr. Darwin's and Mr. Wallace's great books on the modification of species through their competition with each other for the means of living ; but it showed also how clearly he understood that there is a competition among historical and national institutions of which those who mould and work those institutions are quite unconscious. In other words, Mr. Bagehot proved that the competitive principle is at work long before men are conscious of any rivalry or struggle with each other in relation to institutions which are really on their trial, and that venerable customs, and even superstitions, had a great advantage over liberty and free speech in an age of the world in which liberty and free speech were not yet consistent with strong organisation, settled order, and a ready capacity for self-defence.

And this brings me to Mr. Bagehot's still more characteristic services to economical and financial science, which, great as they were, it must ever be a subject of permanent regret, were not all that Mr. Bagehot had intended and proposed. His book on *Lombard Street* is, indeed, one of the best illustrations of the complete union in him of a real knowledge of life, with a clear grasp of scientific principle. His familiarity with the banker's and bill broker's business is made at every point to give life and meaning to the monetary and economical theory on which alone the chief facts of that business can be explained. This book threw a flood of light on the relation of commercial life to currency and the medium of exchange, and enabled men to see plainly the working of economical principles in a labyrinth of transactions even more complicated, and to most people more confusing, than even the British Constitution becomes, when closely studied, to foreigners who have wrongly got it into their heads that it is merely a simple application of the abstract principles of popular government. Yet *Lombard Street*, though a powerful and effective essay on the principles of banking, was but a beginning of what Mr. Bagehot could have done in the service of political economy ; as, indeed, his many papers in the *Economist* on the principles of land tenure, the disputes between capital and labour, the causes of commercial panics, the danger of Government interference in commercial enterprise, the folly of lending the savings of civilised nations to Governments really semi-barbarous, and quite unable to give more than the semblance of security for what they borrow, and on a host of other financial and economical questions, sufficiently show. The book so ably begun, of which the "Postulates of Political Economy" were to have been the first chapters, would in itself have been —and I hope that not a little of it may be found to be already in existence—a contribution of the highest value to economical science. In the preliminary essay Mr. Bagehot showed to how many of the nations of the existing world the fundamental assumptions of our economical science are quite inapplicable; in how many there is no free circulation of labour and capital, between employment and employment; in how many there is no Government capable of maintaining order and securing both labour and capital in their transactions; in how many, again, there is the disturbing competition of involuntary or quasi-servile labour still to be allowed for; and thus he illustrated his point that while even to modern Europe and the United States the abstract principles of political economy are only partially applicable, there are still vaster regions in the world to which they are hardly applicable at all, and where we must not expect to find illustrations of its principles, but rather illustrations of principles which are related to it, as the art of the stone or the bronze age is related to the art of our own day. In all these discussions Mr. Bagehot showed the great vividness and vitality of his mind. Take up any of his books—however abstract the subject may seem—and you are constantly coming upon remarks that deserve to be remembered for their intrinsic wisdom, sagacity, and humour. For example, take this as illustrating the scientific uselessness of an exhaustive survey of facts without the help of a plausible hypothesis on which to explain them : "The discovery of a law of nature is very like the discovery of a murder. In the one case you arrest a suspected person, and in the other you isolate a suspected cause." Or again, as illustrating the mischief and folly of the loans to half-barbarous states : "We press upon half-finished and half-civilised communities incalculable sums ; we are to them what the London money dealers are to the students at Oxford and Cambridge. We enable these communities to read in every news-paper that they can have ready money almost of any amount on personal security." Or again, this, on the commonplace character of too many of our public men, "The most benumbing thing to the intellect is routine; the most bewildering is distraction; our system is a distracting routine . . . It is rather wonderful that our public men have any minds left, than that a certain unfixity of opinion seems growing upon them." Or once more, take this on an analogous subject, as illustrating the need under which Parliamentary statesmen live of reflecting the opinions of the masses, "Politicians live on the repute of the commonalty. They may appeal to posterity, but of what use is posterity? Years before that tribunal comes into life your life will be extinct. *It is like a moth going into Chancery.*" Here was Mr. Bagehot's forte. He brought so graphic a knowledge of real life to illustrate his theories, that, in his writings, abstract doctrines lost their dulness, and imaginative power lost its appearance of being unpractical and capricious. He makes his abstractions vivid, and he makes his real life instructive. Political and economical science both owe him quite incalculable obligations.

THE POPULAR EDITION OF WALTER BAGEHOT'S WORKS

THIS is a very clear and pleasant edition, in five volumes, of the best known and, on the whole, perhaps (with three exceptions) most remarkable of Mr. Bagehot's works. It does not contain the striking essay on *Physics and Politics*, nor the book on *The English Constitution*, nor the volume called *Lombard Street*, which, for copyright reasons, I suppose, it was not in Messrs. Longman's power to reproduce. But, with these exceptions, it has all the writings by which his original genius was made known to the world, and by which, in the sixteen years since his death, his power as an author has been more and more universally recognised. Mr. Bagehot was just the writer of whose works a popular edition was eminently desirable. He is fascinating enough to become really popular, and he is original enough and sufficiently "caviare to the general" to need a little effort on the part of his publishers to make him so. There are plenty of his essays which are so lively and impressive that once read they are never again forgotten; and there are also not a few which, if taken up at random, without their more popular companions, might be thought on a hasty glance to need more careful study than ordinary readers are disposed to give. In other words, there is much in his writings which will attract ordinary readers on the first glance, and yet much also which needs a good deal more than a first glance in order to take its proper hold on the mind of the reader. That is just what a book should be to make a proper edition of it of the highest general use to the reading public. Without a very lively and brilliant touch in any author, a popular edition of his works would hardly repay his publishers at all. And yet without much that is by no means superficially attractive in his writings, the gain to the reading world in general of giving the most attractive form to his works, so as to extend the knowledge of him beyond the class which reads only for amusement, would not be nearly so beneficial as it is in the case of a writer who is by no means always amusing, though he is always either amusing or instructive, or both. I fully expect that this edition of Mr Bagehot's most important works will induce many to read him, and to read him with pleasure, who have never read him before, and besides, will induce many who have hitherto read only his more brilliant essays to master those more solid studies in which Mr. Bagehot put forth all his power as an original thinker, and broke new ground on which it takes something like close attention to follow him adequately.

Let me first illustrate Mr. Bagehot's charm as a purely amusing and fascinating writer—one who carried the most buoyant spirits and the gayest humour into the subjects that would generally be thought too recondite to admit of humour at all.

Take this admirable and lively passage, for instance, on Gibbon's historical style :—

In the great histories there are two topics of interest —the man as a type of the age in which he lives—the events and manners of the age he is describing; very often almost all the interest is the contrast of the two. "You should do everything," said Lord Chesterfield, "in minuet time." It was in that time that Gibbon wrote his history, and such was the manner of the age. You fancy him in a suit of flowered velvet, with a bag and sword, wisely smiling, composedly rounding his periods. You seem to see the grave bows, the formal politeness, the finished deference. You perceive the minuetic action accompanying the words. "Give," it would say, "Augustus a chair : Zenobia, the humblest of your slaves : Odoacer, permit me to correct the defect in your attire." As the slap-dash sentences of a rushing critic express the hasty impatience of modern manners, so the deliberate emphasis, the slow acumen, the steady argument, the impressive narration bring before us what is now a tradition, the picture of the correct eighteenth-century gentleman, who never failed in a measured politeness, partly because it was due in propriety towards others, and partly because from his own dignity it was due most obviously to himself. . . . Another characteristic of the eighteenth century is its taste for dignified pageantry. What an existence was that of Versailles ! How gravely admirable to see the grand monarque shaved, and dressed, and powdered ; to look on and watch a great man carefully amusing himself with dreary trifles. Or do we not even now possess an invention of that age—the great eighteenth-century footman, still in the costume of his era with dignity and powder, vast calves, and noble mien ? What a world it must have been when all men looked like that ! Go and gaze with rapture at the footboard of a carriage, and say, "Who would not obey a premier with such an air ?" Grave, tranquil, decorous pageantry is

a part, as it were, of the essence of the last age. There
is nothing more characteristic of Gibbon. A kind of
pomp pervades him. He is never out of livery. He
ever selects for narration those themes which look most
like a levée, grave chamberlains seem to stand throughout ;
life is a vast ceremony, the historian at once the dignitary
and the scribe.

No one can deny that the man who wrote that
is eminently a popular writer. Again, take this
passage in the essay on Bishop Butler concerning
the religion of scrupulosity, the religion of fear :—

Now of the poetic religion there is nothing in
Butler. No one could tell from his writings that the
universe was beautiful. If the world were a Durham
mine or an exact square, if no part of it were more
expressive than a gravel pit or a chalk quarry, the
teaching of Butler would be as true as it is now. A
young poet, not a very wise one, once said : " He did not
like the Bible, there was nothing about flowers in it."
He might have said so of Butler with great truth : a
most ugly and stupid world one would fancy *his* books
were written in. But in return and by way of compensation for this, there is a religion of another sort, a religion
the source of which is within the mind, as the other's
was found to be in the world without : the religion to
which we just now alluded as the religion (by an odd yet
expressive way of speaking) of *superstition*. The source
of this, as most persons are practically aware, is in the
conscience. The moral principle (whatever may be said
to the contrary by complacent thinkers) is really and to
most men a principle of fear. . . . You are going to
battle, you are going out in the bright sun with dancing
plumes and glittering spear ; your shield shines, and
your feathers wave, and your limbs are glad with the
consciousness of strength, and your mind is warm with

glory and renown—with coming glory and unobtained
renown for who are you, to hope for these, who are *you*,
to go forth proudly against the pride of the sun, with
your secret sin and your haunting shame, and your real
fear ? First lie down and abase yourself—strike your
back with hard stripes—cut deep with a sharp knife as
if you would eradicate the consciousness—cry aloud—put
ashes on your head—bruise yourself with stones, then
perhaps God may pardon you ; or, better still,—so runs
the incoherent feeling—give Him something—your ox,
your ass, whole hecatombs, if you are rich enough ;
anything, it is but a chance—you do not know what will
please Him—at any rate, what you love best yourself—
that is, most likely, your first-born son ; then, after such
gifts and such humiliation, He may be appeased, He may
let you off—He may without anger let you go forth
Achilles-like in the glory of your shield—He may *not*
send you home as He would else, the victim of rout and
treachery, with broken arms and foul limbs, in weariness
and humiliation.   Of course, it is not this kind of
fanaticism that we impute to a prelate of the English
Church ; human sacrifices are not respectable, and Achilles
was not Rector of Stanhope.

Again, is it not obvious that the writer of this
passage had in him a good deal more than the full
buoyancy of a very popular writer ? Indeed, lively
and amusing as Mr. Bagehot is, he almost always
manages to be striking and original too.   You
cannot read even the most temporary and occasional
of his essays without being taken into some train of
thought which is at once lively and yet also unexpected, and while it seems remote from the theme
with which he was dealing, is yet most essentially
connected with it.   Take this, for instance, from the
very admirable essay on a statesman now almost forgotten, the late Sir George Cornewall Lewis.   Mr.

Bagehot holds that Sir George Lewis had studied the great jurist, Mr. Austen, till he copied his faults of style, and wrote as if it were quite as necessary to insist elaborately upon what everybody knows, if it happens to be illustrative of a great principle, as it is to insist on what almost everybody forgets :—

It is not advisable to begin with a principle and to work steadily through all its possible applications at the *same* length. If you do, the reader will say : " How this man does prose ! Why, I knew that " ; and he did know it. Some of the applications of a principle are new, and should be treated at length too ; but all the consequences should not be worked out like a sum. An atmosphere of commonplace hangs over long moral didactics, and an equal expansion of what the world knows and what it does not know will not be read by the world. Sir George Lewis did his fame serious harm by neglecting this maxim. He wrote, for example, *An Essay on the Influence of Authority in Matters of Opinion,* which was described by a hasty thinker as a book to prove that when " You wanted to know anything, you asked some one who knew something about it. " This essay certainly abounds in acute remarks and interesting illustrations ; and, if these remarks and these illustrations had been printed separately, it would have been a good book. But the systematic treatment has been fatal to it. The different kinds and cases of authority are so systematically enumerated, that the reader yawns and forgets.

That explains exactly why one of the wisest political thinkers of this century is so soon forgotten. But Mr. Bagehot will not soon be forgotten. One of his greatest powers was the power of fixing attention on those critical features of any great subject which are apt to escape notice, but which are really so characteristic of it that if they do escape notice the whole subject is obscured, and again, the power of diverting attention from those obvious aspects of it which can hardly be missed by any one, and which therefore need no elaboration at all. What can be better, for instance, than his humiliating demonstration in the first political essay he ever wrote (1852), that the reason why politics go well with England and badly with France, is just this, that Englishmen are stupid enough *not* to be misled by plausible and fallacious reasoning, while Frenchmen are acute enough to be captivated and carried away by any kind of plausible and fallacious reasoning :—

Why do the stupid people always win, and the clever people always lose ? I need not say that, in real sound stupidity the English are unrivalled. You hear more wit, and better wit, in an Irish street row than would keep Westminster Hall in humour for five weeks. Or take Sir Robert Peel—our last great statesman, the greatest Member of Parliament that ever lived, an absolutely perfect transactor of public business—the type of the Nineteenth Century Englishman, as Sir R. Walpole was of the Eighteenth. Was there ever such a dull man ? Can any one, without horror, foresee the reading of his memoirs ? A *clairvoyante*, with the book shut, may get on ; but who now, in the flesh, will ever endure the open *vision* of endless recapitulation of interminable Hansard ? Or take Mr. Tennyson's inimitable description :—

No little lily handed Baronet he,
A great broad-shouldered genial Englishman,
A Lord of fat prize oxen and of sheep,
A raiser of huge melons and of pine,
The patron of some thirty charities.
A pamphleteer on guano and on grain,
A quarter sessions chairman, abler none.

Whose company so soporific ?   His talk is of truisms and
bullocks ; his head replete with rustic visions of mutton
and turnips, and a cerebral edition of Burns's *Justice*.
Notwithstanding, he is the salt of the earth, the best of
the English breed.   Who is like him for sound sense ?
But I must restrain my enthusiasm.   You don't want me
to tell you that a Frenchman—a real Frenchman—can't
be stupid ; *esprit* is his essence, wit is to him as water,
bonmots as *bonbons*.   He reads and he learns by reading ;
levity and literature are essentially his line.   Observe the
consequence.   The outbreak of 1848 was accepted in
every province in France ; the decrees of the Parisian
mob were received and registered in all the municipalities
of a hundred cities ; the Revolution ran like the fluid of
the telegraph down the *Chemin de fer du Nord* ; it
stopped at the Belgian frontier.   Once brought into contact
with the dull phlegm of the stupid Fleming, the poison
was powerless.   You remember what the Norman butler
said to Wilkin Flammock of the fulling mills at the castle
of the Garde Douloureuse : " That draught which will but
warm your Flemish hearts, will put wild-fire into Norman
brains ; and what may only encourage your countrymen to
man the walls, will make ours fly over the battlements."
Les braves Belges, I make no doubt, were quite pleased to
observe what folly was being exhibited by those very
clever French, whose tongue they want to speak, and
whose literature they try to imitate.   In fact, what we
opprobriously call stupidity, though not an enlivening
quality in common society, is Nature's favourite resource
for preserving steadiness of conduct and consistency of
opinion.   It enforces concentration ; people who learn
slowly, learn only what they must.   The best security for
people's doing their duty is, that they should not know
anything else to do ; the best security for fixedness of
opinion is, that people should be incapable of com-
prehending what is to be said on the other side.

That is not only approximately true, but it is really

the explanation of most of the special difficulties of our modern politics. Education is removing the top layer of our popular ignorance, and rendering us alive to a number of arguments to which we were densely and stolidly obtuse before. But it has not gone deep enough to educate our popular *judgment*, and the consequence is that we are much more open to the tyranny of superficial errors than we were before.

I believe that the popular edition of Mr. Bagehot's chief works will be of the utmost benefit to this generation of thinkers. We are just beginning to find out how wise was the slow Conservatism of English instincts, and how dangerous is the revolutionary enthusiasm of minds that are audaciously eager for a leap in the dark. Mr. Bagehot's practical caution is at least as remarkable as his literary dash. The latter familiarises us with a multitude of wise securities which the former alone could have suggested. He is the most brilliant of apologists for the policy of avoiding both obtuse obstinacy and eager precipitation.

THE RARITY OF HEREDITARY POETS

THE publication of a thin volume of very graceful poems by Lord Houghton reminds us how seldom it happens that the son of a poet is himself a poet. It does happen occasionally. The most remarkable case is undoubtedly Hartley Coleridge's. Hartley Coleridge was not his father's equal in genius. He could not have conceived or written either "the Ancient Mariner" or "Christabel"; but the "Lyrical Cry" in him was even more exquisitely pure and tender than it was in his father. Then there is the case of Sir Aubrey de Vere and of Mr. Aubrey de Vere, two very genuine poets, and singularly resembling each other in attitude of mind, though there is not a trace of imitation of the father by the son. Again, there are the three Roscoes, grandfather, father, and son—the philanthropist and historian whose poetry was of the slightest and most fanciful order (he wrote "The Butterfly's Ball" and "O'er the Vine-covered hills and fair Valleys of France, See the day-star of liberty rise"); William Stanley Roscoe, who wrote "Vala Crucis" and a few other poems of exquisite beauty and delicacy; and again his son, William Caldwell Roscoe, who has written five or six sonnets which would take rank with the best of those of Hartley Coleridge himself for brilliancy and loveliness—to say nothing of a fine drama and some very beautiful miscellaneous poems.   But these are almost the only instances, except the one which suggested these remarks, that I can recall of the apparent transmission of poetic genius.   Amongst the greatest poets, I know of no instance of inheritance of this particular faculty.   There is no tradition that even David, or Isaiah, or Homer, or Aeschylus, or Virgil, or Horace, or Dante, or Petrarch, or Tasso, or Goethe, or Schiller, or Béranger, or Hugo, or Chaucer, or Shakespeare, or Milton, or Spenser, or Burns, or Scott, or Shelley, or Byron, transmitted any spark of their poetic genius to descendants.   Not very frequently does there appear to have been any special power even of another kind in the descendants of poets.   Byron's daughter was a considerable mathematician, which seems a curious transformation for force like Byron's to undergo.   Chaucer's son was Speaker of the House of Commons and Ambassador to France.   Many of Coleridge's nephews and grand-nephews were distinguished as lawyers and writers.   More than one of Wordsworth's sons, brothers, and nephews were, or are, worthy divines and college teachers.   But, except in the case of the Coleridges, the De Veres, the Roscoes, and the two Lord Houghtons, we can trace no transmission of poetic genius.   Mr. Galton, in his book on heredity, says that "Poets are clearly not founders of families," but goes on to account for this on the abstract principle that poets have, as a rule, strong sensuous tastes, and that people who have strong sensuous tastes are apt to go astray in life, and squander whatever power they have.   But

that is not a reason which applies at all to the
great Hebrew prophets, who were among the
greatest poets of earth, and yet in not one instance,
I believe, is there a Hebrew prophet who transmitted
his gifts to a descendant.   Again, there is no reason
of the kind referred to by Mr. Galton why
Aeschylus, or Sophocles, or Virgil, or Dante, or
Milton, or Scott, or Wordsworth, should not have
founded a family inheriting their great poetic gifts.
And it is very remarkable in relation to the Wordsworths, at least, that while there is no trace of the
transmission of a spark of the poet's higher faculty
to descendants, the serious and didactic impulse
which sometimes exalts, and more often injures his
poetry, was transmitted to his descendants.   In
fact, nothing seems clearer than that the didactic
attitude of mind is very frequently inherited, and
inherited in a very emphatic form.   The Edgeworths,
the Wordsworths, the Stanleys, the Wilberforces,
and most of all the Arnolds, show us how singular
has been the reproduction of the didactic attitude of
mind from father to son ;   and this, too, even in
cases where, as in that of Matthew Arnold, there
was hardly anything which the father believed that
the son also believed for him to teach, though the
teaching posture of mind, and the energy which
teaching needs, were reproduced with strange
exactness, the whole character of the lessons taught
being utterly different.   It was the same with the
Coleridges.   Charles Lamb, when asked by Coleridge
if he had ever heard him preach, replied with his
usual stammer, that he did not think he had ever
heard him do anything else.   And yet, while the
poetical gift was transmitted to Hartley, and Hartley
alone, the didactic animus of Coleridge was trans-

mitted to Sara Coleridge, Derwent Coleridge, and
to remoter descendants.   There is probably no
turn of mind which is so often transmitted from
father to son as the didactic turn of mind.   On the
other hand, imagination and fancy are not often
transmitted, though there are not a few cases in
which father and son, or mother and son, or father
and daughter, have had the same gift for holding
the mirror up to society.   There is Dumas *père* and
Dumas *fils*, for instance; there is Mrs. Trollope
and Anthony Trollope, who not only both drew
characters with great skill and humour, but drew
characters after a fashion in which it is impossible
not to recognise the same mould of mind.   Again,
there is the case of Thackeray and his daughter,
though there the type is greatly modified.   And
there is the case of Nathaniel Hawthorne and his
son.   In all these instances there is, in the case of
a definitely imaginative gift, a transmission of
power as distinct as in the case of the engineering
genius of the two Brunels and the two Stephensons.
I should have been disposed, in the case of the two
Stephensons and the two Brunels, to regard education as the main factor in the reproduction of the
father's type of ability in the son.   But education
cannot count for much, if for anything, in such a
case as that of writers of fiction, and therefore I
think it is to some extent open to doubt whether
education should be credited, in any large degree,
with the marked capacity of the younger Brunel
and Robert Stephenson for the prosecution of their
father's work.   Certainly it must be the transmission
of an original faculty, and not education, which can
alone account for the reproduction in the second
and perhaps greater Pitt, of the statesmanlike

qualities and attitude of Lord Chatham. And, on the whole, we cannot attach anything like the weight which Mr. Galton evidently does attach to his explanation of the ordinary failure of poets to transmit their genius to their children. It is the rarest thing in the world for a poet like the late Lord Houghton to transmit to his son, with the social ease and sympathetic insight into feeling and character, that are often transmitted, just that measure of fancy, imagination, and delight in the sounds and associations of characteristic words and rhymes and rhythms, which go to make the poet. The general attitude of a character—in the sense in which we speak of a didactic attitude, or an ironic attitude, or a self-conscious attitude, or a humorous attitude, or a matter-of-fact attitude—is, I believe, more frequently transmitted from father to son, or daughter, than any other mental quality ; but it is very rare indeed for two poets who, without a trace of imitativeness, resemble each other even as much as Sir Aubrey de Vere and Mr. Aubrey de Vere, or as Mr. W. Stanley Roscoe and Mr. W. Caldwell Roscoe, or as Richard Monckton Milnes, the first Lord Houghton, and the second Lord Houghton, to be in the relation of father and son. In none of these instances are there wanting very marked differences ; but still, with all the real difference, no one would have been very much astonished if the poem on Mr. Stacy Marks's "Bookworm," for instance, by Robert, Lord Houghton, had been produced from the remains of Richard, Lord Houghton. I quote the last three verses, not to prove any very striking likeness (for the likeness is not very striking), but to show that the general type of ease and *savoir-faire* and lightness

which gave to Richard Monckton Milnes the
sobriquet of "the cool of the evening," is the
same :—

> He never read Dame Nature's book—
>   The finch's nest, the moldwarp's burrow,—
> Nor stood to mark the careful rook
>   Peer sidelong down the newest furrow ;
> He never watched the warbler dart
>   From stem to stem among the sedges,
> But, hands behind him, paced apart
>   Between the tall-cut hornbeam hedges
>
> And so his blameless years rolled by,
>   To-day the double of to-morrow,
> No wish to smile, no need to sigh,
>   No heart for mirth, no time for sorrow ;
> His forehead wore a deeper frown,
>   Eyes grew more dim and cheeks more hollow,
> Till friendly Death, one day stepped down,
>   And lightly whispered, ' Rise and follow.'
>
> But Fame, victorious maid, resists
>   The doom for which grey Time intends us,
> Immortal titles crowd the lists
>   Which Mr. Quaritch kindly sends us !
> 'Twixt Drelincourt and Dryden thrust,
>   What name confronts you lone and chilling ?
> " *The Works of Gilbert Dryasdust ;*
>   *Quarto ; 3 vols. ;—old calf : a shilling.*"

That last touch is more like Mr. Locker-Lampson
or Mr. Austin Dobson than the first Lord Houghton ;
but the general ease and sentiment and lightness of
touch in the first two verses quoted are not very
unlike the first Lord Houghton's handiwork.

But the greater poetical gifts are, I do not say
untransmissible, but exceedingly rarely transmitted.

Like the inspiration of the prophet, or the self-forgetfulness of the saint, they are apparently the unique product of a fusion between the creative Spirit and the individual human being to which He communicates some spark or flash of His own unapproachable thought or spirit of self-forgetfulness (if I may properly impute such a quality to the Infinite Mind), and it does not seem His will or habit to produce replicas of genius in any of its highest forms.   Even in the exceptional cases I have noticed, there will be found to be variations so remarkable, that it is rather the constitutional poetic temper which is inherited than the individual genius. Still, it is rare enough for even that to be inherited. As a rule, there is a curious correlation amongst the forms of genius, and the poet's descendant is more likely to turn out a barrister or a judge or an artist, or even an antiquarian, than a poet.   A portion of the energy remains, but it takes to new channels. "The light that never was on sea or land, the consecration, and the poet's dream," is the rarest of all inheritances.   Tricks of the brow and of the fingers, habits of methodical arrangement, habits of careless and unmethodical forgetfulness, attitudes of mind, moral or unmoral or immoral—all these are constantly more or less inherited ; but the highest of all gifts are rarely indeed family heirlooms, and when they are, they should be cherished, since the continuous, or even discontinuous inspiration of any family is a sign to the ages such as is seldom given. There would, indeed, be a divine right for kings if the sons of great kings were to inherit their father's gift ; and even that has happened much oftener than the inheritance of poetic power.

WILLIAM CALDWELL ROSCOE'S POEMS

MISS ROSCOE has done well in republishing, through
Messrs. Macmillan, her father's poems in a separate
volume, for to my mind, of all the minor poets of the
Victorian reign William Caldwell Roscoe is one of
the most fascinating. There is a refinement about his
genius that is not due to fastidiousness or delicacy of
taste, but rather to the vividness of his spiritual discrimination. It is the refinement which gives us
the sense not so much of shrinking from what was
false or extravagant, or ambitious or sentimental
or discordant, although he evidently did shrink from
all these faults, as of a rich and ardent love of true
beauty which lends a grace of form and a flush of
delicate colour to all his thoughts and conceptions.
Mr. Roscoe had no leaning towards the school of
brusque and crude, not to say headlong expression,
of which Mr. Browning has been the greatest
representative in the English literature of the last
forty years. Beauty of form was with him as much
a condition of real poetry as truth of apprehension
and depth of feeling. His thoughts never came
helter-skelter like a succession of boys playing at
leap-frog, treading on each other's heels, till you
have the sensation of being almost mobbed by the
eager scramble of the poet's conceptions. His

imagination was saturated with the Elizabethan
stateliness, though his own mind was essentially
modern on its intellectual side, and full of those
suspensive moods, those questionings, those arrests
of judgment, which have marked the poetry of
Tennyson and Clough.   Mr. Roscoe's ear for rhythm
and for the expressiveness of metre was very fine,
as fine, I think, as Hartley Coleridge's ; and exquisite
as many of Hartley Coleridge's sonnets are, there
are hardly any of the five-and-twenty or so contained
in the present volume (except one or two which
never received the finishing touches) which would
not stand beside the best of Hartley Coleridge's
without losing by the comparison.   Indeed, the
many which have been included of late years in
those selections of the best sonnets of which we
have had so many admirable specimens, sufficiently
show that it is not a mere partial judgment that
rates Mr. Roscoe's sonnets so high.   Perhaps the
most exquisite of all the sonnets is the Epilogue to
the play of " Violenzia," but at least half of the whole
number of sonnets appear to me to be works of as
true a genius as, in a different realm, Mendelssohn's
"Songs without Words."   What, for instance, can
be at once more bright in vision and more lovely in
its cadences than the following ?—

DAYBREAK IN FEBRUARY

Over the ground white snow, and in the air
Silence.   The stars, like lamps soon to expire,
Gleam tremblingly ; serene and heavenly fair,
The eastern hanging crescent climbeth higher.
See, purple on the azure softly steals,
And Morning, faintly touched with quivering fire,

Leans on the frosty summits of the hills,
Like a young girl over her hoary sire.
Oh, such a dawning over me has come,—
The daybreak of thy purity and love ;—
The sadness of the never-satiate tomb
Thy countenance hath power to remove ;
And from the sepulchre of Hope thy palm
Can roll the stone, and raise her bright and calm.

Bryn Rhedyn, 1854.

There are other poems, not sonnets, and somewhat more airy and radiant in their effect than any sonnet (which in its perfection always seems to be most beautiful when it is most reticent), that give a more adequate impression of the grace and ease of Mr. Roscoe's imagination — the following, for example, which for spiritual beauty has always seemed to me one of the airiest, tenderest, and most truly spiritual of the poems of its class :—

TO LITTLE A. C. IN THE GARDEN AT EASTBURY

Come, my beauty, come, my bird ;
We two will wander, and no third
Shall mar the sweetest solitude
    Of a garden and a child,
When the fresh elms are first in bud,
    And western winds blow mild.

Clasp that short-reaching arm about a neck
    Stript of a deeper love's more close embrace,
And with the softness of thy baby-cheek
    Press roses on a care-distained face.

What ? set thee down, because the air
Ruffles too boldly thy brown hair ?

Walk, then, and as thy tiny boot
    Presses the greenness of the sod,
Teach me to see that tottering foot
    Uplifted and set down by God ;

Teach me a stronger, tenderer hand than mine
    Sways every motion of thy infant frame ;
Bid me take hold, like thee, and not repine,—
    Weak with my errors and deserved shame.

How ? home again ? ah, that soft laughter
Tells me what voice thou hankerest after.
Run, run, with that bright shining face,
    And little hands stretched forth apart,
Into a mother's fond embrace,
    Close, closer to her heart.

I too will turn, for I discern a voice
    Which whispers me that I am far from home
Bids me repent, and led by holier choice
    Back to a Father's open bosom come.

Or, again, the poem to his wife called "The Year of Love" is at once one of the tenderest and of the most lovely of its class. With children and flowers Mr. Roscoe seemed more thoroughly at home than any of those Elizabethan poets whom he so much admired, and with whose imaginative conceptions he was so familiar.

As regards the two tragedies, it is more difficult to speak with perfect confidence. They are both of them rich and beautiful poems, though in the early and youthful one, "Eliduke, Count of Yveloc," there is here and there a little trace of the Elizabethan extravagance of passion, of the passion torn to tatters at which the satirists who assail that school very justly point their ridicule, for instance, in Eliduke's address to the apparently dead form of Estreldis, in pp. 202-3. But "Eliduke"

was written when Mr. Roscoe was almost a boy,
and it is full of beauty and spirit from beginning
to end. Take, for instance, this passage on the
brilliancy of the Breton knights as dancers, when
they are received at the comparatively rude Court
of Cornwall :—

Lar.   Oh, let me dance to-night,
And go to heaven happy, having tasted
Earth's best felicity.
    Est.   Dancing, Lardune ?
    Lar.   Oh, with these Breton knights,
         that make the air
Heavy in pace behind them, and still tread
With such a delicate feeling of the time,
As if the music dwelt in their own frames,
And shook the motion from them. Oh, divine !
    Est.   Is it so charming ? I remember me
Dancing was ever your delight, but now——
    Lar.   I never danced till now. Our
         Cornwall sirs
We thought were adepts ; but compared to these
They're dull and heavy, and lack ears to mark
The proper grace of movement. Say these walk,
Then you may stint the breath of commendation,
And say these strangers dance. Let our knights dance,
These others fly and ride upon the air ;
Or flattering, call our Cornish motion flight,—
These Bretons are the untied elements
That in their airy and fantastic course,
Joining and now disjoining, mingling now
In fresh variety of curious shapes,
Hold dancing revelry in Nature's halls.
    Est.   Thou'rt mad, Lardune ;—tell me,
         Azalia,
What think you of these strangers ? will they wear
As fairly in the trial as they show now ?

Lar.   Oh, I'll be sworn for 't ; trust me,
    outward bearing
Glasses the man within.   True gold, that shines most,
Is in itself more costly and more noble
Than duller seeming brass.   That agile force,
That trains their feet i' th' dance, will in the fight
Show bravely in their arms, and their bright swords
Tread such quick measure on the heads of foes,
The ringing helms their music, that Dismay
Shall seize them at the force of 't, and Defeat,
Ever his follower, clear the field of them.

That is not a specimen of the best poetry in
" Eliduke," but it is a fair specimen of the fire
and spirit with which the play abounds.   The
subject of the two plays is in essence the same—
the struggle of a fine nature, full of noble instincts
and high resolves, with the temptations of life,
those temptations naturally centring in the
relations between men and women.   In the early
play, Eliduke, noble as he is by nature meant
to be, succumbs to passion ; in the later one, Ethel,
equally noble, obtains the victory over the most
overwhelming of all the temptations that could
beset the heart of man.   I do not hesitate to say
that " Violenzia," though it hinges on a most painful
subject, the subject of outrage, is an exceedingly
fine drama, sustained in its interest from first to
last, overwhelming in its tragic close, and full of
the most genuine poetry.   I do not know that I
should call either play in the highest sense dramatic.
The plots are full of power and passion, and the
reader's mind is never once allowed to lose its
high-wrought suspense till the play ends ; but for
all that, but few of the characters are powerfully
delineated, and the whole real passion of either

play is concentrated in the hero. Mr. Roscoe, I need hardly say, had written both plays long before Lord Tennyson's "Idylls of the King" had ever been heard of. But Ethel, Earl of Felborg, is in many respects an anticipation of Tennyson's Arthur, and will be charged by many readers with the same defect which has been brought against him—namely, that he is too much of a preacher, that he is more of a saint with a sword in his hand than a soldier and statesman. It is, indeed, far from easy to paint a great ideal character under circumstances in which almost all men would flash into the fiercest passion of loathing, without giving room to the charge of a certain spiritual priggishness. It is the common accusation brought against Tennyson's Arthur, though I myself have never felt its truth. And it will be brought again against the still higher and more spiritual character delineated in this striking play, "Violenzia." I doubt whether any attempt to paint a character that, in such circumstances as these, was perfectly victorious over temptation, could fail to be liable to such objections. But for my own part, I believe that such a character as Ethel's, if it had been long trained in the school of true Christian faith, would be quite possible, and that the picture of it here given is thoroughly inspiring, though it will undoubtedly give occasion to sneers at its too perfect and solemn virtue. That the picture is not wanting in the highest poetical vividness, a single extract will sufficiently show. It is the morning of the day on which a great battle is to be fought :—

Eth.   'Twill not be till noon.
O peaceful morning-tide, with what rude deeds

Will they deface thy evening ! Is it not heavenly ?
The air is cool and still ; soft dawn shoots up
Into the fleecy heaven, that, like a mother
Uncovering her rosy naked babe,
Looks down upon the tender new-born day.
Strange prelude to a battle.

 Cor.   True, it is piteous,
And best not thought of.

 Eth.   Piteous it is indeed,
And yet not best not thought of, so is nothing.
We dare not faint at woe and violence,
When we are sure our cause is with the right.
And gaping wounds, and the red skeleton death,
Painted in blood of many slaughtered men,
Though they may stir our gorge more, are in
  themselves,
And should be to our spirits, less abhorrent
Than living men, walking like sepulchres
Of their dead spiritual lives.

 Cor.   I have seen such men.

 Eth. So sick, I have seen many, and some dead.
He is noble that can hang a shield of patience
Between himself and injuries, but most base
That sees injustices unremedied.

 Cor. That did you never.

 Eth.   No, nor you, Cornelius,
Nor any man who doth believe in heaven,
But when he sees a wrong must war with it—
By sufferance, if sufferance best abates it,
But only then.   And always in his spirit
Eager antagonism, not passive spirits,
Oppose the dangerous devil's mastery ;
But sworded and aggressive warriors,
Who with swift charge beat down his mustered ranks,
And all day long maintain the weary war,
And die in faith of unseen victory.

 Cor. Warriors of God ; servants of God ;—great titles.

Eth. Oh, that we might be worthy to be such !
Our youth is like this morning, and we stand
Between the night of our unconscious childhood
And the world's monstrous battle, whose loud roar
Grows in our ears.   Well, when we mix in it,
God keep us in His hand !

I should add that the picture of Malgodin, the true tempter of the play, is extremely vigorous.   He is a Mephistopheles who surpasses Goethe's Mephistopheles in sardonic evil, and I think, even in resource.   When Goethe set himself to delineate the tempter, as in the scene with the medical student, or the scene in which he prompts Faust to compass the ruin of Gretchen, Goethe's touch is very fine.   But Mephistopheles too often seems to forget his main object in cultivating Faust so closely, and rambles off into disquisitions which are not specially satanic.   Malgodin is as evil a tempter as ever entered into the heart of man.   Mr. W. C. Roscoe's poems should win him a permanent, if a modest place, in the English literature of the nineteenth century.   His genius was not fertile, but it was singularly true and discerning, and, what is more, it was a genius that worked in the finest material, that translated its conceptions into the most perfect and expressive forms of human speech.   Mr. Roscoe worked in cameo, not in wood or brass, and the execution is at least as beautiful as the imagination.

SELF-CONSCIOUSNESS IN POETRY

Professor Courthope, in his Oxford lecture on "Poetical Decadence," insisted very earnestly on the recent "vast growth of individual self-consciousness" as one of the main causes of the poetical decadence which he finds in the last generation of our literary life. Professor Courthope has steadily maintained that, without a universal element as well as an individual element in poetry, there can be no poetry of the higher kind. And no doubt he is right if he interprets the universal and the individual elements in poetry with subtlety and accuracy. But I doubt whether he does not greatly underrate the universal element contained in what may yet be fairly termed "individual self-consciousness," and overrate that petty and egotistical element in it which unfits it for the purposes of the truly great poet. The poets whom he picks out for the purpose of illustrating the decadence in our most considerable recent poetry are Matthew Arnold, Algernon Swinburne, and Rudyard Kipling. I understand what he means in thus distinguishing Matthew Arnold, though I disagree widely from his judgment, but with regard to the two other poets I should not have thought that, whatever their faults may be, there was any exaggerated element of individual self-consciousness in either of them.   Mr. Swinburne, except when he held fast to the lines of the Greek tragedy,—which he has not done since his poetical career was almost in its infancy,—has hardly been a considerable poet at all, unless we regard his vast command of musical and impressive words as constituting a considerable poet.   And of Mr. Rudyard Kipling I should say with Professor Courthope that he hardly knows "the difference between the life of poetry and the life of verse."   Yet this can hardly be true of any great poet, though it is true of Mr. Rudyard Kipling, vigorous as his verse certainly is.   But with relation to Matthew Arnold, I should absolutely deny that his defective definition of poetry—he defines its essence to be, as Professor Courthope reminds us, "the criticism of life"—and his attacks on the imperfection of the middle class ideal of life, in the least injure the character of his own poetry, which is neither made up of criticisms of life, nor of attacks on the imperfect ideal of middle class taste.   No doubt his definition of the essence of poetry shows that one of his prose essays is not inspired by a high standard of critical principle.   But it does not show that his own poems were not very much more perfect than his own criticism.   To my mind his poems are undoubtedly marked by a "vast growth of individual self-consciousness"; but that vast growth of individual self-consciousness was not of the kind fatal, or otherwise than exalting, to his genius as a poet. The kind of individual self-consciousness which is fatal to poetry is that which throws up the oddities and unmeaning eccentricities of individuals, instead of bringing out more fully the characteristics of human nature at large.   I should even say that

Wordsworth is oftener guilty of this mistake than Matthew Arnold—though, of course, when he does dwell on the higher characteristics of human nature he soars far above Matthew Arnold,—as, for example, in painting the "Resolution and Independence" of the "Leech-gatherer on the lonely moor," or in painting the influence of nature over the mind of the child of whom he said that:—

> The floating clouds their state shall lend
> To her, for her the willow bend,
> Nor shall she fail to see
> E'en in the motions of the storm
> Grace that shall mould the maiden's form
> By silent sympathy.

But, nevertheless, Wordsworth wrote many more poems that were really flat and entirely deficient in what Professor Courthope calls the universal element needful for all the higher poetry than Matthew Arnold. Matthew Arnold never wrote anything so utterly wanting in any universal element as the lines to the "Spade with which Wilkinson hath tilled his lands," or "Jones, as from Calais southward you and I," or "I hate that Andrew Jones, he'll breed his children up to waste and pillage," or some scores of pieces which come far below the true level of his marvellous genius. No one, however, could truly say that Wordsworth often showed that "vast growth of individual self-consciousness" which Professor Courthope regards as the signal of the recent decadence of our poetry, for Wordsworth is seldom self-conscious at all except when he rises to his highest level, as, for example, in the magnificent lines written "Near Tintern Abbey," or in "There was a boy; ye knew him well, ye Cliffs and islands of Winander," or in "The Fountain : a conversation." If Professor Courthope had wished to write down self-consciousness he certainly would never have chosen Wordsworth to illustrate his view. When Wordsworth is at his worst he is not in the least self-conscious, but only deliberately common-place and dull ; but, when he is in the highest plane of self-consciousness, he is also in the truest and noblest sense a poet.

In the same sense I should say that Matthew Arnold is one of those poets who help us to see how largely what Professor Courthope terms the universal element in poetry enters into the adequate exposition of self-consciousness. Of course individual self-consciousness may be made one of the poorest and least poetic of themes, not because it stamps an individual rightly, but because it fails to stamp him rightly, since it is impossible to stamp an individual rightly unless you bring out the universal element in every man as well as the individual element in one man. But that is precisely what Matthew Arnold does. He hardly ever delineates, if indeed he ever delineates, a mere accident in human nature. When he deals with human nature he always gives you not only that which distinguishes a man or woman from their fellows, but also that which unites them to their fellows, by showing us the universal as well as the distinctive aspect of their nature. Take, for instance, the lines in "The Scholar Gipsy " in which he dwells so exquisitely on the craving of the Oxford student for a life plunged in the calm and the passion of a contemplative lot, and also tells us what it is in the life of half-study and of half-belief which so profoundly disappoints the soul, and makes it eager for that "spark from heaven" that alone

can light up the intellect and give it back the full
energy of a vivid life :—

For early didst thou leave the world, with powers
    Fresh, undiverted to the world without,
        Firm to their mark, not spent on other things ;
    Free from the sick fatigue, the languid doubt,
        Which much to have tried, in much been baffled,
            brings.
            O life unlike to ours !
    Who fluctuate idly without term or scope,
        Of whom each strives, nor knows for what he
            strives,
        And each half lives a hundred different lives ;
    Who wait like thee, but not, like thee, in hope

Thou waitest for the spark from heaven ! and we,
    Light half-believers of our casual creeds,
        Who never deeply felt, nor clearly will'd,
    Whose insight never has borne fruit in deeds,
        Whose vague resolves never have been fulfill'd ;
            For whom each year we see
    Breeds new beginnings, disappointments new ;
        Who hesitate and falter life away,
        And lose to-morrow the ground won to-day—
    Ah ! do not we, wanderer ! await it too ?

Perhaps, however, Professor Courthope is thinking
of "Empedocles on Etna" when he charges Matthew
Arnold with illustrating that "vast growth of
individual self-consciousness" which has tended to
destroy the vitality of our recent poetry.   Now I
should be sorry to assert that "Empedocles on Etna"
is one of the finest of his poems, because, except in its
few though lovely lyrics, it has unquestionably much
less of the wonderfully delicate description of
Nature's beauty, which was one of Arnold's greatest

gifts as a poet. "Empedocles on Etna" is indeed a poem intended to embody a Stoical moral philosophy, and one which actually embodies it with the greatest possible subtlety and force. But no one can justly say that it is self-consciousness which spoils it as a poem. There is no doubt a sort of self-consciousness which is deleterious to poetry, a self-consciousness which dwells on what is petty and egotistic in the poet's mind, and which excludes that universal element in all poetry that lifts and expands and illuminates the mind. But there is no such petty egotism in "Empedocles on Etna." It is full of the finer elements of the Stoic philosophy, but there is not a trace in it of the narrowness and poverty and self-occupation which spoil a poem. Take, for instance, this rebuke to those who complain of the little store of happiness which they have achieved in life :—

> Fools ! That so often here
> Happiness mock'd our prayer,
> I think, might make us fear
> A like event elsewhere ;
> Make us, not fly to dreams, but moderate desire.

> And yet, for those who know
> Themselves, who wisely take
> Their way through life, and bow
> To what they cannot break,
> Why should I say that life need yield but *moderate* bliss ?

> Shall we, with temper spoil'd,
> Health sapp'd by living ill,
> And judgment all embroil'd
> By sadness and self-will,
> Shall *we* judge what for man is not true bliss or is ?

> Is it so small a thing
> To have enjoy'd the sun,
> To have lived light in the spring,
> To have loved, to have thought, to have done ;
> To have advanced true friends, and beat down baffling
> foes ?

Whatever may be said of the comparative tameness of these lines, no one can say that they are full of that narrow and dreary self-consciousness which Professor Courthope regards as the very antithesis of true poetry. On the contrary, there is great force and great keenness in these stanzas, and in fact they throw out in fine relief those exquisite lyrics of Callicles which constitute the great beauty of the poem. The last thing I should say of Matthew Arnold is that he spoils his poetry by a narrow self-consciousness. No doubt his greatest poems are those in which he paints scenery and expresses emotion with a unique power of his own. But even when he *thinks* in verse instead of feeling in it, he gives a power and a delicacy and vividness to his thought which but few other poets of this century have fully attained.

DECADENCE IN POETRY

PROFESSOR COURTHOPE, in the lecture which he delivered at Oxford on "Life in Poetry," began to consider the causes of decadence, or in other words, want of life in poetry, and asked whether the rise of a school of poetry which is evidently artificial and wanting in force and spring, is due to a failure in the genius and methods of the poets themselves, or to the failure of vitality and freshness in that section of society to which they belong, or to a drying up of the sources of ideal life in the nation at large. Surely it may well be due to any one or all three of these causes, and it would be more complete in those cases in which all these causes were combined. There are many cases in which a decadent poet lives in an age in which he might have found, had he had the larger social sympathies in himself, a new spring of ideal life, but failed to find it from the want of elasticity and spiritual force within himself, just as Byron, in spite of his magnificent powers and genius, was, in the exhaustion of his ideal life, a decadent poet in the very same age in which Wordsworth struck new and rich sources of poetic inspiration. Again, I may say, that the very same poet, and sometimes even a great poet like Goethe, has had both a fresh and decadent epoch in his own poetry.

In Goethe's case, it was a vital period in which he wrote his lovely lyrics, and his "Goetz von Berlichingen," and the first part of "Faust," and a decadent period in which he wrote his "Elective Affinities" and his "Roman Elegies," and the second part of "Faust," when not only the sources of his ideal life as a poet were evidently drying up, but his sympathies with the most vivid hopes of his own people were narrowing and giving way to his somewhat supercilious scorn for the deeper and stronger impulses of his country, and when he was becoming hopeless of German national life, and out of sympathy with the purest sources of moral inspiration. And, again, we see in such a poet as the late William Morris, one whose sympathies quite outran, as it were, his finer tastes, and who became "the idle singer of an empty day," even at the very time at which he was eagerly seeking to extend the range of the moral life of his own class and to lead it to drink at new springs of thought and action. While he eagerly desired to make the life of culti-vated thought richer and deeper and more in keeping with the aspirations of the people at large, his poetical genius did not find any natural outlet in the direction in which his moral sympathies led him. As a poet he remained *a laudator temporis acti*, a singer whose imagination dwelt in one world, while his heart and hopes were in another.

Decadence in poetry, indeed, as often perhaps betrays a purely personal as a social or political origin, but it may betray any one of these sources. I do not suppose Fletcher, the poetical ally of Beaumont, to have been a poet of the decadent type, for he was a great dramatist, but evidently he had seen and studied those who were decadents in his own time. It would be hard to find a poem of more definitely decadent a type than the little poem on *Melancholy*, which Mr. Palgrave in his *Golden Treasury of Songs and Lyrics*, has placed immediately before Sir Walter Scott's lines, "To a Lock of Hair," in which Sir Walter shows us how he himself was led to open up a region of poetry in which he was not only very great, but the leader of a great school of vigorous life and genius, by the very same causes which have so often betrayed feebler and fainter spirits into the poetry which I should call more or less decadent. Here is Fletcher's praise of melancholy :—

> Hence, all you vain delights,
> As short as are the nights
> Wherein you spend your folly :
> There is nought in this life sweet,
> If man were wise to see't,
> But only melancholy,
> O sweetest Melancholy !
> Welcome, folded arms, and fixéd eyes,
> A sigh that piercing, mortifies,
> A look that's fasten'd to the ground,
> A tongue chain'd up without a sound !
> Fountain heads and pathless groves,
> Places which pale passion loves !
> Moonlight walks, when all the fowls
> Are warmly housed save bats and owls !
> A midnight bell, a parting groan !
> These are the sounds we feed upon ;
> Then stretch our bones in a still gloomy valley ;
> Nothing's so dainty sweet as lovely melancholy.

That is very delicate die-away poetry, but, except as a pure dramatist, no one could ever have written it who was not more in sympathy with that which was dying out of life, than with that which was coming

into being. Now turn to Sir Walter Scott's lines
which Mr Palgrave has placed in immediate sequence
to Fletcher's poem, lines which show us not only
how melancholy had bred in Scott a reaction into
the eager life which kindled his genius and made him
the most buoyant of poets, but which had planted a
new literature amongst us, and spread, as it were, " a
forest on the hills, fast as the seasons could make
steps " :—

TO A LOCK OF HAIR

Thy hue, dear pledge, is pure and bright
As in that well-remember'd night
When first thy mystic braid was wove,
And first my Agnes whispered love.

Since then how often hast thou prest
The torrid zone of this wild breast,
Whose wrath and hate have sworn to dwell
With the first sin that peopled Hell ;
A breast whose blood's a troubled ocean,
Each throb the earthquake's wild commotion !
O, if such clime thou canst endure
Yet keep thy hue unstain'd and pure,
What conquest o'er each erring thought
Of that fierce realm had Agnes wrought !
I had not wander'd far and wide
With such an angel for my guide ;
Nor earth, nor Heaven could then reprove me
If she had lived, and lived to love me !

Not then this world's wild joys had been
To me one savage hunting scene,
My sole delight the headlong race
And frantic hurry of the chase ;

To start, pursue, and bring to bay,
Rush in, drag down, and rend my prey,
Then—from the carcase turn away !
Mine ireful mood had sweetness tamed,
And soothed each wound which pride inflamed :—
Yes, God and man might now approve me,
If thou hadst lived, and lived to love me !

This passionate out-pouring of Scott's momentary despair should show us how dangerous it is to trace what seems to be decadence in any one poet to general, social, and political causes. We never know whether that which drives one poet into artificial and morbid strains, into histrionic attempts to simulate passions which he does not really feel, may not drive another into those "fresh woods and pastures new" which renew a decadent world. Scott became the originator of a great and healthy literature through an attack of melancholy, which was due to a purely personal grief.

Critics would generally, I suppose, be inclined to call the poetry of Crashaw and Cowley decadent poetry. There is a fondness for languid conceits about both of them which certainly suggests a half-exhausted ideal life. Here, for instance, is a portion of Crashaw's reflections on that "not impossible she" in whom, if he ever encountered her, his soul would delight :—

Till that divine
Idea take a shrine
Of crystal flesh, through which to shine :

Meet you her, my Wishes,
Bespeak her to my blisses,
And be ye call'd, my absent kisses.

I wish her beauty
That owes not all its duty
To gaudy tire, or glist'ring shoe-tie :

Something more than
Taffata or tissue can,
Or rampant feather, or rich fan.

A face that's best
By its own beauty drest,
And can alone command the rest :

A face made up
Out of no other shop
Than what Nature's white hand sets ope.

That surely, with all its elegance, or rather by
virtue of its elegance, is decadent in spirit. There
is no real life or spring in it. It is long-drawn and
sickly. And here, again, is Cowley asserting that
the strings of his lyre themselves make "a kind of
numerous trembling" though "the moving hand
approach not near," when he is proposing to sing of
the object of his love :—

A SUPPLICATION

Awake, awake, my lyre !
And tell thy silent master's humble tale
In sounds that may prevail ;
Sounds that gentle thoughts inspire :
Though so exalted she,
And I so lowly be
Tell her, such different notes make all thy harmony.

Hark ! how the strings awake :
And, though the moving hand approach not near,
Themselves with awful fear
A kind of numerous trembling make.

Now all thy forces try ;
Now all thy charms apply,
Revenge upon her ear the conquests of her eye.

Weak lyre ! thy virtue sure
Is useless here, since thou art only found
To cure, but not to wound,
And she to wound, but not to cure.
Too weak, too, wilt thou prove
My passion to remove ;
Physic to other ills, thou'rt nourishment to love.

Sleep, sleep, again my lyre !
For thou canst never tell my humble tale
In sounds that will prevail,
Nor gentle thoughts in her inspire,
All thy vain mirth lay by,
Bid thy strings silent lie,
Sleep, sleep, again, my lyre, and let thy master die.

That surely is full of conceits and as unreal as
the poetry of a man of a certain genius could
possibly be. Yet the age when Crashaw and Cowley
flourished, if they ever really flourished, was the
age of Milton, and the age in which Dryden began
his work, and where could we find the promise of
new kinds of poetical life and genius, if not in the
age of Milton and Dryden ? We shall often find
poets with signs of decadence, poets who are
strained and artificial in their efforts to be sublime,
contemporary with other poets who are as natural
and fresh as if they came straight from the heart of
Nature. Perhaps the poetry of Gay was as poor,
manufactured, and artificial as that of any poet in
our literature, for with his liveliness there was
hardly any kind of true idealism, and his senti-

mentality was ostentatious. Nothing, for instance, could be in worse or more artificial taste than the metaphor in which he likens the sailor lover in his "Black-eyed Susan" to a lark, because he dropped so quickly from the shrouds of the ship to the side of his mistress :—

> William, who high upon the yard
> Rock'd with his billow to and fro,
> Soon as her well-known voice he heard,
> He sigh'd and cast his eyes below ;
> The cord slides quickly through his glowing hands,
> And quick as lightning on the deck he stands.

> So the sweet lark, high poised in air,
> Shuts close his pinions to his breast
> If chance his mate's shrill call he hear,
> And drops at once into her nest ;—
> The noblest Captain in the British fleet
> Might envy William's lip those kisses sweet.

Yet Gay was the contemporary of Pope, who though certainly not a poet whose mind was in any high sense ideal, still had a buoyancy of satiric life in him which furnished a whole generation with a rich stock of keen and piercing poetic wit such as we could ill spare from English literature. Whatever may be said in depreciation of Pope's poetry, no one could justly call him a decadent. Indeed, decadence is hardly consistent with the brighter kind of intellect. It always implies that want of deep sagacity which disposes a writer to dwell at disproportionate length on an unhealthy class of thoughts. And from any habit of that kind, so keen and scimitar-like an intellect as Pope's effectually diverted him. Decadent poets are more often decadent because they have not had the judgment, or the breadth of sympathy, to find out the healthier instincts of their age, than because they live in a society which is deeply infected with a morbid taint.

LIFE IN POETRY

POETRY, said Mr. Courthope in the lecture which he delivered in the Taylor Institution, is "the art which produces pleasure for the imagination by imitating human actions, thoughts, and passions in metrical language." Poetry, said Matthew Arnold, is "the criticism of Life." Is either of these definitions adequate? Is it not truer to say that poetry is a real addition to the life of man, or at all events, an emancipation, a manumission of that life, wherever it is prepared for emancipation, and needs only the signal to go free? Imitation, "criticism," these are sadly inadequate and limiting words. In every true poem, life as surely rushes into a new form of mental existence, as when the child lets loose his heart in his first free scamper over the hills, or as when "the young light-hearted" masters of the waves "snatched at the rudder" and shook out more sail,

> And day and night held on indignantly.
> O'er the blue Midland waters with the gale,
> Betwixt the Syrtes and soft Sicily,
> To where the Atlantic raves,
> Outside the Western Straits.

All poetry is an act of emancipation, even the poetry of elegy, even the "lyrical cry," even the poetry of satire and invective. There is no mere imitativeness in poetry. It is a liberation of the true mind. Even when Pope exclaims in his half-histrionic fashion—

> Awake, my St. John, leave all meaner things
> To low ambition and the pride of Kings,"

he is trying in his own artificial way to break a sort of bondage—not to impose a new bondage, the bondage of literary fetters. Every great poem has been a great stroke for freedom, for the freedom of the heart and mind. Professor Courthope said well that when great poets like Milton and Dante (why did he not begin with Homer?) introduced their poems with a solemn invocation to the Muse, they held that the life "and much even of the form of their work" was "contained germinally in their matter." It was of the first importance that they should direct their thoughts to a subject on which they could speak with authority and freedom, on which, in fact, they could strike away some fetters by which the mind of man had previously been bound. That was what the invocation to the Muse meant; it was a prayer to be directed to the region in which they could most effectually set free their own souls. And when Professor Courthope says that it is a condition of true poetry not only that the subject should suit the singer, but that it should also suit the audience, that it should be one in which the listeners themselves are eager for the password which will set their imaginations on fire, that it is only another way of saying that poetry should not only liberate the mind of the poet, but also the minds of those to whose more or less constrained and over-burdened hearts the poet brings a new im-

pulse of free and buoyant movement. That is the
real essence of poetry. Even the least popular poet,
the most "caviare to the general," even Shelley and
Spenser, and Arnold and Clough, and the poets who
are said to be rather the poets of the poetic, than
the poets of the mass of mankind, loose some fetter
on the mind or heart of their readers which had
weighed heavily on their predecessors. Such a
poet as Gray, for instance, a recluse, fastidious,
academic almost, gives a profounder sense of
emancipation to the world of tranquil, meditative
musers in his famous elegy, than any other poet of
his century, unless it were Burns or Wordsworth, of
whom the latter really led the way into a new
century of poetry, and shot back a bolt in the
human breast which almost the whole of the present
century has busied itself in securing against any
recoil. All poetry is emancipation, is a new life, a
new freedom ; and it is quite true, as Professor
Courthope asserts, that even satire, even such a
poem as Pope's letter to Mr. Arbuthnot, with the
profound scorn of its vivid portraiture, seems to
open to us the way into a fresh world, and thereby,
as I believe, to strike the characteristic note of all
poetry, by inspiring a new current of indignant
and scornful emotion. Of course satire opens the
narrowest of these avenues to fresh life. It only
destroys those artificial barriers which really never
hold back any but purely conventional natures from
the "fresh woods and pastures new" of the human
spirit. Still even satire does that, and does it
effectually. It is only an artificial bondage that it
breaks, but since many of our worst fetters are
artificial fetters which we have fastened upon ourselves, and which the true man does not feel, satire

has its liberating influence, and often sets us free from fetters which we have welcomed in the inmost recesses of our own souls.

Professor Courthope holds that the great vein of pessimism in modern poetry is more or less due to the tendency of poets to "think of nature and society in those romantic moulds of the imagination which no longer corresponded with the reality of things." I should not have thought that the poetry of the present day exhibited any such tendency. In fact, it has been too realistic, and shown signs of revolt not only against romantic conceptions of life, but against all those restraining influences which are the very secret of true freedom. For freedom and emancipation cannot be secured without willingly submitting the heart and mind to those natural restraining influences which are bred in the inmost recesses of our being. I should have said that far from showing any tendency to conform too closely to the old romantic moulds of human thought, and to fret at the discrepancy between the world of romance and the world of reality, the tendency of the present day had been to ignore altogether the moral limits within which alone we can be truly free, and to attempt to liberate ourselves from the authority of the truest self within us, and seek after an unnatural freedom which is really the most galling bondage. After all, freedom is a relative word. You cannot be free *from* your nature, you can only be free *in* your nature, in you highest nature. And no bondage is more cruel, more intolerable, than the bondage which comes of fighting against the very law of your own true nature. It is there, as it seems to me, that the pessimism of the newer poetry arises. It springs from a reluctance to bear the only yoke with which we cannot dispense without ceasing to be our true selves. Even the great poet who endeavoured so vainly in his prose writings to accomplish the impossible task of reconciling the scepticism with the faith of the day, even Matthew Arnold, felt keenly that there was something in man, as well as in the Universe outside man, which rendered it impossible to attain the highest freedom without submitting himself to the mysterious yoke within him—a yoke which he would not ignore, though he would not welcome it, and he ended his wonderfully impressive lines on " Resignation " in this half-heartedly reluctant strain :—

> Enough, we live !—and if a life,
> With large results so little rife,
> Though bearable, seem hardly worth
> This pomp of worlds, this pain of birth ;
> Yet, Fausta, the mute turf we tread,
> The solemn hills around us spread,
> This stream which falls incessantly,
> The strange-scrawl'd rocks, the lonely sky,
> If I might lend their life a voice,
> Seem to bear rather than rejoice.
> And even could the intemperate prayer
> Man iterates, while these forbear,
> For movement, for an ampler sphere.
> Pierce Fate's impenetrable ear ;
> Not milder is the general lot
> Because our spirits have forgot,
> In action's dizzying eddy whirl'd,
> The something that infects the world.

Surely the " something that infects the world "—our modern world at least—is the unhealthy reluctance to resign ourselves to the will of that Divine Power which " built this fabric of things," and which has found it essential for us to administer to us suffering in many forms in order to open our shrinking and limited nature to larger issues than any to which the natural man is ready to adapt himself. We recoil like a sensitive plant from the first rude touch, and yet it is only through these rude touches, and many of them, that our natures can be taught to expand to the craving for higher ideals and the appreciation of nobler efforts. We want to shrink to the dimensions of poorer natures, though we are destined to find our only true happiness in the evolution of a greater fortitude and of loftier hopes.

POETRY AND LANDSCAPE

In a delightful book on the place of landscape in poetry, by Mr. Palgrave, formerly Professor of Poetry in the University of Oxford, published by Messrs. Macmillan, we have an exquisite series of illustrations, from Homer to Tennyson, of the curious significance of landscape in the expression of human emotion. On his title page Mr. Palgrave quotes from Beethoven this motto for his Pastoral Symphony, "*Mehr Ausdruck der Empfindung als Malerei*"—"More an expression of emotion than Painting"—and a better motto he could hardly have found for a series of exquisite illustrations of the significance of landscape in poetry. And yet, surely nothing can be more curious than that the emotions of man's heart should, from the first dawn of his intellect, have written themselves indelibly, as it were, on the natural scenery by which he is surrounded, so that from Homer to Tennyson it is next to impossible to express any feeling or passion, however profound, without the aid of those external scenes with which they are not so much associated as absolutely identified, and on which they are inscribed as though language were nothing but a series of hieroglyphics sculptured on the rocks or painted on the clouds. From what is almost Mr.

411

Palgrave's earliest illustration of Homer's love for landscape, in the wonderful picture of the Trojan Camp as Tennyson himself translated it for us with a magic touch, to his last charming illustration of the mode in which Tennyson pictured for himself his own passionate feelings of delight at the coming of Spring, it seems nearly impossible to express emotion at all, without a consent of Earth and Heaven to embody it, or to appear to us to embody it, in the external scenes with which it claims a mysterious affinity.   Here is the celebrated passage from Homer in which he has given to the Trojan Plain and watch-fires a sense of mystery and pathos which I doubt if he ever gave to the Camp of the Greeks.   It is a pity, I think, that Mr. Palgrave did not quote enough of the passage to bring the landscape before us, instead of only one exquisite fragment :—

> And these all night upon the bridge of war
> Sat glorying ; many a fire before them blazed ;
> As when in heaven the stars about the moon
> Look beautiful, when all the winds are laid,
> And every height comes out, and jutting peak
> And valley, and the immeasurable heavens
> Break open to their highest, and all the stars
> Shine, and the shepherd gladdens in his heart ;
> So many a fire between the ships and stream
> Of Xanthus blazed before the towers of Troy,
> A thousand on the plain ; and close by each
> Sat fifty in the blaze of burning fire ;
> And eating hoary grain and pulse, the steeds
> Fixt by their cars, waited the golden dawn.

And here again is the wonderful passage in which Tennyson most nearly expressed, as Mr. Mackail

and Mr. Palgrave both hold, "the actual process
through which poetry comes into existence":—

> Past, Future, glimpse and fade
>   Through some slight spell,
> A gleam from yonder vale,
>   Some far blue fell,
> And sympathies, how frail
>   In sound and smell!
>
> Till at thy chuckled note,
>   Thou twinkling bird,
> The fairy fancies range,
>   And, lightly stirred,
> Ring little bells of change
>   From word to word.
>
> For now the Heavenly Power
>   Makes all things new,
> And thaws the cold and fills
>   The flower with dew;
> The blackbirds have their wills,
>   The poets too.

"The poets have their wills," but not without the
help of that external scene, that conspiracy of
Earth and Heaven to give them their wills, which
impresses on them this necessity for identifying
their wills with some strange, and at first sight
almost arbitrary, background of bright or dreary
scenery.   Surely this love of landscape, which seems
so inseparable from all human emotion, is a very
notable phenomenon deserving of more thought
than it usually receives.   Who can explain why
Tennyson himself finds it impossible to speak of

those "tears, idle tears," of which he says that he knows not what they mean, without picturing to himself the "happy autumn fields" on which he gazes through their blinding mist, or to recall the "tender grace of a day that is dead," without imaging to himself the breaking of the sea at the foot of the cold grey stones with which that dead day was in his mind identified? Why cannot Matthew Arnold realise to himself the existence of that "Something which infects the world" without dwelling on—

> The mute turf we tread,
> The solemn hills around us spread,
> The stream which falls incessantly,
> The strange-scrawled rocks, the lonely sky,

all of which seem to assure him that the world has had inscribed upon it a deep trace of suffering, if not of ruin?

Why should Wordsworth insist that—

> Amid the groves, under the shadowy hills,
> The generations are prepared, the pangs,
> The internal pangs, are ready ; the dread strife
> Of poor humanity's afflicted will
> Struggling in vain with ruthless destiny.

Yet without the "groves" and the "shadowy hills," "the pangs, the internal pangs," would not have fully imaged his thought at all, for to have some glimpse of the scene of these pangs as it presents itself to the imagination of the victim is at once an essential part of the suffering, and also, I suspect, something of an alleviation of its rigours. To realise that the "groves" and "shadowy hills" are witnesses of the anguish which pierces the heart of the generations who are undergoing the discipline beneath their shelter, makes it both more visible to the imagination, and perhaps a little more tolerable, just as it is more tolerable to know that your sufferings are not the only reality, than to imagine that beyond the dark centre of the tortured nerves there may be no refuge, no real existence at all. And not only does realising a great world external to the "internal pangs" partially alleviate these pangs, but to realise a great world external to the vividness of individual life and energy, lends a new flavour and intensity to that life and energy. Is it questionable for a moment that when Homer compared to the spectacle of the starry heavens breaking open to their highest, while the shepherds were gladdened at the exquisite tranquillity and brilliance of the night, the gladness of the Trojan host as they rested by the blazing watch-fires and waited for the dawn, he shed a new glory over the hearts of those who rejoiced in the prowess of the besieged, and in the great deeds of Hector, and in the flushed hopes of the warriors who had done so much towards driving the Archæan invaders from their shores? When the poet contrives to make external Nature join as it were in the exultation of the happy warrior or warriors with whom he is dealing, he places the crown on their heads and gives a new splendour to their achievements. Indeed, the art of making any landscape smile with human happiness, or darken with human woe, is and has been in all ages one of the greatest triumphs of the poet. Who can doubt that even the suggestion of a certain sympathy between the beauty of a landscape

or of a summer sky and the beauty of a woman,
adds infinitely to the sense of that beauty ; as, for
example, in such a verse as this ?—

> Her eyes like stars of twilight fair,
> Like twilight, too, her dusky hair;
> But all things else about her drawn
> From Maytime and the cheerful dawn.

And who can doubt that when St. Paul enlarged on
the sufferings of all created things,—" For we know
that the whole creation groaneth and travaileth in
pain together until now,"—instead of adding to the
burden of the individual sufferer, he rather alleviated
it by representing that all creation shares it, and
that whatever pierces the gloom for one may pierce
it for all, by virtue of the unity which binds
together the diversified lots of men ? Is not this
really at the root of the poetical impulse which
renders it so inevitable to draw landscape into the
very heart of human emotion, or, if that be the
truer way of expressing it, to spread human
emotion so liberally over the face of the landscape ?
It is not true, of course, that individual joy diffuses
itself widely over the external world, or that individual anguish darkens it. But it is true that there
is a unity at the heart of things which makes it
natural for man to seek some reflection of his
happiness and of his misery in the great object of
his faith and hope. And is not this the source of
the impulse which drives him instinctively to attri-
bute his exultations and his pangs to the external
world, as a mode of stretching out towards that
great centre of power and life which is beyond his
own reach ? He snatches at the face of the visible
world as an infant snatches at what is bright or

glistening, and tries to draw it within the sphere of his own feelings. But the dim impulse which makes him seek this reflection of his own feeling in the world beyond is the keen sense of a larger and deeper Sympathy which lies behind this visible scene and enters into all the life which everywhere pervades it.

THE END